MAN EAST AND WEST:
ESSAYS IN EAST-WEST PHILOSOPHY

Howard L. Parsons

Philosophical Currents

Vol. 8

David H. DeGrood
Editor

The important views expressed by our writers are represented without necessarily implying concurrence of either editors or publisher.

B. R. GRÜNER B. V. — Amsterdam 1975

Man East and West:
Essays in East-West Philosophy

Howard L. Parsons

B. R. Grüner B. V. Amsterdam — 1975

Library of Congress Catalog
Card Number 73-81622

ISBN 90 6032 020 4
Printed in Hungary

MAN EAST AND WEST:
ESSAYS IN EAST-WEST PHILOSOPHY

Howard L. Parsons

PREFACE

This work is a philosophical and somewhat historical study of ideas about the nature, values, and fulfillment of man. ("Man" is a species term including women and children.) But going beyond these ideas as such, it tries to describe some of the generic features and values of persons and societies as revealed in the literature of some philosophies and religions in East and West, as well as in some findings of the sciences. It traces briefly the rise of some of these ideas about man. It sets forth some significant differences in the philosophical and religious traditions of East and West, as well as conditions correlated with these differences. "East" here means chiefly India and China; "West" means chiefly western Europe and North America.

As a species, mankind has been on this planet for more than a million years, has occupied a great variety of environments – tropical forest and savanna, temperate plain and valley, mountain and seacoast, semidesert and winter region – and has created thousands of different cultures and 4,000 extant languages. Mankind is a complex thing. No one person or book can hope to comprehend everything important about man or to appraise and synthesize all the evidence about man. This book concentrates in a philosophical way on a portion of the evidence about man.

I take philosophy as method to be an analytical, critical, synthetic, and constructive inquiry into certain categories or questions embedded in all human living. The purpose of such inquiry is to formulate the categories and to take a reasoned stand on the questions, so as to help man to live and to live well. Three of these categories are man, value, and fulfillment – the subject of this work. If he deals with these categories, nothing human can be alien to the philosopher, as material for reflection. Personal observations and analysis can provide many data for understanding. So can observation of several cultures. Even so, such data are limited. Most of the data for philosophical inquiry must come of necessity from secondary sources – from the recorded expressions of philosophies, religions, arts, and other modes of symbolism of human cultures, and from the conclusions of the natural and social sciences pertaining to human activity. In parts of the present study I have tried to combine some of the insights of traditional philosophies and religions in East and West with the more precise data of the relatively modern sciences. Ancient philosophies and religions have had much to say about man, value and fulfillment; those indeed were their main subjects, though what they said was often expressed in mythical form. Moreover, they were formulated under and for social conditions quite different from contemporary conditions. Hence their truth and relevance must be refined and recast to fit contemporary conditions. Since the sciences grow out of contemporary conditions and in their own ways are intended to deal with them, they afford fresh data relevant to the nature of man, value, and fulfillment. But as the insights of ancient philosophies and religions must be stated anew and be, so to speak, modernized, so the findings of the particular modern sciences must be generalized and systematized within a philosophical scheme in order to be rendered relevant and useful to the problem at hand – the problem of understanding man's nature, value, and fulfillment. I have tried to do both. Thus the philosophical method here has aimed to identify, assemble, analyze, compare, appraise, and synthesize some important data from the philosophies, religions, and sciences, in order to take a stand on basic human questions. It has aimed to *humanize* these data by signifying their import for the theory and practice of being human.

In scope, this work to some degree attempts to take account of similarities and differences among persons and societies with regard to physique, temperament, individual and social values, patterns of culture, and social conflicts. While I have been guided by a conviction in a generic structure of man, I have also laid stress on the diverse symbolized or "conceived" values of people, as Charles Morris has called them, and his Maitreyan ideal of dynamic unity in diversity informs my work. Also, I have been more concerned with concepts than with individual and social practices, though the latter are assumed in the background and are referred to. A fuller treatment of the subject of man would take greater cognizance of the wide variety of persons and cultures actually displayed on the planet, as cultural anthropology has revealed these in empirical detail.[1] James Harvey Robinson has pointed out that man is animal, savage, and child; and therefore a proper study of mankind is of man from the standpoint of biology, cultural anthropology, and child psychology. Man is also physicochemical, social, historical, economic, ecological, symbolizing, valuative, etc. Comprehensive study of man would embrace the well established conclusions of all disciplines directed to these aspects of the human way of being.

The essays comprising this work were first written during the past decade and a half and reflect some of the major social concerns of the author during this period as well as the state of scientific knowledge then. As I have recently reread and revised the essays, I can see that now, in 1972, some of these concerns have taken on more urgency with myself and others than they had

1. Clifford Geertz, "The Impact of the Concept of Culture on the Concept of Man," in *New Views of the Nature of Man*, ed. John R. Platt. Chicago: University of Chicago, 1965, 93–118.

then – e.g., the concerns about the nuclear war, armaments, population, ecology, and world-wide poverty; and the U. S. war in Indochina from the 1960's into the 1970's has etched with increasing clarity the roles of imperialism, socialism, national liberation movements, and Asian anti-colonial struggles on the world scene today. In addition, as is well known, scientific knowledge about the world and man continues to grow at a rate that outruns the capacity of most people, even scientists, to assimilate and make good human use of it. It has been estimated that eighty per cent of the scientists who have ever lived are living today – though it may be doubted that all these are true scientists – and each second 30,000 words are added to scientific literature. Much of this literature bears directly on the subject of this work (though much else is trivial), but because of its mass and growth it has not come into the purview of this work.

Yet the urgency of the needs and concerns of mankind and the growth of knowledge related to mankind are not reasons for turning aside from the effort to satisfy these needs and concerns and to understand and use the knowledge well. They are, on the contrary, reasons for a renewed struggle to understand how man might survive and live in ways that commence to help man to consummate his human powers. Moreover, this understanding does not depend entirely on the indefinite Baconian accumulation of data. The data must be selected under the guidance of some leading hypothesis, and at some point they must be analyzed and criticized to determine to what extent they support that hypothesis and to what extent the hypothesis must be modified or discarded. Such guidance, analysis, and criticism are the function of philosophy.

Parts of the earlier essays show a theoretical emphasis and somewhat lyrical tone that may not seem suited to a world today crying out for practical measures and immediate remedies. However, theory and lyrical imagination concerning man can furnish needed perspective on the quality, direction, and ends of such practice. They can show man mixed with the elements and endenizened in the milieu of planetary, biological, and historical evolution. They can hold up in vivid form man's possibilities, both terrible and wonderful, for the future. They can offer a requisite antidote and contrast to mere pragmatic action, ungoverned by adequate theory and uninspired by deep feelings for man both real and ideal. Between the time of the writing of the first of these essays and the present, my own interests have shifted increasingly to concrete social questions. But a rewriting of the chapters with these interests dominant would result in another book quite different from this one. I offer it as an expression of that earlier period.

Since most of these essays were first written, many works have appeared in the field of comparative and East-West philosophy. I have not, however, taken the time to rewrite the present volume in the light of these works.

Such rewriting would entail modifications of the theses presented here – perhaps not so thoroughgoing as to issue, if carried through, in a new work, but not so total, I trust, as to extinguish all of the theses. One of the richest and most valuable of the new works is Hajime Nakamura's *Ways of Thinking of Eastern Peoples: India-China-Tibet-Japan* (Honolulu: East-West Center, 1964). With erudition and clarity Nakamura brings out the specific and unique characteristics in the thinking of each of these cultures, carefully differentiating them from one another. He expounds India's preference for universals over particulars and individual selves, for the alienated, introspective personality, for the negative, for a transcendental and unitary metaphysics, and for tolerance. China, by contrast, is portrayed as emphasizing nature (the concrete, the particular, the human individual), conformity to the classics and the past, social hierarchy, practicality, complex concrete multiplicity, and harmonizing tendencies. Tibet stressed absolutism and individualism, while Japan inclined toward phenomenalism, a "limited social nexus," and the non-rational. There are important differences between these cultures, though Nakamura's way is not the only way of stating them. For example, Nakamura passes over the dionysian factor in India, and in my view he seems to accentuate Confucianism in China and to underestimate the role of Taoism there. I have written about the thought of these Eastern cultures in order to clarify not their differences from one another but their differences from the thought of the West. It will be evident that one of my purposes here is to expose to criticism the appallingly inhuman capitalism of the West.

Given the limitations of this work, the reader will, I hope, take these *essais* as attempts and testings of answers to questions that concern him or her and all mankind. Insofar as they are philosophical and formulate and focus upon the philosophical questions inherent in social problems and concerns, they are directed to issues that outlast passing conditions and knowledge. Above all, the questions of the nature and fulfillment of man are questions that confront us all, in good times and bad, and we all share in the obligation to formulate the questions and search for the answers, in both theory and practice.

HOWARD L. PARSONS

ACKNOWLEDGEMENTS

I wish to thank the editors listed below for their kind permission to reprint in revised form the articles that have appeared in their publications:

The editor of *The Aryan Path*, for "Man in East and West: His Division and His Unity," Vol. XXXII, Nos. 1, 2, and 3 (January, February, March, 1961), pp. 4–9, 52–57, 101–106.

The editors of *The Philosophical Quarterly*, for "The Meeting of East and West in Philosophical Method," Vol. XXXI, No. 2 (July, 1958), pp. 73–94.

The publisher of *Krishna Chandra Bhattacharyya Memorial* Volume, ed. S. K. Maitra et al. (Amalner: Indian Institute of Philosophy, 1958), for "The Unity of Man and Nature in East and West," pp. 151–182.

The publisher of *S. Radhakrishnan Souvenir Volume*, ed. B. L. Atreya et al. (Moradabad: Darshana Printer, 1964), for "Man East and West", pp. 337–352.

The publisher and editorial staff of Verlag Herder, for "Man, Nature, Value, and Religion," which first appeared in German in *Internationale Dialog Zeitschrift*, 2 Jahrgang, 1969, 1, pp. 35–60, and then in English in *Concurrence*, No. 4, Fall, 1969, pp. 265–285.

The substance of Chapter II here first appeared as "The Natural Roots of Popular Religion," in *Mankind*, Vol. II, Nos. 11–12 (June-July, 1958), pp. 1–19. Though my present efforts to reach the editors to secure permission to reprint have failed, I would like to acknowledge my thanks to them *in absentia*.

Finally, I would like to record with thanks the assistance of the following: the Wenner-Gren Foundation for Anthropological Research, which contributed a grant in support of some of the research done for this volume, particularly the research whose results appear in Chapter I; the Kavir Institute, whose grant made possible the research in Chapter VII; and the University of Bridgeport's Committee on Grants from the Faculty Research Fund for 1972–1973, which provided a grant to help defray the expenses of the project.

Neither these organizations nor any persons connected with them are to be held responsible for any of the views expressed in this study, which as the author's own work is his own responsibility.

Mrs. Elsie Havanich typed portions of the manuscript, and my colleague and editor of this series, Professor David H. DeGrood, has taken a continuing interest in this work. I wish to record my indebtedness for their kind help.

Chapter I

MAN IN EAST AND WEST: HIS DIVISION AND HIS UNITY

The problems of man in our world in our times are often conceived in terms of the separation between the cultures of the East and those of the West. No doubt there are many differences, and an examination of them can be fruitful. But they point to a deeper problem. That is the problem of man himself. Who is man? What are his source and destiny? What are and ought to be his relations, as an individual, to his fellow man, to his society, and to his historical heritage? What are and ought to be his relations, as an individual and a race, to nature? To the cosmos and values?

In this chapter I would like to approach some of these problems through an analysis of certain distinctive and contrasting characteristics of East and West. The analysis makes the contrasts seem sharper than in fact they are, particularly as East and West interact and modify one another. But deeper than the cultural contrasts lie human ones. And human contrasts must be variations on generic themes. Contrasts, moreover, can become antagonisms, so that man as an individual species becomes a problem to himself, threatening his own very existence. Therefore, the problem to which we gain entrance through the idea of "East" and "West" is the problem of human differences and antagonisms – the problem of how man is divided, and why, and how he can be united as an individual person, as a social species, and as a species in relation to the rest of nature.

The terms "East" and "West" are difficult to define precisely, for the earth is round, and geographical as well as cultural east and west lie on a continuum. However, if we follow for the moment A. J. Toynbee's classification of civilizations, we can make explicit the meaning of these terms as they are used in this work. "East" shall mean here the Sinic civilization that arose from unknown origins on the lower valley of the Yellow River c. 1500 B. C. and that gave rise to subsequent Chinese civilization and influenced Japanese-Korean civilization; and Indic civilization, beginning c. 1500 B. C. in the Indus and Ganges River valleys and producing Hindu civilization. "Western" here shall mean the Hellenic civilization which was partially derived from the Minoan in the Aegean before 1200 B. C.; Judaic culture, which was the offspring of Syriac and Babylonic civilizations in the first millenium B. C.; and Orthodox Christian civilization (exclusive of the Russian Orthodox offshoot) in its western European development. Judaeo-Christian and Hellenic (Greco-Roman) elements fused to form what is called "Western" here,

1

and "the West" geographically means generally western Europe as it was influenced by these cultural traditions as well as North America which was colonized initially and primarily by western Europeans.

For one not familiar with this usage – which is currently common among United States scholars – this specialized usage of "East" and "West" may seem confusing. Are not all of Asia and Australia in the east? Is not Latin America in the west? Where is Africa to be placed, with its own east and west divided by the Sahara? What about the "Near East" and Palestine, which is one of the cradles of "western" civilization but also produced the Orthodox Christianity that went into Russia? And what about the Soviet Union, which stretches from a decidedly western Leningrad (as Peter the Great made sure) on the Baltic, to the Bering Sea, thousands of miles north and east of China, Korea, and Japan, and which extends even east of a portion of Alaska, now a part of the United States?

In the West the terms "East" and "West" have had an imprecise and changing history. "Asia" was the name of the first Roman province east of the Aegean, formed in 133 B. C., so that even then the distinction was arbitrary. We know that in the third millenium B. C. the cities of Sumer on the Tigris were in commercial contact with the civilization on the Nile to the west and with the civilization on the Indus in the east. Salt from northern India was traded between Syria and the Persian Gulf before Alexander's time, and silk was imported at the Greek port of Kos before classical times. Such trading relations continued through the centuries. The Muslim domination of the Mediterranean from the 7th to the 11th century produced a sudden and sharp separation between the Christianity of the West, which was driven into northwestern Europe, and the Byzantine Christianity of the East. This separation vivified the idea of a dichotomy between east and west.

With the decline of this domination, and the renewal of overland and oceanic trade from the Mediterranean to India, Cathay, and other parts of the Orient, the idea of East and West acquired a new meaning. Vasco de Gama's voyage to India in 1498, culminating after some 50 years of exploration for such a route, marked the beginning of a new period and a new attitude. (By 1417 Cheng Ho had guided the great naval fleet of the Chinese emperor to Kenya.) During the subsequent western colonialization of the East, the terms "East" and "West" became invidious; they reflected, as they still do in the West, the narrow commercial interests of European and North American capitalism. With the shift in the center of commercial power from the Mediterranean to Atlantic and Baltic Europe, and, since World War II, to the United States, the meanings of these terms have also shifted. In addition, modern means of communication and travel have brought all nations into much closer contact than ever before. East and West have met, mixed and changed one another, so that the old distinctions hardly seem to hold.

2

Moreover, these definitions of "East" and "West" leave out of account several civilizations: the Egyptiac, Andean, Sumeric, Mayan, Yucatec, Mexic, Hittite, Iranic, and Arabic – though the latter two, which fused to produce Islamic civilization, are included in the "West" to the extent that they are associated with the Judaeo-Christian tradition. However, of the 21 civilizations that Toynbee describes, only five now exist – the Western, Orthodox Christian, Islamic, Hindu, and Far Eastern (Chinese, Japanese-Korean) – and all of these come into consideration in the definitions here. Any fully adequate description and evaluation of mankind must consider these as well as primitive societies for the light that they throw on the generic character and problems of mankind.

Finally, it must be emphasized that the present work is not a history or philosophy of civilizations but principally a comparative study of philosophical ideas and attitudes. These have arisen and developed in the cultural contexts of the civilizations mentioned. It would be a mistake to believe that the contrasts that appear among these ideas and attitudes consistently appear in all facets of the circumambient cultures, though they do appear in some. From time to time reference is made to the cultures for illustrations of how the ideas and attitudes have worked themselves out in practice. It is true, also that one can cite quite different practices which belie the contrasts illustrated, so that the contrast in this regard must be qualified. But I have used the terms "East" and "West" here because they provide a handy vehicle for developing important comparisons and contrasts in the domain of philosophical ideas about reality, values, and knowledge. Neither the terms nor the contrasts associated with them are intended as absolute.

Let us begin with a well known distinction. Eastern cultures have been relatively simple, unspecialized, and unitary. Western cultures have been complex, highly differentiated, and fragmented. To make this distinction stick, we would have to modify it so severely that perhaps it would disappear. But it is useful. In sociological language,[1] the East has been "tradition-directed," agrarian, status-oriented, and dominated by "ritual, routine, and religion." Social continuity has characterized the ancient civilizations of India and the Far East. The West, in modern times especially, has been "inner-directed" and "other-directed." Manufacturing and trade have been its material and social base. Orientation has been supplied to the individual person through his own "psychological gyroscope" or his "need for approval and direction from others." The essential problem of the West – in recent centuries, with expansion – has been the material environment, and the regulation of the behavior of large groups of mobile people.

1. David Riesman, Nathan Glazer, Reuel Denney, *The Lonely Crowd.* New Haven: Yale University, 1950.

3

The simple unity of Eastern cultures is ancient. As we trace it historically, it recedes into the Neolithic past. In India, the beliefs in *ahiṁsā* and *karma* date back to distant pre-Vedic times. The aboriginal Indians believed in a Mother Goddess. They were aware, with all the vivid realism of the primitive imagination, that nature gives and takes away; that all things are formed and transformed in the great creative and destructive cycles of nature; that man lives and dies; and that passing into his children, his cult's memory, and the soil itself, he seems to be reborn. Like all primitive peoples, these people were cryptic naturalists. And their world-view, as it developed, was monistic, mystical, and democratic, even in the early stages of the urban revolution, before cities became separated from farmers and specialized technology rent culture with class struggles.[2] This profound sense of unity that men had with one another and with the powers of nature is reflected in the earliest known religion of India. It is also reflected in the early philosophies which echo, and, in urban times, endeavor to recover that primeval unity which they dimly divined the innocent primitive mind to possess.

Our records for China do not carry us as far back as do those for India. Nonetheless, the emphasis on man's interdependence with nature and with one another is unmistakable.

> It is to be noted [says one writer] that 'Earth' and not 'Heaven' is regarded as the Giver, the source of life, from whom comes the abundance of crops and the fecundity of women. . . . The connection between the human body and the soil was also very close. . . corpses were deposited near the dwelling place during decomposition, thus fertilizing the family soil, and. . . each new member of the family was regarded as a reincarnation, not of any special ancestor but of the actual substance of all his ancestors.

> In these agricultural communities the rhythm of life followed that of Nature, and from this sprang some of the basic ideas in *li* (ritual propriety) and *ho* (social harmony), two concepts deeply rooted in Chinese life. Customs, or taboos, must be followed with due propriety in order that the whole life of the community may be kept in harmony with Nature and thus the blessing of Nature be assured.[3]

The unitary character of Indian and Chinese thought, while not by any means intact or unchanged through the centuries, has remained remarkably constant. As in India, the universal facts of struggle, suffering, sacrifice, and rebirth – the subordination of the individual person to social and cosmic purposes – have long since been recognized, so in China thought has similarly

---

2. Gordon Childe, *What Happened in History*. Harmondsworth: Penguin, 1942. Lokāyata was an ancient and popular materialism in India. See Debiprasad Chattopadhyaya, *Indian Philosophy*. Delhi: People's Publishing House, 1964, ch. 28.
3. E. R. Hughes and K. Hughes, *Religion in China*. London: Hutchinson's University Library, 1950, p. 15.

reflected cultural practice. A typical attitude is that of the Neo-Confucianist Chang Tsai: "All men are my brothers; all things are my relatives." Of course Indian and Chinese philosophers differed in their approaches. The Indians tended to seek to transcend the unity of man and nature through a philosophical sublimation which identified the self with the embracing divine spirit. They transmuted the palpable unity of natural experience into the impalpable unity of idealism. The Chinese sages, on the other hand, sought to transcend the distinctions of the natural world by a human identification with the maternal source of all things, the great *Tao* of nature.

The contrast between this Indian and Chinese view of man and man's relation to nature, and that which developed in the West, is striking. Just how Western thought developed its peculiar dualism between body and soul, and between nature and man, is too long a story to recount here. For Western thought was not always supernaturalistic. The point, however, is one of contrast. For Western supernaturalism man's soul is essentially a wanderer in an alien land and a pilgrim in a vale of tears. In the West man's unity and salvation consists – not in refining nature and in bringing her along as the gross but necessary baggage in the journey of the spirit; not in taking her multitudes with an air of detachment, humor, or resignation, seeing they are mortal children poured forth from her inexhaustible cornucopia – but in abandoning that old "nurse of generation" and leaving her behind in preference for the forever virginal, angelic, and unproductive mistress of heaven.

Western science has carried forward this dualism that developed in the early days of urbanism as in part an endeavor to cope with the diversities of the old sensualism.[4] Law, the *logos*, reason – all separated man from a direct, qualitative relation to nature. And so Western science assumes what much Western religion assumes: that little man is the center of nature around whom all things should revolve, before whom every other creature should bow; that man has a destiny which he can achieve by deliberate manipulation and control of nature; and that nature as such has no rights but is merely a neutral and inert addendum, or at best a medium to our human desires. It was a Western nation which discovered atomic fission, which pursued a systematic policy of bombing cities in World War II, which was the first (and thus far the only) nation to drop atomic bombs on civilian populations,[5] which has been charged with and has been guilty of genocide and

4. L. L. Whyte, *The Next Development in Man*. New York: New American Library of World Literature, 1950, p. 68.
5. Compare, for example, the publications of the United States Strategic Bombing Survey – which stresses the long-range, strategic bombing of factories, cities, etc., in World War II – and the military strategy and tactics of the Chinese as laid down in the writings of Mao Tse-tung. Or compare the bombing practices of the two belligerents in the Korean war.

germ warfare, and which has plundered its natural resources with a selfish and self-centered technology.

Consider some further consequences of this philosophical dualism. A science which alienates man from nature is destined in the end to alienate man from himself. Disregard for plant and animal life, for the environing principle of unity in nature at large, is apt to mean disregard for human life and for the principle of unity in society; whereas sympathy for the small and growing things of nature will mean sympathy for the children of men. The social science of the Western nations, as applied, for example, to colonial peoples, has tended to proceed on the basis of the principle, *Divide and rule*. Bureaucratic fiat, propagation of the magical Word, dogmatic decree, arbitrary enforcement, mechanical plans–all are necessitated where the governing relation in a society is exploiters vs. exploited. Colonialism is in some aspects a recrudescence to feudalism, and so easily makes common cause with local feudal lords, as the military arm of colonialism makes common cause with local war lords.

By contrast, the indigeneous revolutionary movements in Asia have been generated at the grass-roots and rice-roots and carried out by broad masses of people whose leaders went to the people, stayed with the people, learned from the people, and helped lead the people along the line of their natural fulfillment.[6] Socialism, which has developed chiefly in industrially backward countries, has tended in places like China to carry forward men's sense of mutuality with nature. The great hydro-electric projects in the Soviet Union and the People's Republic of China are examples: they incarnate and lift to a new creative level the unity of man and nature. We can expect research in the constructive uses of atomic energy also to proceed apace in those countries.[7] Is it true that in the East life is cheap? Rather, the opposite seems true. That life in the East in cheap is a judgment coming out of the mouths of Westerners who have bought and sold Oriental lives so cheaply.

Man *in* nature is man caught up in the natural processes of transforma-

6. Robert Payne (*Mao Tse-tung, Ruler of Red China*. New York: Henry Schuman, 1950) contrasts the mobile guerrilla tactics and fluid character of Mao with the rigid positional warfare and static character of Chiang Kai-shek. In this difference many other contrasts are brought to focus: Eastern agrarianism and "Westernized" and urban bureaucracy, country and city (Mao went to the peasants to learn from them, Chiang stayed in the cities to rule them), service to the young and allegiance to the old, communistic Taoism and oligarchic Confucianism, the feminine orientation and the masculine. Mao has a generous complement of what W. H. Sheldon has called "gynandromorphy" – "the degree or prominence of feminine characteristics in a male physique."
7. India and China are, of course, industry-wise, comparatively backward, but are rapidly expanding industry, with all of industry socialized in China and one-half of capitalist assets being state-owned in India. And the peace-time usage of atomic energy in the next century, untrammeled by the entanglements of private monopoly and profit, may be expected, in those countries, to bypass some of the major problems of development with which other modern industrial nations have been faced.

6

tion; he is the Great Evolution in embryo, recapitulating, anticipating, helping to advance that universal process of creation. Man is nature herself naturing in a differential way, but always exhibiting the universal process of mutual transformation of interacting events: dream and action, hypothesis and experiment, detachment and attachment, mystic seizure and scientific analysis. With the medium of his perceptions and symbols, the conscious magic of his imagination, the unconscious chemistry of his symbolic creativity, and the expanding control of his experimenting, man transmutes his world as plants, in Moleschott's phrase, are "woven out of air by light." Man is ceaselessly transliterating his experience so that "transactions" may be effected. His science is a deliberate control and weighting of this interaction on the side of man: science widens man's sphere of interaction with events. But it may tend, by emphasis on perecision and specific foresight, to impoverish and make lopsided the full play and richness of interaction. A science that is logically rigorous, factually exact, and empirically useful, will have its day, but may find that it cannot accommodate itself to the demands of a new day.[8] The unknown novelties and depths of nature are too vast to be totally known or predicted in any scientific or symbolic scheme; consequently, if science is to be perennially creative it must run its roots down into the subsoil of the creativity of nature herself. It must undertake to create conditions of "change in the direction of increase in the range, variety, and efficacy of adjustment of the organism to its environment"[9] – conditions which will transform itself.

But if the traditional West has fallen into the dualism of quantitative science, as L. L. Whyte[10] has described it, the traditional East has been guilty of an opposite though similar error. Dominated for centuries by the dead, the past, the ritualized, the massive and regular, the deeply laid in nature, it has felt under the burden of its round of unrelieved days an indescribable affinity with nature – an animal or mineral sympathy with all that endures, moves, or throbs in the infinite throng of finite things that arise and pass away. It has sensed that man's common lot with all of nature is the brute and monotonous destiny of mere habitual existence. Man's works and days proceed in the purblind burrow of animal sentience and instinct. According to Eastern teaching, to recognize this unconscious substratum of our lives, this primal blindness, this "suchness" as weak and strong as water, is the beginning of man's liberation and the source of his fulfillment. But this simple naturalistic mysticism of animal man, while basic, is not enough; it is

8. R. B. Braithwaite, *Scientific Explanation*. Cambridge: Cambridge University, 1953.
9. C. Judson Herrick, "A Biological Survey of Integrative Levels," *Philosophy for the Future*, ed. Roy Wood Sellars, V. J. McGill, and Marvin Farber. New York: Macmillan, 1949, p. 227.
10. *Op. cit.*

the mysticism of self-centered introspection, of immobility, of cyclical movement, or static bliss, of the *status quo*. Nature or some Spirit of nature is naively taken to be good in her elemental unity; and so her distinctions, along with the classes and castes of man's cruel inhumanities of man, are conveniently suppressed from awareness and forgotten. For while it is true that the East has been closer to the fertile unitary center of nature and life, India's caste system and China's landlordism have mocked that natural unity. Yet the mockery, though deflecting men from life, has not completely undermined their attachment to it. The *Gītā* and the Chinese sages counsel attachment to nature and action in it as well as detachment from it.

The contrasts between the Eastern and Western views of nature and man are evident if we observe, for illustration, the differences between Calcutta and New York City. In Calcutta rhesus monkeys inhabit buildings and marketplaces, and cows roam the streets. Lepers are isolated and go untreated, and their children, forced to live in the colony, acquire the disease. During the rainy season the excrement of cattle blocks the sewer canal, and at every dawn the bodies of the dead are picked up by trucks and carried off to the ghats to be burned. The death of the body for most Hindus is an interlude in a round of rebirths, and life is viewed as an illusion to be lived out in passiveness and resignation. Hunger, poverty, disease, and illiteracy are accepted facts of life for most of the eight million people living there. Forty per cent of them live in subhuman conditions, and the ruling religion of mysticism suits both those condemned to squalor and those privileged to affluence. It gives comfort to the suffering and justification to the fortunate ruling groups. Against such conditions and attitudes, technology makes slow headway: in order to provide work for many, the labor unions oppose mechanization and maintain the primitive pace of village life and activity. In the midst of this disorder and death, family life goes on, cohered by religious faith and the glue of tradition. Although Calcutta's agony is the consequence of the imperialism of the English East India Company, the attitudes of its people illustrate both the affirmation of man's unity and the impracticality which mark Indian mystical religion.

In New York City, that steel and brick and concrete monument to technology, wild human nature has been driven into the confines of a few parks and zoos. Often the air is barely breathable, heavy with auto exhaust fumes and industrial gases. The rivers flow with filth. Dwelling places and office buildings tower upward over dark and impersonal canyons. On the streets, in the alleys and subways, robbers mug innocent victims, seeking money to feed their drug habits. Violence lurks around the corners, and the lurid forms of pornography leap out from the printed page and theater marque. A few manage to amass great wealth; "welfare" is doled out to a million people. Automobiles, trains, ships, and planes move continuously in and out of the bedlam. The sights and sounds of applied science assail the senses. The human heart, with its need for social feelings and creative social relations, must fight against being overwhelmed and silenced. A few take refuge in religious supernaturalism; most, however, "look out for number one" and aggressively struggle against the pervasive aggressiveness. The ideology that justifies it all is the atomic individualism of scientific mechanistic materialism and capitalism. Such ideology tends to confirm things as they are, both for the exploited and the exploiters.

These cities illustrate the two extremes in Eastern and Western ideologies. That science which idolizes man in abstraction from nature and his fellow human beings, and that mysticism which meekly loses itself in the acceptance or worship of nature, are both partial and pinched. The one gives man all the power and glory, the other gives that to powers beyond individual or social man; the one is arrogant, the other is submissive. Man deserves a riper development than each alone can yield. Yet implicit within each lies the germ of man's fulfillment: that principle of dialectical interaction of man and men, of man and nature, the social power that draws man into nature and nature into man through a science that releases man's capacities for perception, for feeling, for thought, for sympathy, for memory, for love, and for devotion to the whole creative enterprise of man, of nature's creatures, and of nature herself. Such power it is that creates that emergent society embracing animals and plants and even minerals, creatures which in their interaction of reinforcing one another are evolving a planetary community. In that natural home and garden, in that city of brotherly and sisterly comradeship, men and women and children may be detached, but not without attachment; clearly rational, but not without reverence for life. There man may live, and live well, and live sacrificially, so that when he comes to die he may know that his death is not only a testimony that he has fought the good fight but also a promise that he has kept faith with the multitude of lives to come.

So the ideas and attitudes of East must interact, integrate, and evolve with those of the West if a whole and creative mankind is to arise. It is true that East and West are not perfect opposites or complements: the East has produced humanistic mystics and the West unitary naturalists. But the East has lacked the tools of science, and the West the resources of sensitivity and unitary feeling. Combine the cycling of the *Tao* or of *Brahman* with the linear history of the West and you have the spiral of creative mankind. Mate the mothering of the East and the fathering of the West and you have the children of intelligent love. We need one another, and, as lovers cry one to another, we cannot live apart. As Nature herself is the interacting of opposites and the transformation of differences into higher contrasts, so man, as icon and participant in nature, when he is true to his nature, cherishes and develops this dialectic in himself and with other natures. Thus the attitudes of receptivity and control, of undergoing and doing, of unifying and separating, are mutually indispensable. As the hand guides the eye, giving its vision depth and solidity, so the eye can guide the hand, giving it the proper touch, foresight, and uncompulsive delight; or in the figure of the Sāmkhya, blind matter and lame spirit cooperate in getting out of a forest; so man East and man West need each other, as one hemisphere needs another to constitute a rounded and symmetrical globe. Huntington has said that a primary factor in man's creativity has been "cyclonic storms with their constant alternation between masses of warm, moist, tropical air, and cool, dry, polar air."[11] So man must be wrought in the tension of peaceful void and vigorous form, combining in evolving opposition the moist, low mysticism of the East and the dry, high science of the West.

To go forward East and West must go backward, recovering that dynamic center, that integrative principle, that stabilizing source of life which prevents perversions, harmonizes diversities, coordinates individuations, heals breaches, socializes retreat, and gently transforms brute power into works of art. Yet as these lines are written this process is occurring: the East, which has never been wholly mystical or ascetic, has grasped the tools of science and is commencing to transform flood into electricity and waste into fruits; and the West, whose poets at least trusted Nature, and could say

> He prayeth well who loveth well
> Both man and bird and beast,

is turning back to nature. Even America has bred and nurtured her romantics, and if Thoreau and Emerson and Whitman had no vast hearing in the press, pulpits, and platforms of the big cities, still the ponds and the woods and hills from which they borrowed all the beauty of their hues and the reasonance of their notes, now echo back to us of later time their moods and messages, as if these were returning to us with intensified meaning and power, much as a child on entering into maturity suddenly realizes the richness of his ancestry. Under the influence of professional philosophers as diverse in their emphases as Peirce, James, Dewey, Santayana, and Whitehead, Western philosophy has tended to turn away from the metaphysical flight that is content with nothing less than resting on the uppermost roost of the Supernatural. We may say that Santayana's sonnet on the Icarian metaphysician is the most ironically gentle if not the last epitaph written to the genteel tradition and its grandiloquent patriarchs. The poet could well afford to smile, for he himself was a patriarch of the realm of spirit, all too sensitively conscious of his origin, his participation, and his destiny in the realm of matter.

11. Ellsworth Huntington, *Mainsprings of Civilization*. New York: John Wiley and Sons, 1945, p. 369.

Even Western science, though sporadically, as in the TVA, has returned to rely on and carefully utilize its natural springs. So thought returns to resume its role as the natural associate of bodies, as mind (Whitehead points out) has been put back into nature by modern biology. "The purpose of philosophy," wrote Whitehead, "is to rationalize mysticism."[12]

"Reversal is the movement of the *Tao*." So the West like the East is changing in the direction of its opposite. Whitehead's philosophy of organism is touched at every point by the influence of modern science and the distinctive realistic and empirical temper of Western philosophy. Yet he could write that it "seems to approximate more to some strains of Indian, or Chinese, thought, than to western Asiatic, or European, thought."[13] And it is not without significance that one of the most important early expositions of his philosophy is that by an Indian, Ras-Vihary Das, in *The Philosophy of Whitehead*.[14] Whitehead's speculations at times sound like those of one in the grand tradition of Indian Idealism. "I certainly think," he wrote, "that the universe is running down. It means that our epoch illustrates one special type of order. For example, this absurdly limited number of three dimensions of space is a sign that you have got something characteristic of a special order.... All the effects to be derived from our existing type of order are passing away into trivialities. That does not mean that there are not some other types of order of which you and I have not the faintest notion, unless perchance they are to be found in our highest mentality and are unperceived by us in their true relevance to the future. The universe is laying the foundation of a new type, where our present theories of order will appear as trivial.... This is the only possible doctrine of a universe always driving on to novelty."[15]

On the other side, philosophers of modern India have begun to incorporate the naturalistic, realistic, and vitalistic emphases of recent Western thought.[16] Men like Sri Aurobindo and S. K. Maitra have assimilated and transformed the Western notion of evolution, and in some ways are in advance of Westerners in their grasp of the spiritual implications of evolution. The "dynamic idealism" of Sri S. Radhakrishnan, the richly integral approach and the bold cosmic scope of Sri Aurobindo, and the delicately differentiated lacework of K. C. Bhattacharyya's idealism, represent syntheses of Western and Eastern tendencies which, like Whitehead's in the West, are tentative models from whose spirit all subsequent philosophers, aiming at a world

12. Alfred North Whitehead, *Modes of Thought*. New York: Macmillan, 1938, p. 237.
13. *Process and Reality*. New York: Macmillan, 1929, p. 11.
14. London: James Clarke, 1938.
15. *Essays in Science and Philosophy*. New York: Philosophical Library, 1947, pp. 118–119.
16. See D. M. Datta, *The Chief Currents of Contemporary Philosophy*. Calcutta: University of Calcutta, 1950, Appendix, "The Contribution of Modern Indian Philosophy to World Philosophy."

philosophy, might learn. For example, Bhattacharyya's realistic relativism (the unique "subjective form" of each Whiteheadian "actual entity" – fundamentally "self-enjoyment"); his absolute or "indefinite" constituting the matrix out of which determinate subjects and objects are precipitated (Whitehead's creativity or concrescent process, together with the primordial principle of concretion which in itself, as the unchanging vision of God, is the negation of all facts, like Bhattacharyya's absolute); his grades of consciousness or stages of perception – inanimate object, body, (psychical) presentation, (spiritual) feeling, introspection, and finally de-individualized absolute freedom – a process paralleling the phases of any organismic concrescence; his definition of freedom as progressive self-transcendence – Whitehead's *causa sui*, or mentality, "lying beyond all determinations;" his conception of metaphysics as the analytic elaboration of what *is*, self-evidently, in pure consciousness – Whitehead's "sheer display"; and his pluralistic view of alternative symbolic systems in religion: all these and other emphases deserve serious attention from those who wish to describe the basic categories of man's experience.

Nor can the world-philosopher of the present or future neglect the important changes now taking place in Chinese philosophy, in which the method of Western science, as mediated through Marxism and Western industrial technology, is now being mated with the humanistic naturalism of centuries past. Fung Yu-lan says the "Taoist philosophy is the only system of mysticism which the world has ever seen which is not fundamentally anti-scientific."[17]

The spirit of the Chinese *Book of Changes*, necessary changes being made, is modern, as the Indians have pointed out that their age-old view of the world of matter as the restless interaction of relatives and the transformation of opposites is now precisely confirmed in physics and biology. Accordingly, the adoption of modern science, both as theory and practice, in the East, cannot come as a mystery to us. Whatever we think of that "science of society," dialectical materialism, its general presuppositions and procedures are by no means incompatible with much of the tradition of the Orient. Joseph Needham says of classical and medieval Chinese thought that it is "in extraordinary congruity with the ideas of dialectical materialism, descended from Leibniz through Hegel," and that it almost restores "to the Chinese people something profoundly their own...."[18] That is why I believe

17. As quoted in Joseph Needham, *Science and Society in Ancient China*, Conway Memorial Lecture. London: Watts, 1947, p. 10.
18. Joseph Needham, reviewing *Chinese Thought from Confucius to Mao Tse-tung*, in *Science and Society*, XVIII, 4 (Fall, 1954), p. 375. See also the Ph. D. dissertation of Shen-Yu Dai, *Mao Tse-tung and Confucianism*. Philadelphia: University of Pennsylvania, 1952. Mao's transformation of the *Tao* of nature into the "fountainhead" of the people may be seen in his *Problems of Art and Literature*. New York: International, 1950. As a

that Northrop in *The Taming of the Nations* is unwarrantedly pessimistic in his denunciation of Chinese Communism as rigidly theoretical. He does not grasp its ancient and modern roots in the lives of the people and the philosophy of the sages. His judgment is theoretical and not concrete, verbal and not empirical, static and not dialectical. In 1945 Ralph Linton wrote:

> . . . the bulk of the world's population still lives under the relatively stable, integrated cultures which have been erected on the basis of the second mutation [food-raising]. . . . Most of these "backward" peoples do not share our own fixation on technological improvement for its own sake. If the pressures which the Western nations are now able to exert are removed, it seems highly probable that these people will profit by our errors, take over the new technology at a slower rate and exercise much greater selectivity. Their aim, conscious or otherwise, will be to adapt the machine to man rather than man to the machine.[19]

Western man is mechanized and specialized to such extremes that whether he be factory worker, financier, general, or analytical philosopher, he cannot tell you the why of life and nature and history or the purposes for which his own superb tools are designed. Far indeed has he wandered from the fertile, sub-tropical centers of life in Near-Asia. His scientific and technological explorations have been multitudinous, and the main technique he knows for coordination is massive power – the monopoly, the bomb, the police state, the loyalty oath. The mysteries of life and of nature are no more; for many a Western man, they are all dissolved in the clear glass of television and the smooth, post-prandial cocktails of new commentators served up for him daily. But the East has stayed closer to the stabilizing forces of life – closer to the land, the plants, the animals, the home, the family, the village. It has maintained the attitude of reverence, and a sense of man's dignity. Consequently, it is less advanced materially, less specialized, less complex, less urbanized, less strong. But that very weakness is its strength, as its sages discerned long ago; its deprivation these many centuries has been a blessing in disguise, while we of the West, having gained the whole world and its basic secrets, so far as non-human nature is concerned, are on the brink of

---

type of organicism Marxism is inherently opposed to the mechanistic presuppositions and class uses of modern Western science; while Marxism is humanistic, it is a deepened humanism set in the context of a unitary history and nature. It is therefore not surprising that a British biologist who is also a Marxist should write: "Have we any duties to plants and inanimate nature beyond preserving them for the delight, instruction, and use of our own species? I do not know the answer to that question, but I suspect it is yes. It is a poor man who does not love his country, which is not the same as loving his countrymen. That is something in addition. If we love it, then I think we have a duty to it". J. B. S. Haldane, *What is Life?* London: Lindsay Drummond, 1949, p. 260.

19. Ralph Linton, "Present World Conditions in Cultural Perspective," in *The Science of Man in the World Crisis*, ed. Ralph Linton. New York: Columbia University, 1945, p. 221.

losing both our bodies and our souls. The East has not learned the policy of "Get Tough," "Operation Killer," "Massive Retaliation," "Positions of Overwhelming Strength." How could it? It has been too weak in power and tender in ambition. It has been forced under historical exigency to manage with meager resources, and so has tended to remain master of its means and ends. The advent of modern technology in the East will test whether its people can keep human values at the center of their life. The development of scientific socialism in the People's Republic of China, in the Democratic People's Republic of Korea, and in the Democratic Republic of Vietnam indicates success in this regard.

We of the West, though increasingly chastened by our own excesses and weary of an obsessive, frenetic adventure in expansive capitalism which ends only in depressions, wars, and mass death, must not forget our unique gift at the new council of the nations. Our ancestors ate of the tree of scientific knowledge and stole the fire of power over nature from the gods. These we may bring – and have brought – to the East and to all mankind. In turn we can exchange them if we are sensible for the natural and human wisdom of our Oriental neighbors. As specialists and analysts, dominated by an individualistic male orientation, we of the West need the unitary, whole-hearted, intuitive, outlook of the East. We need the more slow, stable, social, nature-revering philosophy of Mother India and of the Good Earth of China. We need to repair a divisive process going on in our species since civilization appeared and to recover on a higher level the unity which our species once possessed and enjoyed. This divisive process has its origins in both the evolved biology and the culture of the human species.

For a million years and probably longer, the members of our species roamed over the earth in small bands, the males bonded by their collective hunt for game and fish with crude stone weapons, the females bound to temporary settlements with the children and gathering fruits and berries and roots in the environs. This way of life, developing from the general line of hominids established in the Miocene period, evolved by way of genetic adjustments and basic anatomical changes in the species, such as upright posture, developed legs for running, rotatable forelimb, hand, binocular eyes, recession of the jaw, modern-sized brain, pharyngeal space, and sexual dimorphism. The functional result was the development of language and the communication and cooperation that mark family and social life, both in productive work and in domains freed from the pressures of physical survival – talk, play, art, religion, day-dreaming, and puttering with materials by means of primitive tools.

This way of life with its demand for certain functions among members of the human group evolved a sexual differentiation which is distinctive among anthropoids. In general the males are larger and more mesomorphic

14

than the smaller females. The male physique, with its specialization in larger shoulders, muscles, lungs, and heart, its larger and less breakable bones, its more numerous red blood corpuscles, its higher metabolism, its higher level of blood sugar, and its higher level of testosterone (the aggression-producing hormone), especially at adolescence, is adapted for the exertion of power, agility, and bursts of energy. From birth the male physique appears to be more active and aggressive, matures more slowly, and is less socialized.

In general the female physique is smaller, with greater endomorphy, wider pelvis, permanent breast, and year-round menstrual cycle. The female physique matures more rapidly and at all ages is physically more mature than the male. Physically it is more viable, both *in utero* and throughout life. Its metabolism is slower, and the balance of female sex hormones and male sex hormones which it shares with the male prior to adolescence is not overturned in puberty as it is in the male physique by the great rush of testosterone into the blood stream. The female physique is more highly fetalized than the male: it resembles the child more and accordingly is closer to the general line of human development. From birth it is quicker to respond to physical and emotional stimuli, is more stable emotionally, is more communicative, and is more adaptable to its social and natural environment. Its physique has developed it to adapt to tasks that center around child-bearing, child-rearing, and the interpersonal relations requisite for family and social life.

However, these differentiations of physique should not be taken as absolute and dichotomous. For they are differentiations on a basic ground plan of *human* characteristics, and every individual human being of each sex shares in the common structures and hence functions that characterize the species. The influence of culture, moreover, demonstrates that the functions deriving from these structures can be greatly modified.

When the cooperative life of the dimorphic male and female of the Paleolithic period was replaced by Neolithic agricultural settlements some 8,000 years ago, and was then succeeded by the first large urban civilizations some 5,000 years ago, the primitive communism in production and consumption of the early period was dissipated and displaced by the rise of a system of social organization based on private ownership and private consumption. There is some evidence that in many Neolithic communities, whose outlook was influenced by the association of the female with agricultural activities and by the magic of the maternal or nurturing principle, matriarchy prevailed. With the onset of private property, patriarchy came to be the dominant form of political rule, and this was accentuated as class societies developed and, in the Western world, passed from slavery to feudalism and thence into the various stages of capitalism.

Asia (and Africa), being much less developed along class lines during this same period and therefore being closer to the primitive forms of human relations and attitudes, have remained nearer to the sources of integral human life and community.[20] The Western world, dominated by a male, abstract, Faustian surge of activity, has wandered away from such sources, in the same way that the aggressive male, oriented to conquest in the external world, has been separated from the female oriented to the stabilities of human relations in society and nature and to the continuties of history maintained by nurture of the child and care of the old.

However, the problem of healing our division, of removing the excesses of our differentiations produced by social organization, of getting ourselves together in creative synthesis, is not limited to any one region or sex. Man is now estranged from woman, as West from East; and this enstrangement is expressed in the male, urban, technological differentiation of the West and the female, agrarian feudalism of the East. As institutions make persons and persons in turn make institutions, changes must be made both at the level of personal attitudes and interpersonal relations and at the level of institutional structures. Furthermore, while male and female are physically differentiated, anatomy is not our whole human destiny. We are symbol-creating creatures, and we have the power to direct the actions of our bodies by means of ideas and ideals. The question is whether we can modify (not overcome) within a planetary urban environment the tendencies of dimorphic physiques evolved to deal with a Paleolithic environment.

The male must come home again, acquiring some of the concreteness and life-nurturing interests and skills traditionally centered around women and the home – the care and education of children, the relaxation of talk and game and play, the tending of plants and animals, the domestic arts, the detached and non-possessive enjoyment of nature, the warmth of close primary relations. The male must moderate his anxiety-driven compulsion to "prove" himself in the public arenas of politics, economics, science, technology, and war. The male must regulate his swings of mood, his bursts of furious energy and violence punctuated by spells of indifference, his pride and intransigence in interpersonal and international affairs. He must learn the receptivity, stability, and periodicity native to women and heretofore accented in many Eastern cultures. He must learn the social skills, intuitiveness, empathy, and concern for others developed more by women then by men through history. He must lose his narrow, severe, compulsive, hard, impersonal ways, his mechanical science and his myopic, dehumanizing habits of work acquired in the mills of Mammon.

More endomorphic, more affined to the life-creating and life-preserving powers of nature, more sensitively social, the female in both East and West

20. For an exposition of the sense of unity of the spiritual world and the physical universe among African peoples, see John S. Mbiti, *African Religions and Philosophies*. New York: Praeger, 1969.

must put off her role of conservative conformist to patriarchal patterns, plaything, slave, mere housekeeper and propagator and puppet of soldiers, politicians, and scientists. Depending on her endowment, temperament, and interest, as well as the needs of society, she must emerge, at least in part, out of the home into the tasks and opportunities of the public domain. She must liberate herself from "the idiocy of rural life," the more subtle narotizing of urban and suburban diversionary patterns, and the exploitation of her energies and talents in business and industry. She must be freed from her status as parasite under patriarchal monogamy, assuming her rightful place in the institutions of education, industry, and politics. The female must lose some of her diffuse, easygoing, sentimental, soft attachments – her idolatrous commitment to her little household gods, her ritualized vanities, her madness for fashion, her compliant adaptability to the crowd or the leader. She can usefully learn to incorporate the analytical power, the independence of judgment, the potency and spontaneity heretofore more often the province of the male.[21]

In this process male and female will transform one another, and the strength of each will then reinforce the strength of all. None will cease to be what he or she truly is, but in becoming what he or she can be each person will become more human and more unique. Sex will no longer be a major defining characteristic of the person; the person and his or her contribution to the world-wide community of persons will be the primary category by which people are perceived, known, and judged. Females and males, children and adults, will become *human* beings, equal *as human,* and, as need and ability determine, equally participating in the opportunities and fruits of culture and history. In this process the East will teach the West the lessons of a humanistic past which have not yet been forgotten in the cultural patterns there, while the West will make accessible to the East its scientific knowledge of human nature and nature.

Confirmation for many of these generalizations can be found in a book by Charles Morris, *Varieties of Human Value.*[22] This is an empirical study and statistical analysis of the actual preferences of contemporary college and university students in various parts of the West and East, with special reference to India, China, and the United States. While it is true, as pointed out by Morris in correspondence with the writer, that the present study is grounded in the "wisdom" literature of the past whereas his work measures the values of youth today, still the present reflects the past and partially repeats its deeply laid and slowly changing patterns. Some of Morris' conclusions, which lend credence to the contrasts set forth in this paper are as follows.

21. Margaret Mead, *Male and Female.* New York: William Morrow, 1949, ch. 10.
22. Chicago: University of Chicago, 1956.

The West is more self-centered, the East more society-centered. India ranks considerably higher than the United States in the factor of self-control and social restraint, and China ranks higher than both in receptivity and sympathetic concern. The East is more tolerant of cultural diversity, the West of individual or psychological diversity. In India the constitutional opposition between mesomorphy (roughly, muscularity and skeletal strength) and ectomorphy (fragility and linearity) is not so extreme as in the U. S. A. And in China mesomorphy is associated with an active and energetic way of living which includes receptivity and sympathetic concern. As for women, they show a higher score than do men on the factor of receptivity and sympathetic concern and a lower score on the factor of enjoyment and progress in action.

The new human being will thus unite opposites in creative synthesis. He will be complete because forever unfinished, the orchestral development of many tendencies. His temperament will be a tempering of arctic and tropical extremes and the childlike fusion of male and female elements – a being eternally young but as old as nature's streams and hills, avoiding the excessive differentiations of a rigid and specialized adulthood. The new person will be a father-mother god, a *trimūrti* of masculine, feminine, and neuter, a holy trinity, a creature whose full stature is adumbrated in those representations of Maitreya in India, China, and Japan, in the Mahāyāna Avalokita and his maternal female equivalent, and in many of the Western portraits of Jesus: a being both masculine and feminine in character, universal but concrete and particularized.

And how is this new Jerusalem to be ushered in? That chapter is yet to be written in the plays and works of men and women. As the aim and solution of man's problem is complex, and as the divine according to wisdom both East and West incarnates and fulfills itself in many ways, so the pathways and procedures must be plural and flexible. Men and women must undertake to effect physical, biological, economic, artistic, philosophical, and religious transformations in their whole mode of living if human beings are to become those creative beings which they are fitted to be. To achieve this fulfillment, men cannot ignore their social, natural, and cosmic setting with impunity. Society, history, and nature are holy to us insofar (and that is very far indeed) as they support and advance us. We are what we are, we become what we might, and our goodness endures, so far as what we do accords with the great economy of nature. C. H. Waddington, the British geneticist, has pointed out how nuclear explosions, disturbing the numerous bacteria and viruses necessary to nature's web of life and evolved over some billion or more years into their hard-won and needed niches, might profoundly alter the beneficent balance of nature and hence the evolved stability of man. If as Santayana said piety is man's "reverent attachment to the source of his being and the steadying of his life by that attachment,"[23] then what is required of the man who wishes to be true to his being is that he be true to that being which is his source and stay. What is required is not only justice, love, mercy, humility, and peace among his fellow human beings, but also a "reverence for life" and for the creative and sustaining power that lies below life and leads life on beyond itself – what Nietzsche called the power of self-surpassing.

The intuition into man's unity with nature, his dependence on her, and his required cooperation with her, is a primitive one. The naive man, ancient or modern, thrown back on his elemental resources as he strives to come into commerce with things and forces and to relieve his imperious impulses – such a man, unspoiled by an urban life that isolates him in awareness from the vast motions and orders of nature, can see how his welfare is implicated with the welfare of living and non-living things. Such is the intuition of animism and totemism, man's oldest and deepest religions. Describing the religion of the American Indians John Collier has said:

> The primitive group required of its members intensity, plunged each of them into much of the whole of the social heritage, applied itself to the personality development of every man, and in immemorial ritual transfigured each of its individuals into a partnership with the forces of the universe.[24]

The direction of human nature was thus implicated with the direction of plant and animal life and of inanimate things. Men felt a kinship with the gods: "We shall be one person," said the Pueblos when they prayed. The security that man feels in this kind of relation is difficult to convey to the individualistic "self-made man" of the Western world. The theme of Western civilization is man's ceaseless quest for a garden from which he has been expelled, for a home from which he has been cast out, for a land from which he has been exiled. It is not unnatural that he should in his wandering return to the East; that is where he started, and that has not lost its intuition of wholeness.

Individualism preys on itself; it is self-defeating. In the West individualism has produced the intensest forms of class struggle and war, crime, delinquency, neurosis, psychosis, monopoly, and dictatorship. It is like a wild, cancerous growth that issues only in death, for it has not even the good sense, like most bacteria, to preserve its host or the other conditions of its life. But the Eastern cultures, for all their recent turmoils, have a kind of

23. *The Life of Reason*, Book III, *Reason in Religion*. New York: Charles Scribner's Sond 1905, p. 258.
24. *Indians of the Americas*: *The Long Hope*. New York: New American Library of Worls, Literature, 1947, p. 21.

19

stability and serenity. Why is that? Kluckhohn, the anthropologist, has written that a culture

> where the child's attachments are spread among many relatives and where dependence is focussed upon the group as a whole rather than upon particular individuals, is peculiarly resistant to leaders of the Hitler type.[25]

It is a special Western culture that has formulated and criticized the concept of "authoritarianism." This is an effort on the part of a rational segment of the community to combat the arbitrary and pathic authority of an individual or institution with individual autonomy. But the tendency of Western rationalists is to throw out authority entirely, not making Erich Fromm's distinction between rational and irrational authority.[26] The excess of anti-authoritarianism has called forth the excess that rejects all authority and leads to anarchism. Eastern philosophy, rooted in the "great family" and in a tradition-directed culture, has paid the utmost respect to the authority of the past and of common sense, without always becoming enslaved by it. "Authority," say two scholars of Indian philosophy, "forms the basis of philosophy"; and reasoning follows the lead either of ordinary experience or authority or both.[27] This gives a stability to analysis and speculation which is impossible to a philosophy whose context is social fragmentation and rampant individualism.

We have already observed how Chinese culture and thought developed from the root metaphor of man's harmony with his fellow man and with the land. Similarly, classical Indian philosophy is rooted in the doctrine of *ahimsā*. An adequate world-view must surely incorporate something akin to this deep natural piety; for man cannot become himself unless his environment is properly secured. And he cannot violate that environment as he pleases; he has grown up out of it and with it; it is fit for him and responsive to his purposes – within the limits *it* sets. Man may for a time deplete or erode the soil, denude the forests, pollute the streams, kill the wildlife, make numerous species extinct, spread atomic radiation, and even poison his own food with insecticides and herbicides. But what he sows he will at last reap; his *karma* will accumulate destructively. To live, and live creatively, therefore, man must deepen his sense of the holiness of nature. This is what Western man can learn from the East.

At the same time, this dim and diffuse sense of identity with nature and her living creatures must be informed and directed. *Ahimsā* must be retained

25. *Mirror for Man.* New York: McGraw-Hill, 1949, p. 217.
26. *Man for Himself.* New York: Rinehart, 1947, pp. 8–12.
27. Satischandra Chatterjee and Dhirendramohan Datta, *An Introduction to Indian Philosophy*, 4th ed. Calcutta: University of Calcutta, 1950, p. 8.

as a basic attitude, but must be qualified by the demands of history, of the whole life-process, and of nature's economy. Of the three phyla or basic types of animals living on the planet today which constitute the great bulk of the million extant species, man's main enemies are to be found, not among the Mollusca, which are aquatic, nor among his own phylum, the Chordata, but among the Arthropoda and in particular, a few groups of insects which destroy man's food supply and spread disease. The proper control or elimination of these pests would not alter the beneficent balance of nature and would remove untold human suffering. The Jaina and Hindu practice of *ahiṁsā* was aimed at respect for life and the equality of souls; but destruction or incapacitation of the *Anopheles* mosquito, malarial parasites, the lice transmitting typhus, flies transmitting sleeping sickness, the dysentery amoeba, etc. would have prevented a few single-celled (or small) units of life from destroying millions of organisms themselves having each a hundred million million cells. From the point of view of sheer increase or abundance of life-energy – "the most nearly universal phenomenon of evolution," according to George Gaylord Simpson – such a decision can be justified. "A balance" of the other criteria advanced for progress in evolution "warrants the conclusion that man is, on the whole but not in every single respect, the pinnacle so far of evolutionary progress."[28] While *ahiṁsā* incorporates the truth that every unit of living substance (whether called "soul" or "matter") has the right to life and fulfillment unfettered – the doctrine contains an inherent contradiction, for it makes no distinction between the variations in intrinsic and extrinsic worth of living things. The absolute idealism of Hinduism seems to be a better defense of an unqualified *ahiṁsā* than is Jainism; for since, under classical Vedānta, there exist no distinctions in reality, we ought not to invent discriminations in our ethical choices: the ultimate demand is the demand of the World-Soul for being throughout the length and breadth of its endless run of appearances on the world's stages.

Evolved as an advanced mammal in the last million years, man as a species has achieved strategic dominance over his environment, so that the course of the evolution of life on the planet now lies largely in his hands. The pre-eminent question is whether man will use his power destructively or constructively. Since 1600 man has destroyed more than 125 distinct species of birds and mammals and nearly 100 subspecies, races, or varieties.[29] He has destroyed most of the members of his own species through war, oppressed labor, slavery, poverty, and other forms of exploitation. What is the way of constructive action? Eastern cultures have retained a sense of man's unalienated unity with nature and his fellow man; but they have tended toward simplicity, passivity, and stagnation. While Western men have been more

28. *The Meaning of Evolution*. New Haven: Yale University, 1950, p. 262.
29. These are the figures of the Smithsonian Institution, Washington, D. C.

active toward society and nature, controlling it by science and technology and raising human life to more abundant and complex levels, they have also generated profound alienations between man and man and man and nature. The pathway of man's fulfillment is to take the best of East and West and combine them for the welfare of all men. That means that men must cooprate to use their knowledge and power to create conditions for their fulfillment both now and in the long run. Most generally stated, those conditions are those relations between man and man and man and the rest of nature which are mutually reinforcing, since individual man survives and develops optimally only in such relations. For such survival and development, man requires the security and freedom of creative interaction with others, as well as relations with a natural environment of water, food, air, and esthetic quality and order which sustain man's body and generate health and joy. Such relations of man with other men and nature are not static and given; they are dynamic. They involve men and the living and non-living things of nature in continuous exchange and evolving ecological unity. When men began to domesticate plants and animals some 8,000 years ago and then eventually entered into urban living and genuine history, they became controllers of the evolution of spirit and life and matter on this planet. But control does not mean total control, total knowledge, total value, or total being. Man as species and individual came out of a planetary and cosmic environment, and he profoundly depends on it for life and development. Therefore man's short-sighted indulgence, domination, and mystical withdrawal spell his suffering and destruction. But his path of fulfillment is his striving with his fellow men to create an order of man-to-man and man-to-nature mutuality which will differentiate and integrate men, both as persons and as a species, and will do so in the single world of his natural environment. So far as our best knowledge now informs us, democracy and socialism define such man relations; science and art are the ways of his apprehending nature; and a naturalized, creative humanity indicates the direction of his fulfillment.

Chapter II

THE NATURAL AND HUMAN ROOTS OF POPULAR RELIGIONS

A naturalist might ask, "What is more natural than for religion to have roots? And what kind of roots might it have, other than natural and human ones?" For, to a naturalist, everything has its own natural history, including the doctrine of supernaturalism. Yet in the minds of some people, and in the thought of many theologians, religion has come to be linked with a supernaturalistic orientation. And while man's religious quest may have its origins, according to that view, in nature, as man's body does, it has its consummation in heaven, which is the proper aim and home of man's spirit.

The major theme which I wish to develop here is the idea that the popular religions of man's history not only have their roots in natural processes but also have their flowering, fertilization, fruition, and perpetuation there; and, no less important, that in the symbols and stories, myths and rituals of those popular cults, the natural origins and ends of man's religious life are recognized and celebrated. In short, the popular religions are implicitly naturalistic in outlook.

This claim is not new, and perhaps it is not startling. But if one studies the great theologians of all religious traditions one gains quite the opposite impression; for most theology is predominantly supernaturalistic in emphasis. One must qualify that generalization, as we shall see, especially in the case of India (which has been mainly Idealistic) and of China (which has leaned toward naturalism). Nevertheless, I think it is fair to say that Plato's bold figure in the *Timaeus* (90a) – man is a "plant whose roots are in heaven" – epitomizes the tone and temper of much theology, although Plato's implicit supernaturalism is not really developed until Plotinus and the Neo-Platonists.

Hegel, more recently, has expressed a stream-lined version of the view that nature is the working out of the transcendent Absolute Idea. And it is significant that Marx, who voiced the new Titanic commitment of the modern proletariat, instinctively recognized his antagonist in Hegel, and sought to "turn him upside down." Marx was a latter-day Prometheus, who strove to bring the fire of heaven back to earth and to man, where it originated.

Yet the distinction between the popular orientation and the theological one, between naturalism and supernaturalism, is, like most distinctions (as between Hegel and Marx), not in fact a hard and fast one. And antagonism is always a unity of opposites, so that certain elements of each antagonist may be found in both. Moreover, as Charles Hartshorne[1] has pointed out, traditional theology had discerned one side of the divine nature – its absolute, eternal, infinite, necessary, potential, abstract, static aspects – but its mistake has been the failure to see that these aspects are *included* in that side of the divine nature which is temporal, finite, contingent, actual, concrete, and dynamic. The growing realization of this mistake, which has come with the advance of science and democracy, can be found not only in some modern Western theologies (from James through Whitehead) but also in those of the East (as in Aurobindo).

What I propose to do here is to disentangle these two opposites, to sharpen the contrast between them, and to indicate something of their natural origins. My main emphasis is on the natural and human origins of popular religion, and its naturalistic outlook. I shall be suggestive rather than exhaustive, and shall consider in turn the development of religious ideals in the West, in India, and in China.

I.

The course of the development of the divine idea in Western culture, as elsewhere, has been a contradictory one. It is like a counterpoint of bass and treble themes. Many theologians, in the rarefied atmosphere of cloister and academy, have sung with falsetto delicacy of that Platonic heaven of which all temporal things are but passing shadows, and of that Neo-Platonic One of which all multiple, mutable, and mortal things are the putrid excrescences. Such an intellectual distinction between Creator and creation, the One and the many, God and the world, though it may have begun as a simple, single impulse of religion, was destined in the end to issue in a dualism that would divide soul from body and the divine from the natural. It dissociated mind from body, philosophy from matter, and the cerebral religion of the few from the somatic and visceral religion of the many.

At the same time, theologians found themselves echoing willy-nilly the deep and abiding strains of the common religious life and thought. For the early Christians, as for the early Jews, the distinction and separation between God and His creatures did not exist. Jewish symbolism and thought are crudely realistic, materialistic, and practical. Yahweh dwells in specific places – and He *is* the specific powers of spiritual and material deliverance. He is, as Santayana has put it, the brute powers of matter: indiscriminate, blind, potent, terrible, and tender. Particular objects are pregnant with this divine power, and as no distinction is made between the character of Yahweh and His consequences, so none is made between cause and effect or between

---

1. *The Divine Relativity.* New Haven: Yale University, 1948. *Reality as Social Process* Glencoe: Free Press, 1953.

24

symbol and reality: the idol *is* the god, and the blood *is* the soul or the essence of life. Thus all souls are tethered into a bundle of life, and are bound into a living, dynamic solidarity with the life of God. Such union and mutuality is the law of life and history.[2]

The great Jewish prophets built upon the democracy indigeneous in the tight-knit Bedouin tribes of wandering Israel, and their insights were sharpened by class conflict and persecution. Amos and Isaiah, Micah and Hosea and Jeremiah, refined the notion of man's obligation to man and to the whole process of human history as Yahweh works in it to create, judge, and redeem. And so the later Jewish theologians, and certain Christian and Moslem thinkers, could not avoid being affected by this powerful strain of materialistic mutuality among men. They indeed, following the prophets, refined and translated its meaning for men who had advanced from the primitive stage of pre-history and food-gathering and totemism, through the stage of agriculture, and finally to the stage of urban civilization. But the specializations of an urban economy issued in a priestly theology severed from its original popular and natural roots.

Yet the deeper theme of Judaic materialism and primitive sociality persisted and gathered accretions as it rolled on through the centuries. It got reinforced by Ionian hylozoism, Heraclitean materialism, the pantheism of the mystery cults, and the unitary organicism and universalism of the Stoics, all of which influenced the complicated polyphony of the Church's thought structure. The theme persisted, for it reflected something basic to the life of the people; and its basic structure had been preserved and cherished in that most earthy and least celestial of books, the Bible.

Here is a book whose heroes and villains have not only become household words but whose characters and plots have acquired a concreteness that often seems more real and commanding than the lives of its readers, or that lends to the reader, who dreams and suffers as they, an enhanced glory. For the Bible itself had its roots and its rise in the soil of Israel – soil tear-stained, sweat-stained, blood-stained, stained with the memories of a thousand years. The Bible is a child of Adam, red as the clay from which God molded him, and whose name he bears, sprung from the loins of mothering nature. It is a biotic book, the book of life and death and transfiguration, of man's goings out and his comings in, of his rising and descendings. A book of deeds, daring and death-defying, heinous and holy. A book of fastings, scourgings, soul-searchings, wanderings, separations, reunions. A book of wormwood and gall, of milk and honey, of intrigue and peace, of outer storm and sweet solitude, of high precipices and burning sands. It is a book of bodies, and of the animating powers of bodies striving, bodies footsore and weary, bodies anointed with oil, bodies joyfully mounting up

2. Stanley Cook, *An Introduction to the Bible*. Harmondsworth: Penguin, 1945.

on wings like eagles; of bodies born of a woman, bodies of sin and death, bodies broken and bodies resurrected, bodies wizened and wise, bodies from ashes and back to ashes, bodies bound up in the bundle of the life of God. Man sees in this book a giant parable magnifying his own life, beginning with the genesis of things from the waters of the void, proceeding through wars, exiles, prophecies, judgments, and dooms, through dream and visions, poems and gnomic sayings, promises, persecutions, defeats, crucifixions, resurrections, redemptions, and revelations. The Bible speaks to men because it speaks from men; it cries from the depths and extremities of man's existential predicament, deep calling unto deep; it appeals to men eternally so far as it recounts, colors, and makes meaningful the recurrent, eternal conditions of men. As in the great epics of the East, the Bible of the West makes philosophy incarnate. The age-old themes of man, of life and death, of chance and fate, of time and eternity, are woven into events as a living pattern is woven into the strands of a tapestry or rug. The Bible was brewed in the ferment of human passion, in the chemistry of hope and fear; it resounds with the neighs and the moans of battle, and smells of the odor of corpses and the fragrance of babes, and echoes with the cries of the damned and saved, the haunted and blessed. It is forged in the fires of tyrants and superstitions as the sparks of hardship fly upward; it is bathed in the salt seas of despair, and borne aloft on the clouds of hope. It is a book of beginnings, and endings, and new beginnings, without end.

Even Paul, that complex tangle of strands, maligned and misunderstood because he takes into his texture all the chief hues and patterns, threads and knots of his time, even Paul cannot avoid articulating this philosophy of creative flux, this doctrine of decay out of growth and growth forever out of decay, undecayingly. Paul could not, any more than the early formulators of the creed, put aside the primacy of the body. He was a Jew, sensing in his own flesh and bones his kinship with all the children of Abraham, and finding in the mystery cults this natural identity confirmed. And to him the resurrection of the body is real and necessary. Thus, Paul argues, as the bodies of nature assume diverse forms, so with our own bodies at resurrection. And being resurrected by the transforming power of Christ's Spirit, our bodies then compose in communion that new body or new creation, the body of Christ. Martin Luther, a man of peasant stock, of solid biological faith, of direct and earthy impulses, abounding in Brueghel-like warmth and vitality, instinctively rejected the abstractions of the philosophers and instinctively responded to this teaching of Paul's. He pictured God as the sower and man as the seed.[3] And as the seed must perish in order to acquire new

3. Arthur C. Cochrane, "The Resurrection Body", in *Crossroads*, V, 4 (July-September, 1955), pp. 33–35. As to the material roots of early Christianity, see Archibald Robertson, *The Origins of Christianity*. New York: International, 1954.

life, so do our bodies perish to acquire the new bodies or garments given by God. "We shall all be changed": such was the conviction of Jesus and Paul and John, and it was rooted in the observation of how natural bodies, through the necessitous transition of death, are transmuted into new forms. Only an autistic type of thought which has turned away from the sweetness and putrefaction of organic efflorescence and decay could pervert this teaching of natural transformation into the doctrine of a supernatural, unchanging, final, immortal state of the soul, completely divorced from the world of present experience.

The viewpoint of Christianity is continuous with that of Judaism, and to grasp the naturalism of Christianity we must grasp it in its Judaic roots, that is, in the Bible. In the Jewish Biblical view, while God is prior to and transcendent over the world, he is also immanent in it and continuous with it. He sustains it. Thus in the account of the authors of P (Genesis 1: 1–2: 4a) God creates the primal light and divides it from the darkness, the firmament and the waters and the dry land, the sun and moon and stars, all living creatures, and at last man after his own image – "male and female he created them." And at every stage "God saw that it was good" – everything that he creates bears the stamp of his character. Human beings are created needing one another, bodies disposed to seek out one another, to work with one another, to enjoy one another. In turn human beings are charged with dominion over living creatures, on which they must rely for food, as the beasts of the field and the birds of the air require green plants for their food. Here we have sketched the rudiments of an ecological whole, a natural economy whose integrity is regulated by the workings of laws imposed by God, the creator and sustainer of the universe.

This ecological picture is more explicit in Psalm 104, an older account of creation. Here, God is portrayed as covering himself "with light as with a garment," providing waters for the beasts, homes for the birds in the trees, rain for the mountains, grass for the cattle, plants for man to cultivate, mountains for the goats, rocks for the badgers, and labor for man: "in wisdom hast thou made them all." There is a sense of the fitness of the environment for each kind of creature, a wide design of fulfillment: "the earth is satifised with the fruit of thy work." In the majestic lines of Job 38 this picture of felicitous harmony is supplanted by an image of sublime and overmastering power within and above nature, a voice out of the whirlwind:

> Where were you when I laid the foundation of the earth?
> ...when the morning stars sang together,
> and all the sons of Good shouted for joy?
>
> Have the gates of death been revealed to you,
> or have you seen the gates of deep darkness?

27

> Can you bind the chains of the Pleiades,
> or loose the cords of Orion?

Here is expressed a primitive and sure feeling of the powers of nature which antedate man's coming and transcend his powers to understand or command. Nature is a divulgence of God's wisdom and omnipotence – sometimes benign, sometimes destructive. The lines about the mystery and bound-up power of the sea tell of the massive insurgencies toward chaos in the universe – a theme evoked once more in our own day with such moving force in Melville's biblical *Moby Dick*. The poem conveys the counsel that it is man's place not to question and inquire but to accept in awe and wonder. And man must bow in meekness before that mighty cosmic working.

Jewish seers and prophets of the Bible usually combined these two features of nature, the known and the unknown, the evident justice and the unapproachable power, in one being. Nature and nature's God were perceived as both mild and terrible. As social life developed, they conceived of man's moral law as a translation of natural law, or as a species or example of that law: as the rain falls on the just and the unjust, so man is enjoined by Jesus to love both friend and enemy. In the voices of the prophets we hear both warning and hope rising out of discernment of how these laws of God will work: warning that if man violates the law of righteousness, he will be punished, and hope that if he is obedient to the law, or repentant about his disobedience, he will be rewarded. Although the prophets were not uniformly correct in this discernment, their conviction in the existence of objective moral laws, grounded in the nature of things, was a great advance over the previous stage of arbitrary social custom and royal caprice. In the midst of the clash of new urban life, its class divisions, and its alienations with the old tribal solidarity, they strove to forge a new meaning for human living. The result was nationalism mixed with internationalism, and naturalism mixed ambiguously with the notion of a benevolent, purposeful, supernatural king.

The Jewish view of the animals of nature manifests a similar ambiguity. Domestic animals supplied a direct and advantageous tie for man to the rest of nature. For a long period the Jews were a pastoral people, and the sheep, goat, ox, camel, and ass figured prominently in their relations to nature and in their feelings of companionship. As they, like anyone who takes care of animals, found analogues for human qualities and relations there, projecting their own humanized perceptions and taking animals into the circle of their own humanized world, so their concept of society and the cosmos was shaped by these relations of domestication. Not only did the animals represent wealth; they were visible evidence of the original richness of nature, which could be tamed and nurtured and put to human uses, which offered man a link to God's creation, and which prompted the P authors of Genesis to say that God had given man dominion "over every living thing that moves upon the earth." Most households owned one or more animals, were housed in the second floor above them, and considered them a part of the family. Each spring it was customary for the family to buy two lambs, one for Passover celebration and other for a pet for the children. Thus in the Jewish Bible the shepherd-sheep relation became a recurrent and root metaphor for man's interpretation of the world. Yahweh is the patriarchal shepherd of the flock, and the Messiah, the suffering servant, is the innocent sacrificial lamb brought to the slaughter. (Isaiah 53:7) Fatherly protectiveness, motherly succor, and infantile trust became some of the major Jewish virtues, suggested and reinforced by this domestic way of life.

At the same time man's home is set within wild nature, with its wild animals, and the line between the safety and order this home and the danger and disorder of destructive nature is not clear-cut. Hence arises the ambiguity in the attitude toward nature and toward God as the author of nature. While the guileless lamb is symbolic of man's helplessness and child-like loyalty, the wild animals that threaten the flock – the lion and the wolf – symbolize the terror and malignant aspects of nature. Yahweh creates and sustains but he also maims and destroys. As man lives within these two homes in nature, the one set within the other, so he finds within himself two spirits at war with one another, the harmonious, life-nurturing forces and the disruptive, annihilating forces. He has within himself the civilizing dispositions of domestic life and the brute forces of his animality. During the protracted crises of the Iron Age, this inner conflict assumed the form of a clash between the humanizing forces of the people and the ruthlessness of empires coupled with the greed of new commercial classes. In the thought of the prophets the humanized features of God – justice, compassion, forgiveness, nurturing care – were increasingly emphasized, while the Lord of revenge and ruination, though remaining as a contradictory element in response to the contradicting social scene, declined. In Jesus this humanized view reached a new height, rejecting the "eye for an eye" philosophy, and it signified that the polarization of the underlying forces, progressive and reactionary, had reached a qualitatively new stage. Social revolutions were breaking out.

Thought about nature always reveals thought about man, for man is the thinker and leaves the mark of his own "subjectivity" in his "objectivity." Thus we can trace Jewish thought about man through its thought about nature and in particular its animal symbolism. There is the eagle of intrepid strength, the dove of trembling gentleness. The wild lion is frequently portrayed as a roaring, menacing, malefic beast. Yet Daniel's God is represented as delivering him from a whole den of lions – a pacifying influence prevailing over the evil powers of imperious nature and imperial man (Darius). Isaiah delineates the foredoomed devastation of Israel; like Shakespeare, in violent images, he conveys the destruction of men through the destruction of nature, and vice versa, so that it cannot be told where one begins and the other ends. Then he concludes his stormy story with an idyl of peace among wild creatures, including, by way of shocking contrast, a small child among the once ferocious beasts. "The wolf," he says, "shall dwell with the lamb," the leopard with the kid, the calf with the lion, the cow with the bear –" and a little child shall lead them" – the weakest and tenderest one of humanity bringing into order the violent impulses of nature in both human and animal worlds. This is a new and powerful statement not only of the potentialities of man, of the conceivable triumph of man's tender social dispositions over the wreckage of a cruel and bloody age, but also of the sway of a new order of life, kind and gentle, over both human nature and wild nature, that is, over the whole planet. This universalism of a compassionate community among all sentient creatures was duplicated in Buddhism and Taoism. All were groping toward a unity of man with nature that had been broken. For them the concord among animals in nature symbolizes and participates in the restored community among men.

Such ideal concord had been pictured as early as the 14th century B. C. in a painting on the palace chair in the tomb of Tutenkhamon. There, in life-like forms and colors, a scene shows loving affection between husband and wife, blessed by the benign rays of the sun. In yet another painting the king Akhnaton and his wife Nofretete play affectionately with their children while the rays of the sun god reach down like generous arms to fondle and feed the earth's creatures. Indeed, Akhnaton's "Hymn to the Sun" – echoed by St. Francis – appears to have been the prototype for Psalm 104, at least in structure, many centuries later. In reacting against the alienations of city life, these Egyptians and Jews rediscovered the sources of their health simultaneously in the concordant arrangements of nature and the sensitive exchanges of family life.

The Jewish family metaphor for cosmic life was carried still farther in the thought of Jesus. A psalmist (Psalms 23) depicts God as a shepherd who gives guidance and comfort but is nonetheless somewhat impersonal, though Isaiah speaks of God as feeding his flock like a shepherd who gathers the lambs in his arms and carries them in his bosom. "Fear not, little flock," Jesus says assuringly, "for it is your Father's good pleasure to give you the kingdom." (Luke 12:32) God for him is his solicitous shepherd who, having a hundred sheep, leaves the ninety-nine to seek out the one who is lost until he finds it. (Luke 15: 3–7) Jesus speaks of himself as "the good shepherd" who lays down his life for his sheep." (John 10: 11) And John the Baptist hails him as "the lamb of God, who takes away the sin of the world." (John: 1: 29) The lamb, like the child, becomes the symbol of absolute but vulnerable trust. Jesus is viewed as both the protective shepherd and the sacrificial lamb, as both the strong father and the defenseless child. In many of his parables he discloses the relations of separation and reconciliation within such family relations. The parable of the prodigal son, for example, reveals in stark outline the relations between the concerned father, the obedient son, and the alienated son who wanders to a distant city, squandering his inheritance and degenerating to the level of the pigs. This story signifies the precise feelings of the alienated and later restored son as well as the feelings of the forgiving, rejoicing father when the son returns. It is evidence that Jesus felt the pull of the heartstrings on both sides of the parent-child relation. It has been argued in a recent book that Jesus was married. Perhaps he was also a parent. In any case, the prime lessons of Jesus' teaching lie in these stories of person-to-person relations and of our duties within them. Aside from the insurrectionary movement which he led, his call to men to set aside selfishness, wealth, exploitation, ostentation and hypocrisy, and the limited loyalties of family, class, and nation, constituted in itself a revolution. It was a revolution in orientation, replacing the inauthentic, impersonal, reified relations of urban men with genuine I-Thou relations and with mutual aid. At times Jesus took as his model for this "heaven" the unworried life of the birds and animals. Comparing them to his own despised and rejected life, he observed that "foxes have holes and birds of the air have nests." (Luke 9: 58) God does not forget even the fallen sparrows, he thought, and God feeds the carefree ravens, who "neither sow nor reap." (Luke 12) In the same way God clothes the grass and adorns the untoiling lilies. (Matthew 6) There is a deep and touching faith here in the sufficient if not bounteous goodness of God in nature – a sufficiency and harmony which is described in Psalms 104 (with which Jesus was no doubt familiar) but from which men have departed. Those men of the wicked city of destruction excoriated by Jesus were primarily the plutocrats who devoured widows' houses, the hypocritical Pharisees, the literal lawyers, and other vultures who had gathered around the roosts of the parasitic ruling class. But in the ideal good society none will lord it over another; each will be a servant to all others. (Matthew 20: 25–28) In the kingdom of heaven it is not tyrants, soldiers, rich men, or priests who will be the queen bees in the hive of human activity. Rather, it will be the children who will be center of human concern. And this concern for the young and needy will extend to the living creatures of nature, all of whom are God's creatures. As the bird protects her little ones, and as the heavenly father takes care of his brood, so man will shelter the little children in the shadow of his wings.

Although Islam is an extreme instance of conceiving of the divine as the wholly Other, independent of space and time and history, still Allāh reveals his will through a concrete historical man who has never been deified, who possessed no supernatural powers, and who founded no special priesthood. Mohammed is viewed as a prophet to whom Allāh speaks as he speaks to all prophets. But historically he was accepted in large numbers in Arabia because his proclamation of one God, of the unity of God's followers, and of a new ethics of social relations articulated and guided a widespread need for social and national unity. At the time of Mohammed Arabia was a hodge-podge of disparate, superstitious, and sometimes battling tribes – some controlled by governments in turn dependent on external powers such as Abyssinia, Persia, and Byzantium; some ruled locally; some wandering about and keeping alive ancestral traditions; some who were Jews. Not only were the people tired of conflict between clans, tribes, and factions in cities like Mecca; they were suffering from an economic crisis. Arabian commerce in spice was undermined by the re-opening of a rival route through the Red Sea. A new commercial class sought to break out of this.

However, before that class adopted Mohammed's religion to suit their own purposes, Mohammed's promises of material profit and luxurious paradise to the devotees of Allāh attracted Bedouin tribesmen and brought about the conquest of the old commercial and religious center, Mecca. Mohammed's code of conduct anticipated a super-tribal, national, and even international order. He was born into a community of fertility gods and goddesses, of animism and polytheism, of jinn and Satan, of drinking and gambling, of the burial alive of small girls, of religious quarrels and wars among clans and tribes. His monotheism, which he learned from Jews and Christians, provided a general order for that chaos. And his ethics in *The Koran* (II, 172) spelled it out in human relations:

> Righteousness is not that ye turn your faces towards the east, or the west, but righteousness is, one who believes in God, and the last day, and the angels, and the Book, and the prophets, and who gives wealth for His love to kindred, and orphans, and the poor, and the son of the road, and beggars, and those in captivity; and who is steadfast in prayer, and gives alms....

Like their counterparts in 16th century Germany in relation to the Christianity of Luther, the new commercial classes of Mecca and other regions in Arabia found this new ideology exactly suited to their desires. After the death of Mohammed in 632, the Moslem armies launched a series of spectacular invasions which, after a century, resulted in their domination of an area stretching from southern Gaul, Spain, and northern Africa in the west, through parts of Italy, Greece, Byzantium, and Persia, to the Indus River and the border of China beyond Samarkand. Such were the natural roots of this particular religion.

The Moslem notion of the divine as an implacable Oriental despot, immovable and irresistible in his will, and undeterrable in his adamantine decisions about man's destiny, seems too harsh and high for mortal man. But its function was political and patriarchal. As the re-enacting of the old Roman *imperium*, as Toynbee observes, it helped to bring order to an anarchic Arabia and to empires in decay. Moreover, it was softened and humanized by the idea of a succession of prophets, by the camaraderie of arms, by the sensitive mystics of Islam, and by Near Eastern sensuousness, which touched not only the heavenly dream but also the life of the cult. An Arab warrior was promised four-fifths of all the booty he could capture. Thus a committed believer in the war againt the infidel could be assured of material pleasures either in this life or in the life to come or in both.

Although every major religion has strayed from the course which its founder charted, there are often revolts against orthodoxy which strive to recover the original roots in man. In its early years Islam was a martial religion, but subsequently Moslem thought underwent many modifications, from the Mu'tazilites and Sufis to the communist, revolutionary Qarmatians. The history of Christianity has been replete with such heretical movements. Christian Protestantism was an effort to re-assert the human, communal roots of the tradition. It was a recrudescence of natural religion – a mixed peasant-artisan-bourgeois protest against the effete etherealization of a religion practiced by idle feudal lords and predatory prelates. Protestantism, says George Santayana, is "full of rudimentary virtues", boasting of a depth and purity which belong to "any formless and primordial substance": "it keeps unsullied that antecedent integrity which is at the bottom of every living thing and at its core."[4] It is a religion of rebellion and romance, fit for enterprise, empire, and frontier, hungering with an overwhelming obsession for the salt bread and heady wine of life, and thirsting deeply, down to its bones, for the everlasting rivers of water hid in the springs of nature. It is the religion of undistorted impulse wherein it prides itself; and it discerns instinctively that to trust the surface forms of thought and institution – in short, anything but the depths and dim directions of its own drives, intuitions, and sense of steadfast communion with others – is to betray the God within. Protestantism is the sense of totemic affinity of man and man and man and nature, lifted to the level of the insurgent peasantry and the new bourgeoisie of Northern Europe.

II

The unspent dynamic and not-to-be denied urgency of the popular dionysian cults is a neglected fact in the history of philosophy and in the history

4. *The Life of Reason*, Book III, *Reason in Religion*. New York: Charles Schribner's Sons, 1905, p. 115.

of ideas generally. Philosophers themselves have in fact deliberately turned away from sitting "at the feet of the familiar" and drawing their wisdom from the town pump. This has been true in India no less than in the West. Yet the cultural existence of such cults, and the universal facts of human experience which through ceremony and symbol they brought to the fore of man's attention, forced itself upon thinkers and inevitably colored their thought. Those cults have persisted as stubborn and inexpungeable data against which star-gazing and heaven-pondering philosophers might eventually stub their clay feet, or with whose elementary impulses and limited earthly aims they might perchance feel a sense of kinship in themselves. Those cults have been the repositories of our ancient past, our recurrent present, our ever-living future; they preserve the form and color of our basic biological propensities, transmuted into the life of ritual and symbol; they stretch back into the mists of Neolithic time, and out to embrace all men, indeed, all creatures, who live and die on this earth. They represent the vivid and reverent rendering of the vital rhythms of living, which no embodied soul can escape and no philosopher, impelled by comprehensiveness, can ignore. As the gross tropisms and emotions of the body form the basis and frame for all subtler dispositions, like imaginations and dreams, so these cults as the collective unconscious have formed the background of all speculation, willy-nilly; and precisely because they have been so popular and have appealed to the ordinary, the common, the deep, the massive, the mysterious, and the universal in men and women, they have been forgotten or laid aside in analysis as human, all too human, and natural, all too natural.

But whoever hopes to see history as a whole can no more neglect these primal, omnipresent, democratizing forces (filling like warm blood-wine the throats of the god-drinkers) than a physiologist can leave out of account the heart and lungs and bowels of a man. Man is, in his heart of hearts, as the early Hindus tell us, appetite for power, for Universal Power; he seeks to enact the divine drama of creation through destruction, the transformation of dying and rising, the suffering of sacrificial love wherein, by losing himself in the agony of mystical bliss, he brings forth his nature anew. Heinrich Zimmer has explained that this direct and undiluted impulse of bodily abandonment and rebirth has been preserved in India in the "expanding form" of their art – "a stupendous dionysian affirmation of the dynamism of the phenomenal spectacle" – and in the dominant Tāntric (not Vedic) strain of the centuries-old rites of the Indian people.[5] The astuteness of Brāhmanism has been to appropriate, re-present, and sublimate this subtle dialectic of opposites in life and nature; and while "tropical India has adopted the sub-

5. Heinrich Zimmer, *Philosophies of India*, ed. Joseph Campbell. Bollingen Series XXVI. New York: Pantheon, 1951, pp. 598, 602.

lime way of sterilization, the way supremely represented in the teaching of the Buddha and in Śaṅkara's Vedānta... always the power and wisdom of the erotic-paradoxical monism of life – and of the Brāhman understanding – has again successfully reasserted its force."[6]

In the yearning for union with the opposite sex; in that "inalienable delight" of the "Bliss-Self", which persists even through agony; in rejoicing over painful tension; in the peculiar ecstasy that lives within but transcends the gladness and sorrow, want and satiety, and all the other opposites of the soul's high seas and sailing weather – that low calm lamp in the pilothouse that abides through the wrench and rinse of waves and the dark winds racking the sea; in the frenzied dancing feet of sheer unfettered joy, their symbols flung sky-high like syllables kicked free from toes, or airy bubbles, starry bells, that spell no sense save eloquence that grows and grows to some great spell winding us in its melody and shaming that pale shadowy grim and grammatical most unfantastical philosophy; and in the revelation of the divine in the sinful, the dialectic of love's degradation, celebrated in the sacrament of the five forbidden things; and in the Tāntric-Brāhman assertion that "One is both at once"; and in the desireless desire, the ashless fire of the *Gītā*; and in the feeling that all energies or *śakti* are undivided, that all things belong to one holy family, and that in the yea-saying union of sex, man and woman as equals epitomize and substantiate the universal "compassionate void"; and in the intuition that the void (*śūnya*) in all creatures is their wisdom, that their compassion by which they negate their natures is also their fulfillment and enlightenment, and that in the solid-liquid, immutable-mutable, waning-remaining, plain-perplexing love-play of sex (the Mahāyāna "great delight"), with all its tingling of mingling and demurring of fury, lovers perceive and recover their aboriginal identity and, as if to seal and sanctify that eternal restoration, create the eternal child – in such symbols and images, techniques and rites, thoughts and theories, Mother India has nurtured her children for centuries. The many-dimensioned but single-minded doctrine of the *Gītā* – a cosmic tree of multiple fruits – or the "completing opposites of a Perfect-Whole" of Vīra-Śaivism,[7] summarize the sentiment.

All of this melody-making with the notes of nature, this mystical harmony of differences and dissonances, makes inevitably for a democratic mold and direction: equality of the sexes, of caste and class, of old and young, of priest and prayed-for, of teacher and student, of gods and men. It includes the liberty of all natures to be transmuted into the divine, lifted from one afflatus to another; fraternity for freak and phoenix, for friend and foe, without exception; universal and infinite compassion. We are all in the same

6. *Ibid.*, p. 600.
7. Shree Kumaraswamiji, "Vīra-Śaivaism", in S. Radhakrishnan, ed., *History of Philosophy: Eastern and Western*. London: George Allen and Unwin, 1952, p. 395.

boat, the big vessel of Mahāyāna, aboard the globule, the stream-lined rain-drop dissolving into the vast unknowing cloud of Being; or in the figure of a scholar, "in spite of vestigial remains of the archaic snobbism of caste, native Indian life is shot through with the radiance of a realization of universal divinity."[8]

In the beginning was the deed – and the feeling – and the thought was an afterthought. So it is with societies, as with individuals. And so it is that prolific, polyglot, paradoxical India is dyed in deeper inks than we have imagined. The non-Aryan tradition there, which antedates the clear-eyed Vedic philosophy and disappears to us in the darkness of antiquity, is unmistakably rooted in the rhythms and rounds of nature, and imparts to the mature Indian outlook that respect for the dialectic of opposites which is expressed in the cosmic dance of Śiva, the combined violence and compassion of his consort Kālī, the spontaneous sport of *māyā*, the creative clash of the Sāṁkhya *guṇas*, the divine interaction of *śakti* and male, the Tibetan meaning of the Yab-Yum embrace, and the Mother Goddess of popular Hinduism.[9] Both the early Dravidian and Indus Valley civilizations, with the directness and naiveté of the primitive mind, take nature seriously, as well as man's involvement in nature's processes. The notions of *karma* and of reincarnation are intuitions springing immediately from the soil of nature's comings and goings, rising and passings away, waxings and wanings: every agrarian culture very soon learns the iron law that links sowing and reaping and the law that joins in endless and universal cycle the facts of birth, growth, death, and transformation into new life. Motion in space: this is the primal fact of our experience. And the value of experience is its creativity, for itself and for what it produces.

In contrast, the Vedic texts speak of the ascension of the soul into a happier world, and not the return of the soul into new bodily form in the natural

8. *Philosophies of India*, p. 602. While Zimmer regards the Aryan society as patriarchal, in contrast to the matrilinear culture of the Pre-Aryan, Dravidian India, he believes that the Vedic outlook, which gradually dominated the native religion, was fundamentally monistic, while the latter, which gave rise to the Jaina and Sāṁkhya philosophies with their "isolation-integration" ideal, was dualistic. What he fails to make explicit is (1) that Tantra, as pointed out by his editor (p. 62) and by Zimmer himself (p. 569) is rooted in pre-Aryan soil and that both Śiva and Yoga are non-Vedic and probably pre-Aryan; and (2) that the Aryan orientation, being, as he points out, objective, political, aristrocratic, and hierarchical – in contrast to the mystical democracy of Tantrism – has inherent in it the principles of dualism an authoritarianism. India has not suffered as much as the West from the dominance of a priesthood – in part because the control of property remained mainly in secular hands (the Buddhists disappeared because of economic competition, and the brahmins degenerated into illiterate priests in isolated villages); in part because India was tolerant in matters of belief; and in part because many Indians were convinced of the inherent unity of man with the divine, the universality of justice (dharma), and the possibility each man's realizing divinity on his own. On the Buddhists and brahmins, see D. D. Kosambi, *Ancient India*. New York: Pantheon, 1965.
9. *Ibid.*, passim.

realm.[10] The non-Aryans were more simple and concrete in their worship and their religious thought. Their gods are living and warm, with the scent of love and war in their nostrils: they sweat and swear, work and play, and wonder about the world's reaches and origins; they court and commit indiscretions; they love and hate, plot and fight, suffer and enjoy and die, and, with unconfinable fervor, return to act out old roles in new masks. Far, far away dwell the abstract deities of their more sophisticated conquerors. For them Śiva the destroyer and Viṣṇu the preserver are everyday powers who can be felt in the towering terrors and benign numinous nurturings of nature. Viṣṇu inhabits the bodies of fish, tortoise, bear, and lion. Rāma and Kṛṣṇa, Durgā and Kālī, are the personal distillations of the monumental divine ranges and misty motions of nature; they dwell in the hearts of the people as mythic archetypes, mirroring to the beholder the answer to his prayer and fulfillment of his dream and the warding off of his fears. They are beloved babies, victorious youths, heroic supermen, compassionate parents, supremely wise men – confidantes and ideal embodiments, who appear in infinite metamorphoses and with (as Joseph Campbell says) a thousand faces, transformed to fit the needs of their believers, always available and responsive. They have animal bodies, bodies of mouse and elephant, and in such bodies they bear the burdens of this world, and show forth in their own limited niche of activity a fair prefigurement of the life to come.

The universe of Mahāyāna, with divine companions to man in his quest for salvation, furnishes a whole array of radiant saviors for the faithful; like Avalokiteśvara, they serve every generation without wearying, walking by the sides of those in trouble and giving strength to the faint-hearted. It is hard to tell just how much of this living lore is traceable in India directly to pre-Aryan influences; but the spirit is the same. The phallus, and even more the symbols of the Mother Goddess, are the products of this early religion; it gave the Divine Female to Hinduism. How else shall we explain the deeply material strain in the Cārvākas, the atomists, the Sāṁkhya, and the lost sources of the *Kāmāsūtra*, except to say that it was mothered and at least fostered by this early tradition with its matrix deep-laid in nature? Even Vedānta could not escape it, for perhaps as early as the Upaniṣads this classical viewpoint adopted and idealized the creative dialectic of nature. The position accorded animals, birds, trees, and the multitude of living and non-living forms in the non-Vedic civilization reveals its animistic, maternal tendencies. Animals and birds are not only the signs, they are the living vehicles of the gods. While the Vedic gods are averse or temperamentally indifferent to incarnations – being objective they cannot change or suffer or

10. See C. K. Raja, "Pre-Vedic Elements in Indian Thought", in *History of Philosophy: Eastern and Western*, p. 38.

die – the indigeneous gods and goddesses of pre-Aryan India find it second nature to incarnate themselves in animal form and thereby assume the mantle of heroes and heroines in humanity's battles. Gods become men, and men may become gods, or even transcend the gods. The matriarchy of that early Indian culture implicitly permits all men and women to struggle equally for salvation; it lends the helping hand of nature, but is also commissions each to walk alone. Whereas the patriarchal Aryan religion, though it is, at least in the later stages, monistic, subjugates man to the rigid laws of an esoteric pantheon, a divine court veiled in mystery and majesty; man's salvation must be ritualistic and propitiatory, and man must throw himself upon the mercy of what is alien and unknown to him. Man must scorn and escape nature in the large because fundamentally he must scorn and escape his own human nature; he is dependent on the gods because he is discontinuous with them. Moreover, he must be a male, and a member of the upper class. But in the democratic maternalism of early India,[11] man can become god or goddess or both in embrace precisely because he is sprung from Mother Nature, breathes her very breath and embodies in his flesh and blood her own heartbeat and independent tendon of strength. Who else shall save Nature, if not herself incarnated in her own sons and daughters? And since early Indian philosophy is pro-human only through the method and medium of environing nature, it is capable of being trans-human and of aiming, like the Nietzschean rocket, at breaking the gravitational barrier that limits man to being the provincial, earth-bound, unreconstructed creature that he is. But an autocratic philosophy can never be trans-human, for it can never in the first instance be pro-human.

The reason for this is that autocracy always springs from a dissociated and divided self; its gods and their inflexible laws are products of the superego, projected and inscribed with relentless zeal upon the scrolls of the cosmos. Supernaturalism is this attitude writ large; it is an attempt to control the passionate and spontaneous realm of nature, with all its vagaries and unforeseeable effervescences, through the imposition of a law foreign to that realm, and grounded in a "higher" principle. If the vitalities of raw nature be not pressed down and directed in an orderly mold, how then should personality or society fare? Indeed, life would be one grand excess after another, a Mardi Gras without end, mad and unmitigated, an incessant holiday and

11. Heinrich Zimmer in *Philosophies of India* holds that the philosophy of the Vedas-Brāhmanas-Upaniṣads supplies the monism of India. At the same time he acknowledges that the cult of the Mother Goddess, revived in the Tantric movement, was "rooted in the Neolithic past" but "overshadowed for a period of about a thousand years by the male divinities of the patriarchal Aryan pantheon." (p. 569) The monism of India appears to be deeper and richer than the theology of the Aryans. The "isolation-integration" ideal of the dualistic philosophies is probably an urban deviation from this pre-Aryan, primitive, naturalistic monism, with which the Aryan viewpoint later become fused.

carnival without accounting. Man would splurge and splurge, splash and splatter, until he split life and limb, head and heart, yea, the whole world into multitudinous pieces. But there is another attitude, nuzzling close to the body of nature, not so thoroughly nihilistic about man and his fellow creatures, with their needs for enthusiastic expansion and throbbing dilation. In this view the gods are no gray detectives, etherealized deputies guarding the bounds of the unconscious. The gods are rather denizens of that very domain which is despised as evil, impulsive, appetitive, and violent by those abstract guardians of morals and civilization. The gods and goddesses live and move in that dark and bloody deep of joy and sorrow; they strive alongside the whole company of humanity, and like us cry out of those depths, deliverers seeking themselves to be delivered; they lead us through those illumined ranges and darkened dales, in and out and round about in pilgrimage unresting, threading through the world like Theseus in the labyrinth, lights unto our paths and lamps unto our feet. And because like everyman they go with us and become our guides in our most constant need and because they share in our travails and failures and triumphs, we trust them and lean upon their staffs and, when death comes, sink back into their everlasting arms.

Man's itinerary moves through a strange terrain; he picks his way, as it were, through a dim Platonian cave, or through a drama the dénouement of which is uncertain and which is a shifting phantasmagoria of shadows, half-shadows, and half-lights; he is caught up within that wheel of birth and death, the wheel of the *Tao*, forever changing from day to night and back again. There is in that world no player and game, no god and creation, no deity from on high discontinuous with earth and disdaining to mix with her. The gods, as the Upaniṣads pictured them, are all in the game together; their transcendence is a heightened immanence; their virtues of courage, wisdom, and love are superlatives and not perfections. Like their fellow-wayfarers each god carries a torch

> That lights the pathway but one step ahead
> Across a void of mystery and dread.

And when a man-god goes like a comet across the night, and his momentous flash illumines the whole firmament, the whole race is lifted up by the vision: "the people that walked in darkness have seen a great light."

Every large and living religious movement in history has been motivated by this imagery, and has implicitly rejected the autocratic figure of an imperial universe centering in a divine throne, high and lifted up, which radiates its largess to the rabble at the periphery. The gods live and die and are reborn deep in the hearts and heavy-laden works of men; they thrive and overthrow wickedness in high places side by side with mortals; they are incarnate wise warriors in the thick of the battle; they feel in their arteries the waves of emotion that ride with tidal force through men of love and hate, swelling every minute capillary with the magic potion of mortal passion, flooding the organs with the vital liquid for fight, or love, or flight. Man is thus filled with the transfused holy spirit of the gods, and as a flooded river seems then to contain its former banks, so the devotee, raised to a new life by the overflowing inebriation of a god within, becomes a god who appears for the time in the form of a man. So the gods are products of our dark veiled biologies, Titans of time with its foam and mist, heroes swaddled from birth in the mysteries of the Nile, hidden for life in the legend of some epiphany, still concealed in death in some hauntingly irresistible tale of resurrection. What is the Gordian knot? It is that umbilicus that ties our gods to us and that we ourselves, like the Indian squaw in the wilderness, must sever with the keen green edge of detachment. And the gods rise from the wombs of darkness like light from the prison of darkness, like Sol Invictus from the monstrous pit. They are the tongues of fire, that laugh into the future. They are not bolts from the blue, but rather partings, initiations, pushes from below; buds and embryos; expansive, expendable atoms and stars; leading and openings, as George Fox called them.

Men who distrust the divinities in the sacristies of their unconscious distrust themselves, and must people the heavens with the cramped penal forms and ordinances of their own little private, provincial lawbooks. It is comforting for timid men to have a celestial magistrate who has a judgment for every human decision, and to impute a special and indiscernible solution which perpetually puzzles mankind. But a faith in nature and in man's nature and in the creative impulse which prevails there – the demiurge, as the Greeks named it – supplies no specific answer to the mysteries of living, since man is progressively passing from one mystery to its resolution and then to a new mystery in the ceaseless round of creation. The Tāntric tradition in India, which is today the most popular there and in the Orient generally,[12] and which antedates the Vedas, expresses this naturalistic faith, and does so not so much in abstruse philosophical systems as in the qualitatively alive and prolific art of India. It is a faith that is not content with the easy, logical acceptance of the tabus; it strives to conquer the forbidden regions of the divine by exploration, conquest, and absorption[13] of those regions; it aims to deal with the polarities of life, not by detachment but by wholehearted participation; it understands that it can find joy only in suffering, divine knowledge only in the deep benighted energy of creation, unity only in the play of opposites, and holiness only in tabu.

12. Heinrich Zimmer, *Myths and Symbols in Indian Art and Civilization*. Bollingen Series VI. New York: Pantheon, 1947, p. 96.
13. Heinrich Zimmer, *Philosophies of India*, p. 579.

In ancient China, natural piety, involving a sense of man's identity with the universe, appears native to that early historical culture from which emerges our first authentic records. This naturalism, which has continued in China for millennia, and which as Northrop points out, quoting Woodroffe and Coomaraswamy,[14] is distinctive of the Orient, seems, in China, to have been paced in a slower tempo and a less intense mood than India. It was grounded in an unbroken qualitative sense of man's union with nature and of his reciprocal relation with her. Like the Hebrews, who placed man in a legal but living covenant-relation with the ultimate, the Chinese conceived of man as a companion or co-worker in the great tasks and regulations of nature. This sense of reciprocity of course evolved, as man's sense of reciprocity to man – Confucius' "man-to-manness" – evolved. In primitive times man's felt dependency on nature and the specific powers and spirits of nature was dominant: he sought to relate himself aright to the gods of the mountains, streams, clouds, rain, wind, thunder, soil, and crops: and later he concerned himself with the various guiding genii of the family, the state, and other social organizations. He discerned pervading these beneficent and evil powers of nature an over-all cosmic order at first located in the sky (*T'ien, Shang Ti*) and later called the order of the will of heaven. Progressively, *T'ien* dominated religious thought and worship in ancient China, a trend that perhaps parallels and reinforces the progressive unification of an agrarian culture under the pastoral, autocratic, Mongol emperors.

But the order of heaven never fully superseded earth and her gods any more than the male force of *yang* supplanted the female power of *yin*. Indeed, heaven, as the impersonal, universal, moral order which harmonizes and regulates nature, was thought of as somehow inhering in the operations of nature, ideally symbolizing, as some have suggested, the functions of the earthly emperor, and imparting to its local agencies a kind of imperial pattern and morale. And though the notion of a supernatural heaven, with its rewards and punishments, its blessings and terrors, and its susceptibility to human blandishment and violation, became increasingly vivid and effective in popular Chinese religion, it was on the philosophical side assimilated to nature. Hence for Mencius, to know human nature is to know nature and in turn to know heaven; for Hsün-tzu, heaven, earth, and man form a unity; the Confucianist Appendices of the *Book of Changes* adopted the *Tao* and identified it with the movement of *yang* and *yin*; and finally, for the Neo-Confucianists, the will of heaven became equivalent to the *Tao*, the Great

14. F. S. C. Northrop, *The Meeting of East and West*. New York: Macmillan, 1946, pp. 373–374.

Ultimate, the indeterminate *logos* or the *li* of nature.[15] Needham argues that the Chinese "law" of nature, far from being an edict passed down by a divine law-giver, is a "dynamic pattern" or organismic principle which is immanent in the activities of things and processes, and in whose indeterminate matrix all events participate and behave according to the particular internal necessities of their own natures and the general necessities of nature at large.[16] He quotes passages from philosophical writings to show that the sage-king, following the will of heaven, is to "rule" the people in the same gentle, non-directive, but persuasive way that Heaven with its *wu-wei* (do-nothing attitude) exercises sway over nature.

This philosophical assimilation and organicism has not been without its effects upon the popular mind. While it has not produced a perfectly coherent monism among the masses (where indeed can such coherence be found anywhere?) the average person in China, up until recent years, has been able to embrace Mahāyāna Buddhism, Taoist magic, and Confucian humanism and ancestor-worship without any sense of dualism or contradiction. Seemingly incompatible elements seem to be reconciled by an underlying naturalism – a unitary orientation that accepts what comes as an indivisible part of the regularities and imperatives of the good earth and the good sky interacting in productive cooperation.

> From the dawn of China's primitive folk religion, the relationship between man and nature has been conceived as a deep, reciprocal involvement in which each can affect the other.... No boundaries may be drawn between the supernatural world, the domain of nature, and that of man.... characteristically Chinese, this attitude toward nature pervades all of China's poetry, art and religion, and underlies the thinking of its great sages whose philosophy is dominated by the notion of Heaven and man in partnership.[17]

The assimilation of heaven to earth in a unity of opposites is a victory of the concrete over the sheer abstract, of the many over the few, of the agrarian over the pastoral. It is the same kind of interaction and fertilization – between speculative, monistic philosophy and dionysian dependence on nature – to which Zimmer attributes the rich character of popular Hinduism. The original clash in China was a clash between agrarian and pastoral cultures: "Historically, the gods of this class, guardians of regions and localities, genii

15. See Wing-tsit Chan, "Syntheses in Chinese Metaphysics", in *Essays in East-West Philosophy*, ed. Charles A. Moore. Honolulu: University of Hawaii, 1951.
16. Joseph Needham, *Human Law and the Laws of Nature in China and the West*. London: Oxford University, 1951.
17. "Religion in the Land of Confucius", *Life*, XXXVIII, 14 (April 4, 1955), p. 69. See also E. R. Hughes and K. Hughes, *Religion in China*. London: Hutchinson's University Library, 1950, p. 15.

of fertility, belong to the land and its agricultural civilization, while Heaven and the manes are elements of the older religion of the nomadic Mongols."[18] But this clash enriched Chinese culture.

The history of Chinese thought is the history of the active enmity, merging, and mutual transformation of these two tendencies. As in the symbolism of the popular religion, so in the ideologies of the emperors and intellectuals the conflict was never fully resolved: while as early as the Shang dynasty patriarchy won out over matriarchy,[19] and while since the origin of the Empire in the Chin dynasty the principle of paternalism has prevailed from the highest to the lowest social organization, certain feminine traits have persisted – intuitiveness, sensitivity, gentleness, compassion, delicacy, calmness, softness, lightness, balance, a sense of unity and equality[20] – and have shown themselves unmistakably in Chinese philosophy, painting, literature, poetry, sculpture, ceramics, and the episodic social reforms. Thus Chinese culture has waxed and waned, alternating between the harsh rigidities of autocracy, which produced enormities like the foot-binding of women and the inhuman landlordism of recent times, and the mellower, more leisurely, and democratic cultures like the Han and Tang. The natives of the Yellow River valley have from time to time through history conquered and assimilated the nomads from the northwest, and have thus succeeded to some degree in reducing the workings of an imperial heaven to a natural order. Taoism as a philosophy and even in some respects as a religion has implicitly championed a universal democracy; it has been mystical, unitary, equalitarian, anarchical. And when Tao-sheng, the Chinese Buddhist of the 5th century, who was influenced by Taoism, taught that every sentient creature possesses the divine nature – not excluding skeptics and infidels, carps and cockroaches – he was, though rejected by his own colleagues as heretical and revolutionary, pursuing to its topmost branches the traditional tree of Chinese wisdom. He represented the agrarian and grass-roots cultural force in China which has continued, unbroken but at times submerged, in China to this day, and is now being contacted and extended by the Communists. Confucianism, on the other hand, represents the other wing – the urban, differentiated, hierarchical principle of paternal rule; and though it has been inevitably

18. G. F. Moore, *History of Religions*, vol. I. New York: Charles Scribner's Sons, 1941, p. 27.
19. Joseph Needham, *Science and Civilisation in China.*, vol. I. Cambridge: Cambridge University, 1954, p. 85.
20. In what way if any are these traits correlated with the paedomorphic or infantile features of adult Mongoloids – smooth brows, button nose, epicanthic eyefolds, protuberant eyeballs, and hairlessness? Perhaps in none. But at first glance the Chinese appear to have excelled in the development of the psychological traits mentioned. If that is so, the problem is to explain why. For paedormorphic features in the Chinese, see Weston La Barre, *The Human Animal*. Chicago: University of Chicago, 1955, pp. 151–155.

modified through the centuries by the levelling influence of Taoism, it has been in practice a philosophy of determinate relations, of status, of fixed social forms, of unconditional filial piety, of feudalism and imperialism, and of aristocratic and military dictatorship which culminated in the regime of Chiang Kai-shek. Yet the very fact that philosophically classical Confucianism has been transformed into something very different through the course of the centuries indicates that even it could not escape the Taoistic transformation of all things.

The religious orientation of Japan, affiliated with China, has taken a similar but a unique turn. Japan's Buddhism has happily conjoined the cosmic magnanimity of India with the sensitivity toward nature expressed among the Chinese. The result is a peculiar feeling of identity and tenderness toward all living as well as non-sentient things. This feeling of reverent excitement toward things and persons, suffusing and uniting all subordinate sensitivities, is perhaps a generalized and enriched version of what the Westerner feels in romantic and parental love. It originated in China, where Taoism naturalized Buddhism; became intensified in Zen; and then passed on into Japan. There, in Mahāyāna, the supreme Buddhahood always manages to find a "skillful means" (upaya) by which it may incarnate itself in a variety of forms to save all; for the Bosatu has a never-to-be-extinguished desire to save all his fellow-beings and an "infinite compassion" for all his fellow-creatures. This is the doctrine of panentheism taken seriously and personalized. It expresses itself in the Japanese rite of kuyō, in which an offering of homage, reverence, and love is made to persons, dead objects, instruments, insects singing in the field, brushes discarded by painters, needles used by housewives, broken dolls, captured animals, uprooted weeds, or anything whatsoever.[21]

While Western man may reject what seems to be an indiscriminate sympathy toward nature on the part of the Easterner, he might profit from the religious principle implicit in it; for his emphasis on individuation threatens to issue not only in atomic but also in personal and social fission. Individuation springs from a ground of unity, and rightly issues in a greater unity, elaborated and vivified. The creative process, which generates and increases good, necessarily means, in principle, a cosmic democracy; for, ideally, all things are possible, and, practically, whatever has been actualized has some possibility of betterment. Each event is the inheritor of past good and the means for future good; it belongs to itself, in the inviolable present, but it also belongs to the future for appropriation and use, as its past belonged in it. It may realize its own good, but it may also contribute its share of vivid and

21. Daisetz Teitaro Suzuki, *Japanese Buddhism*. Board of Tourist Industry, Japanese Government Railways, 1938, p. 173.

meaningful experience – its feeling, thought, aspiration, labor, and sacrifice – to the experiences of others and the totality of cosmic creation. Every one of the Many is a member and in a sense an epitome of the One; it is also a means for its fellow members and for the One, the Creativity of the universe that is pervasive, inclusive, and integrative. Each contributes to the increase of good by actualizing in its own experience of value and by forming the means for the fulfillment of other's experiences. Thus each man must not only revere himself; he must revere all things, insofar as that means appreciating the possibilities for good in every event and situation, and endeavoring to mold the conditions or materials of creation for greater creation.

Chapter III

THE MEETING OF EAST AND WEST
IN PHILOSOPHICAL METHOD

E. A. Burtt's article, "What Can Western Philosophy Learn From India?",[1] brings into focus one of the main differences between Eastern and Western philosophy. That difference has to do with how man may adequately know and describe his world. Burtt does this by illuminating some of the limitations in Western logic in the light of the Indian approach to the problems of descriptive knowledge. Thus there is posed the double problem – the differences between East and West in this regard, as well as their reconciliation. The result is suggestive, and I would like to pursue some of the implications arising out of Burtt's article.

Since our theory of knowledge about the world depends on our theory of the world, I shall consider (1) the nature of the world, as differently conceived in East and West, (2) some of the logical principles that should govern our knowledge of, or reasoning about, that world, as they have been or might be interpreted by the Eastern and Western world views, and (3) the contrasts between Eastern and Western thought, with (4) a final summary and suggestion for their reconciliation.

I.

Burtt points out that Western philosophy has, with the exception of speculative philosophy, patterned its procedures, aims, and norms after the model of science. It has proceeded by a strict delimitation of its domain of inquiry, by rigorous definition of its terms and assumptions, by the unqualified application of rules of logical consistency, and by an unflinching and complete analysis of the topic before it. It has been distinguished by its work in the criticism of abstractions, in logic and epistemology, in the analysis of language, and in linking its task with the foundations and techniques of mathematics and the sciences. It has been dominated by a substance-attribute view of the world, by a symbolism which with its subject-predicate form reflects that view, and, in recent times, by the doctrine of clear and distinct ideas. The norms regulating its activity, as in science, have been clarity, definiteness, precision, rigor, coherence, elegance, and the like. Logic has become a powerful tool in the West – sometimes, as Burtt indicates, more

1. *Philosophy East and West*, vol. V, no. 3 (October, 1955), pp. 195–210.

powerful in demolishing the arguments of one's opponent and in eliminating generally fuzzy conceptions and invalid reasonings, than in advancing positive truth about traditional philosophical questions.

Accordingly, "the world" for Western philosophers of this kind, so far as they have turned their attention to it, has been conceived as a world that justifies such procedures and norms, both as the ground on which they are constructed and the terminus by which they are used and tested. What kind of a world must that be? A world of discrete, atomic entities – autonomous, isolable, self-identical. A world of distinctions and relations which can themselves be clarified and ordered in the conscious symbolic systems of man's mind. A world of impressions which can be reflected. A world of matter and of mind, of fact and of reason which thinks about fact, of an ordered world and a mental activity which orders its thoughts after that world.

And what about the East? Philosophy there, as Burtt indicates, has taken its rise from another starting point. The philosopher in India is concerned to achieve liberation, integration, fulfillment; and the philosopher in China desires to become a sage, merged with the wisdom of the universe. In both countries, therefore, philosophy becomes a means; exact analysis of limited problems and the rigorous application of logic to certain concepts are never for Easterners the goal of philosophy. Rather, the goal of philosophy is the goal of human living itself, and philosophy is employed as an instrument to facilitate human fulfillment.

This conception of philosophy – "involving new and intriguing possibilities for philosophic thought," as Burtt says – constitutes a contrast to the Western conception, in both procedures and norms. Since in the East men as philosophical have been concerned with more than a logical mastery of certain selected entities and problems, they have turned their attention to the broad aspects, the pervasive wholes, the abiding concretions, the recurrent issues of human experience. The result is the uncovering of complexities and relations which subtend the world of clear and distinct entities and which, in their qualitative richness, stretch away from and elude our perceptual as well as our conceptual grasp and make that first world seem, as Whitehead has said, like a world of abstractions. While the philosophical man must not discard reason, he must recognize that it is effective and valid only within a limited range of experience and that it must be supplemented by other methods which reveal other aspects of experience – by authority, by scripture, by art, and by intuition. A primary philosophical norm is comprehensiveness, or comprehension, to be achieved by subtle sensitivity to the various sources of truth. This norm is itself a species of a generic norm, namely, integration – or, as it is usually expressed, integration with the ultimate principle of reality and value in the universe.

We may characterize these two world-views by listing some of the distinctive entities or attributes emphasized in each:

clear and distinct	vague and undifferentiated
determinate	indeterminate
absolute	relative
space	time
abstract	concrescent
matter	value

What these entities or attributes represent are polar and complementary aspects required together for a more complete world view that either East or West has alone provided. The column of words on the East refers to the world as concrete becoming. It is the world in process, in the making, involving not only the fullness of that process in all its manyness, complexity, and incompatibility, but also the vast realm of possibilities, with its truths and its untruths, its goods and its evils, its diverse data presented to process here and now. This indeed is the world of the East, with its multifarious bazaars and altars and peoples, and with the numberless artistic and metaphysical systems of its fecund imagination. The world symbolized on the West is the world as abstracted from the world of immediate and concrete process. Indeterminate possibilities become, through the process of concrescence, determinate, and these determinations exhibit certain clear and distinct characteristics. They are now achievements, not processes or possibilities, with their distinct identities and differences and relations; and their natures and relations can be etched in the timeless and chaste space of logic, with its strict rules of inclusion and exclusion, and its rigorous orders, ruling out incompatibilities and enthroning pure reason to reign supreme.

While there are many differences to be found among Oriental thinkers, there is a strong consensus on the following points: nature consists in energetic activities or continuous changes; the processes of nature maintain their identity and change relative to other processes and to the whole; nature is marked by difference, opposition, strife, and destruction among the processes composing nature; at the same time these processes are interdependent and organic to the whole; the differentiated processes of nature evolve and are transformed; creation and destruction occur together; the present universe, like all things in it, has come into being and will pass away; the existential world and any process in it in its full concreteness of structure and quality displays an indefinite number of aspects – and, as a consequence, our perceptions and symbolic accounts of natural processes must always be relative and limited and can never, as abstract, fully exhaust that concreteness.

But the logic of the West finds itself more adapted to, and more effective in, another world – or in another dimension of that single world of human experience of which East and West represent hemispheres and perspectives. The logic of the West is most effectively able to deal with that part of the world which is achieved and finished. That is the world of specific objects, precipitated out of the vast realm of potentiality and the onrushing processes of historical becoming: a world of finalities and not of evolution, a world of accomplished matter of fact and not of aspiration and indeterminate aim, a world of space and of definite objects occupying that space and not of time which like Chronos spawns its Titanic creatures of strife. It is a world of peace and compatibility – a world in which "there shall be no more sea." In the worlds of K. C. Bhattacharyya, it is the world of definiteness, arising out of the background of indefiniteness. In Northrop's language, it is the determinate and discontinuous emerging out of the undifferentiated esthetic continuum. It is the world of completion and, in its own way, perfection – the world as finished, worn out, fulfilled. What began as a process and project has now become subject and object for new process – providing data for fresh feeling or fresh thought. The dynamic event has become a "thing." And each thing is what it is (Whitehead's category of "objective identity")[2]; it is distinctively itself, for all realization is finite; it is nothing else. There is no amalgamating or mixing or "confusing" of entities (Whitehead's "objective diversity")[3]. This is the field of autonomous entities, spread out in space and displaying certain unchanging relations to one another – a field of entities abstracted from movement, change, and time, stripped of their historical evolutions and transformations. It is the world of the "specious" present, because, as with a single unmoving picture in a movie film, time is arrested and rendered irrelevant. In that world, therefore, the principles of identity, non-contradiction, and excluded middle rule without exception.

Let us now turn to a consideration of the modes of thought and the linguistic expressions that have been devised to fit, respectively, these two conceptions or perspectives of the world. Following Burtt's example, we shall examine the so-called "laws" of thought as stated in Western logic and the scope of subject matter to which they apply, and, similarly, the modes of thought of Eastern thought and the range of subject matter to which they apply.

The "law of identity" states that $S \supset S$; or $S \equiv S$. With respect to existence, this means that if S, a subject, exists, then S exists; or the existence of S is the existence of S and is not the existence of non-S. ("p", for "property" or "predicate", could be substituted for S.) For symbols, the law of identity stipulates that terms and propositions shall have "fixed" meanings – i.e., a

2. *Process and Reality,* New York: Macmillan, 1929, p. 39.
3. *Ibid.*

proposition with the subject of S or a term signifying a property p shall mean respectively S and p and nothing else. And if such a proposition is true, it is true; if a term signifies a property p, it signifies that property p. Fixed meanings, necessary to valid reasoning and communication, in turn necessitate a fixed subject matter (S's and p's) if there are to be reasoning and communication.

The important thing to note about the law of identity (as well as the other laws of thought) is that it is presupposed in all our thinking[4] that purports to be reasonable. Reasoning – in the deductive sense stressed in Western logic – involves essentially the process of substitution of symbols; and while we may faithfully follow the rules of substitution our conclusions will be untrustworthy with respect to their empirical signification unless by a given symbol we consistently mean the same thing throughout the course of the argument. Shifts in meaning lead to fallacies. But fixity of meaning requires a fixed subject matter. That is to say, logic applies to the world, but it applies to those aspects of the world that are fixed.

Burtt points out that Hindu and Buddhist logic respect the principle that S is S ($S \supset S$) but believe that it does not express the complete truth about S. From one point of view S is S: for not only is a given entity or property distinctively itself and nothing else, but as the Neo-Realists have argued any given perspective of S presents us with a reality distinct from those other "S's" presented in other perspectives. From this point of view the Western position can be sustained.

But, ask the Hindu and the Buddhist, may not S imply more than S – i.e., is it not true that $S \supset -S$? While we may accept the fact, the reasoning goes, that S is S, must this proposition exclude the assertion that the existence of S implies (necessitates, is accompanied by) the existence of what is not S? Empirically, it is plain enough that the existence of S at any given fixed moment necessitates the existence of S ($S \supset S$). But it need not follow empirically that S is the only existent that is necessitated by the existence of S, as is implied when $S \supset S$ is rendered as $S \equiv S$. S may necessitate things other than S; indeed, so far as we find empirically that an individual requires its environment, stretching out indefinitely in space and backwards in time, it requires its universe. Atman is Brahman (the Self is the non-Self); or as Whitehead has said, "Everything is everywhere."[5] In this sense S may be said to necessitate non-S; or, S is $-S$, where "is" does not mean "identical with" in the sense of complete identity with no differences, but does mean "identical with" in the sense of "participate in." This latter meaning provides for the relation of part-whole and for diversity in unity.

4. Morris R. Cohen and Ernest Nagel, *An Introduction to Logic and Scientific Method.* New York: Harcourt, Brace, 1934, p. 182.
5. *Science and the Modern World.* New York: Macmillan, 1926, p. 133.

The question is how S can be participant in $-S$ and still remain S, i.e., retain its identity. The logic of the West precludes the participation of a given subject in its opposite, just as it precludes the valid derivation of something negative (a false conclusion) from something positive (a set of true premises). The principle of identity in the calculus of classes states that S is included in S $(S < S)$ where "S" represents a class. This entails that $S = S$ and that S is not included in non-S (otherwise, a contradiction). Thus the logical product of both S and $-S$ is nothing or a null class $(S-S = 0)$ and the sum of S and $-S$ is the universe of discourse $(S+-S = 1)$. S cannot participate in $-S$ because S is a class, a set of ideal properties, an abstraction, a form, and forms are governed by the principles of identity, non-contradiction, and excluded middle. But if S is considered as a concrete individual then it can participate in what is not itself, because as a prehension or process it is continuously affecting and being affected and thereby is continuously changing into something other than what it now is or has been. Thus, on the side of its general, self-identical form, S retains its identity; on the side of its particular process, it participates in $-S$.

Western logic may reply that when we say S is S we mean that if it is true that a given subject has a certain property (S is p) then it is false that it does not have that property (S is $-p$). If it is answered that S may display p under certain conditions or to a certain observer and $-p$ to another observer under other conditions, then the reply is that what is meant is that S is p only under specified conditions at a specified place and a specified time to a specified kind of observer. But this simply asserts that S is p if S is p, i.e., *if* the specified conditions, etc., are met. It means that one perspective excludes another which is its opposite: it means that the three laws of identity, non-contradiction, and excluded middle apply to single perspectives. What Oriental logic endeavors to do is (1) to take account of and express the multiplicity of aspects from which a given subject may be viewed or perspectivized, and (2) to consider, as indicated above, a given subject in its concrete, dynamic, and relational character and not just in its "simple location." In both cases it may utter expressions which, from the point of view of the requirements of Western logical discourse, could be called "contradictory." S may be both changing and permanent, or, as the Chinese say, finite and infinite. Are these properties contradictories? They may not be realizable in the same person in exactly the same respect and the same way, any more than red and green may occupy the same spot in a painting. But they are compatible as complementary aspects of a given process. Oriental philosophy strives to bring the diversity of the aspects of experience into the unity of intuition; thus the identity that it aims at is the identity that embraces diversity. This is esthetic identity and not the identity of Western logic. It is concrete identity and not abstract identity.

52

Identity or unity of experience, whether the result of concrete reasoning or of esthetic intuition, is always an achievement. It is the synthesis and outcome of *process*, binding together into a whole that which was previously separated. A syllogism, as concrete, is thus a process[6] whose product "follows from" the previous parts according to certain operations (rules) and postulates or "laws of thought." An esthetic experience involves a process of synthesizing certain qualities and the issuance of that process into a unified product which "follows from" the prior parts according to certain operations and regulatory postulates or principles of appreciation. Let us consider two examples.

> This painting in respect a is green of a certain intensity.
> This painting in respect b is red of a certain intensity.
> a and b are juxtaposed in a certain way.
> Therefore, this painting in respects a and b taken
>   together has the quality of contrast; moreover,
>   green becomes *more* intense, as does red.

> All men are mortal.
> Socrates is a man.
> Therefore, Socrates is mortal.

The conclusion in the first illustration adds considerably more than would be logically allowed by its premises. More is inferred about contrast, green, and red than would be warranted by the ordinary logical interpretation of the terms in the premises and by the rules of implication. We may say either that the meanings of the terms "green" and "red" shift from premises to conclusion, or that two different greens and two different reds are referred to in the course of the argument. In either case, we have violated the rule of "fixity" necessary for valid formal argument. But the fact is that these concrete, funding, crescive processes do go on and that we do experience their outcomes as containing qualities and structures not contained in the parts taken severally. It is true that the argument could be stated so as to be formally validly, as

> All juxtapositions (of colors) of a certain kind
>   produce contrasts.
> This is a juxtaposition of that kind.
> Therefore, this is a contrast.

But that way of stating it either reduces the actual esthetic process to a verbal tautology, or it collapses the process of moving from premises to conclusion so as to eclipse the real leap that takes place. And if, moreover,

6. Cf. Whitehead's view of mathematical statements as process, as quoted in A. H. Johnson, *Whitehead's Theory of Reality*. Boston: Beacon, 1952, p. 56.

it is said that this first example is merely a description of what takes place in esthetic appreciation, or a prescription of what should take place, it may be answered that the second example may be descriptive (and must be if it is to be empirically useful) and that as valid it surely prescribes the process of reasoning for an *ideal* reasoner.

Let us turn to the second example. Either this is a tautology or it involves a movement from premises to conclusion that introduces new meaning different from the meanings of the premises. If it is a tautology, aiming at "analytic" truth, it can be nothing more than the precise "explication of our own intended meanings."[7] But some logicians would not be satisifed with that interpretation; and it may be questioned whether even a tautology is entirely devoid of process (a circle goes somewhere) and whether *e*xplication is not a movement of essentially the same kind involved in synthetic arguments and esthetic processes. The line between saying the argument (of the second example) is tautological and saying that the conclusion "adds" meaning is, operationally, difficult to draw. Does "Socrates is mortal" *explicate* or *add to* the prior meanings? If "Socrates" in the conclusion means *exactly* what the term means in the premise, how is there explication? And if it means more ("mortal" added to "man") then is there not progression in the series of propositions?

The difference between the two examples seems to be partly a matter of degree. Esthetic and deductive thought follow parallel patterns. In both, certain materials are given (qualities, and premises). In both, these materials are organized by certain regulatory principles or rules. In both, an ideal is aimed at (unity in variety, and consistency). In esthetic thought, this ideal demands that there be a certain "fitness" or "relevance" between materials and form, means and ends, a certain compatibility of parts with one another and with the whole. But in formal thought, where the meanings of the means (premises) are more rigorously or rigidly fixed, the consistency is defined by explicit and definite rules of implication.

The difference can be drawn more sharply. In deductive reasoning the materials are so chosen that their meanings are relatively definite, unchanging, and mutually dependent; and the ideal logical system then becomes mathematical, where the meanings are made precise and fixed by the constants in the general nature of things. Esthetic thought cannot be so rigorous, for the meaning (or connectedness) of a given element is undergoing transformation within an evolving whole. In art, the meaning attached to elements is variable and flexible, within the bounds of the general ideal, for while our general intention remains the same the specific content or meanings bringing

7. C. I. Lewis, *An Analysis of Knowledge and Valuation*. La Salle: Open Court, 1946, p. 31.

us to its full expression will change as they evolve; whereas in reason the intention is fixed initially and its explication is a matter of psychological necessity.

In art, there are many different ways, using the given materials, to the same end, namely, unity in variety; for there are many ways in which the parts may be unified, esthetically. But in correct reasoning, there is only one path to the conclusion, given certain materials: in a valid process, true premises preclude a false conclusion. In such a case, the end-in-view is consistency, and no other value can interfere with our following the argument wherever it may lead; whereas "qualitative thought," as Dewey has called it,[8] more freely selects and organizes what is given. Esthetic fitness is a more generous ideal than logical consistency.

In both cases the novelty of emergent quality appears in the outcome. When we are engaged in *routine* or ordinary processes of thought, either logical-mathematical (as in the trite and monotonous examples of textbooks) or esthetic, we do not notice the quality which is the outcome of creative process. But children and geniuses do. Esthetic creation has order, different from logical order; and in turn the explication of meanings in logic yields surprises when (as in art) we are genuinely discovering what we do mean.

The question of what meanings can be derived from other meanings is the question of how broad or how narrow the first meanings are. And this question is a matter for human decision, determined by the purposes that the decider has in mind. If as in the West he had valid conclusions in mind, then he will fix and make as precise as possible those meanings. Thus, in the moods of the syllogism of traditional logic, the propositions A, E, I, and 0 are fixed variables (constants) whose values are to be supplied indifferently, i.e., without affecting the structure of the propositions or rules whereby they are combined. The same is true of a "logical truth" in modern logic: "A formula is logically true if and only if it is true *no matter what interpretation we give* to the constant terms in it."[9] Similarly, existential logic cannot be mixed with conditional logic without contradiction. If as in the East a man aims at an intuition of ultimate reality or at the "infinite point of view," then he can afford to entertain the diverse meanings of a given subject S—S in the multiplicity of its internal aspects and relations, S in the multiplicity of its relations to its neighbors and to the universe, and S in the transformations which it undergoes through time. Western logic achieves its aim so far as it treats S simply, i.e., considers it in any given unit of discourse as possessing some abstract characteristic in a specious present: S is p. Eastern thought

8. "Qualitative Thought," in *Philosophy and Civilization*. New York: Minton, Balch, 1931, pp. 93–116.
9. A. H. Basson and D. J. O'Connor, *Introduction to Symbolic Logic*. London: University Tutorial, 1953, p. 111.

endeavors to treat S in the fullness of its qualitative concreteness and of its relations to other events in time: S is p, q, r, etc. and −p.

Our conclusion is that as respects the law of identity Eastern and Western thought are not mutually exclusive. Insofar as one does not accept that law one cannot be logical in the Western sense. To reason correctly about things, to obtain results (forms) which are consistent with one's grounds or premises (also forms), one must fix one's premises, i.e., one must formalize them. The abstract form is all – in logic – for that is what characterizes a given subject S throughout all its manifold changes.[10] We can reason about form because (as in the replication of the units of a crystal) there is a discreteness and constancy about individual forms and a necessity in their order of succession; and reason aims at the duplication of such constancy and necessity in its operations.

But the East for many years has been impressed by the togetherness, inconstancy, and contingency of the events of the world. A concrete subject is multiple in its aspects; it changes; and what follows from it – either within its own nature or within the natures it affects – is not altogether necessary or reasonable (deductively) or predictable with absolute certainty. To be sure, forms exercise some hegemony over the flux in which they participate, and hence some necessity. There are "laws" of change – of decay and growth – which prescribes the general pathway which any activity whatsoever must take. In this sense change is necessary, and is a metaphysical category. But while an individual child – under more or less favorable conditions – *must* grow, the particular rate, direction, and content of his growth are contingencies which can be known only with probability. Western logic has paid its respect to this fact by the recognition of certain fallacies which arise from a failure to recognize the distinction between general forms and individual cases (accident, converse accident), the differences between individuals (inductive fallacies), the distinction between part and whole (division, composition), and the distinction between class-membership and the part-whole relation.

Western logic has shown that valid or necessary thinking cannot proceed if a certain property "living" is predicated of a certain S in the same respect, time, and place. The individual may be both living and dying, but at different times (S_1 and S_2) or in different respects. But these respects cannot be mixed in an act of thought and predicated of S. To think about the world, the East finds this procedure useful within its limits, but inadequate. The approach of the East is alogical, or esthetic. Thus the Easterner may accept the formula that S is S, but ask, "But what is S?" If this is a formula that concerns the question of meaning, then the Easterner may accept the logical grounds on

10. Cohen and Nagel, *op. cit*, p. 186.

56

which the meaning is arbitrarily fixed but point out that a fixed meaning is an abstraction sundered from concrete usage and from concrete referents. If it is a formula that refers to S as a concrete event, then he may point out again that S is multiple, internally and externally, and that S is in continuous change and that *some* changes at least are part of the concrete essence of S. S may be said to possess an abstract identity insofar as certain of its properties, such as manness and mortality, perdure through time and change. But this identity, so far as it participates and is particularized in process, is itself in continuous negation: S is ceasing to be both a man and a mortal. In that sense S is or is becoming $-S$; or the p of S is becoming $-p$. As the general semanticists say, S_1 is not S_2. And so these successive concretions of "S" (the abstract S) rise out of and pass back into "the supreme identity," namely, the universe.

We pass then from the law of identity to the law of non-contradiction, which has already been considered in connection with the meaning of identity. For the negative meaning of "$S \equiv S$" is that S is excluded from $-S [-(S. -S)]$. The law of non-contradiction states that it is impossible that S can both exist and not exist; or, it is impossible that S is p and also that S is $-p$ at the same time and place and in the same way. For symbols this means that the proposition "S is p" and "S is $-p$", where predicated of S at the same time and place and in the same way, cannot both be true; or, that "S is p" cannot be both true and false.

We have already seen that effectiveness in formal reasoning requires the principle of non-contradiction. The process by which a concrete being changes into its negation or "contradictory" must, in formal logic, itself be negated. Concrete changes bring forth, among other things, inconsistencies; but what is aimed at in the processes of deductive reason is consistencies. Thus the principle of non-contradiction excludes such inconsistency at the outset by stipulating specificity and fixity of meaning in its terms and its propositions. Oriental thought is able to accept all this, recognizing that it is limited to the domain of definite and static things; but with its doctrine of "two levels"[11] it asserts that there is another realm which includes this first domain and in which the principles of formal logic do not apply. This inclusive realm has two aspects, the aspect of continuous change and "reversal," and the aspect of undifferentiated unity. Formal logic could grasp neither aspect; rather, esthetic sensitivity and intuition are the appropriate modes of apprehension.

Thus the principle of "both-and," denied in logic, may be effectively used in certain areas of our experience.

11. Charles A. Moore, "Comparative Philosophies of Life," in *Philosophy East and West*, ed. Charles A. Moore. Princeton: Princeton University, 1944, pp. 283–287.

For example, S may be both p and −p where p and −p are different aspects of S, i.e., are prehended into the unity of S. A person may be joyful and sad, loving and hating, simultaneously, as any event is a dynamic equilibrium of positive and negative factors. Formal logic succeeds in fixing its meanings only by narrowing its attention to single and therefore abstract properties of events. But because it has been concerned to encompass wholes – persons, molar experiences, families, societies, traditions, the cosmos – Oriental philosophy has been forced to deal also with what is multiple. The epistemic problem then becomes, Can multiples be grasped as a unit? And the metaphysical problem is, Are multiples in fact unified, and, if so, what is the nature of that unity? Much Eastern thought, supported by recent process philosophy in the West like that of Whitehead, has held that concrete wholes, inclusive of parts, do exist; and it has therefore inclined toward an ultimate monism[12] which has sometimes tended to erase parts or individuals (especially in India), though China has on the whole preserved the person as a union of parts and the cosmos as a union of individuals. In asserting that S is both p and −p, Jaina logic combines two points of view "into one composite point of view"; and "the necessity of such compound judgment lies in the need of a comprehensive view of the positive and negative character of an object."[13] Similarly, the School of the Middle Path in Chinese Buddhism asserted three levels of double truth (*yu* and *wu*; *yu* and *wu*, and neither *yu* nor *wu*; neither *yu* nor *wu*, and neither non-*yu* nor not-*wu*)[14] and thereby showed that by a series of progressively more inclusive perspectives we may at each level unite what was distinct at the previous level, until we reach a unity of perspective that must necessarily deny all perspective, or all distinctions.

Again, it is possible for S to be both p and −p where p and −p are sectors in a continuum such that they are not clearly distinguishable and a transitional sector (dynamic or static)[15] exists which exhibits the properties p and −p. As an example, an organism may be both living and dying, or may be passing from youth to maturity; and again, there is a transitional sector on the spectrum between red and orange which, for lack of a clear-cut dividing line, may be said to be both red and not-red. It has been proposed that the contradiction can be easily removed by a definitional decision which draws a sharp line through the transition and separates the vague sector into two mutually exclusive parts. But what is a "sharp" line? All such lines, on close

12. *Ibid.*, pp. 302–308.
13. Satischandra Chatterjee and Dhirendramohan Datta, *An Introduction to Indian Philosophy*, 4th ed. Calcutta: University of Calcutta, 1950, p. 86.
14. Fung Yu-lan, *A Short History of Chinese Philosophy*, trans. Derk Bodde. New York: Macmillan, 1950, p. 254.
15. V. J. McGill and W. T. Parry, "The Unity of Opposites: A Dialectical Principle," *Science and Society*, vol. XII, no. 4 (Fall, 1948), p. 429.

investigation, turn out to be jagged or fuzzy. The events of nature seem to possess, to our way of perceiving, an ineradicable vagueness or "fringe."[16] And "precision" therefore becomes an ideal which is approximated but never perfectly achieved: "exactness is a fake."[17]

Not only is it true that it is an arbitrary decision to separate in symbols what is in concrete existence joined together, thereby simplifying and falsifying our experience; but the misrepresentation may have practical consequences which make vivid to us the violence done to reality. Some persons have been unwittingly buried alive. It may be said that the physicians simply made mistakes in observation or judgment. But that is the point: it is not always easy to determine where life ends and death beings. Does a youth achieve maturity on his 21st birthday? A wise parent knows that at that age a youth is more or less mature, or is passing into maturity, and that it could be harmful to insist that in certain respects he cannot be both immature and mature. Is it possible for a student to be both passing and failing a course? A student's grade may fall exactly on the borderline drawn between passing and failing; and in that case the grader must make a second decision and draw the borderline anew. Would it not be realistic, in such a case, for the grader to consider the passage or progress that the student has made from the worse to the better?

The principle of non-contradiction rests upon our capacity to make distinctions. Most thinkers, even in the East, accept the existence of distinctions (with the exception of absolute monists); but the difficulty is that distinctions must be made within the background of an undifferentiated continuum which underlies and joins the things distinguished. Can life be distinguished from non-life?[18] So far as life displays emergent qualities and structures, yes; so far as it displays characteristics like prehension, no. The acknowledgement of and emphasis on common characteristics has been the main direction of Eastern thought, and it has ended in mysticism; whereas the West, attending to distinctions, whether aboriginally atomic or creatively emergent, has produced science and scientific philosophy.

While the principle of non-contradiction forbids the conjunction of opposites or contradictories, the principle of excluded middle explicitly forces a choice between existence and non-existence, between truth and falsity. "$S \wedge -S$" means that a subject S either exists or does not exist; or, S is either p or $-p$. By the principle of non-contradiction, the "or" expresses

16. *Ibid.*, p. 428.
17. A. N. Whitehead, "Immortality," Ingersoll Lecture, reprinted in *The Philosophy of Alfred North Whitehead*, ed. Paul Arthur Schilpp. Evanston and Chicago: Northwestern University, 1941, p. 700.
18. See Garret Hardin, "Meaninglessness of the Word Protoplasm," *The Scientific Monthly*, vol. 82, no. 3 (March, 1956), pp. 112–120.

a strong alternation, excluding "both". For symbols, this means that the proposition "S is p" is either true or false. The principle of excluded middle is a formal way of prescribing that the terms and objects of discourse be fixed. It might be called the principle of decision. It calls for arbitrariness in symbols, for only by such specificity and fixity in meaning can we order the factors of our past, present, and future experiences deductively and inductively. If experience did not have such order, or something approximating to it, then our arbitrariness with symbols would not work as applied pragmatically. But it does work. To reason, to communicate, to live one with another, we must be consistent in our use of meanings, and in our combining of meanings. But it is an equally plain fact of experience that we do change our minds and that we ought to insofar as the world changes and our fulfillment is contingent upon our adjustment to those changes. Eastern thought, by and large, has long been aware that the symbolic stipulations and orders of man are abstractions drawn like a "net of words" from the teeming, churning sea of concrete and immediate experience, and that to be adequate in their reference they must adumbrate the massive and vague presences of that larger setting. The world is a vast, complex, oppositional world with respect to which man does not always feel forced to simplify, to speak or think consistently, or to choose as between alternatives. Man may wish to be receptive to the whole alogical concourse of things, renouncing his thought-control of the world and accepting it for what it is:

> Do I contradict myself?
> Very well then I contradict myself,
> (I am large, I contain multitudes.)[19]

As the principle of decision, the law of excluded middle does, as indicated, have some ground in experience; for it is presupposed in sound reasoning, and sound reasoning, if it is initially premised on fact, may reliably lead us to other facts. There seems to be a structure of the world of facts which persists in the midst of change, and this structure is the ground and presupposition of logic, and is formulated in the so-called laws of thought and other logical principles.[20] If logic is the science of this structure of fact, then what is fact? A given fact, to be treated as a unit in a logical structure or operation, must be unchanging. It must be a fixed element within its universe of discourse. A fact is an aspect of the flux of things – a fixed aspect. A fact is flux as finished; it is something done, a deed, the *factum* of *facere*. The doctrine that universals are real could account for *general* facts but foundered

---

19. Walt Whitman, *Leaves of Grass*, Book III, "Song of Myself," 51.
20. See, for example, Bertrand Russell, *The Problems of Philosophy*. London: Oxford University, 1912, pp. 72–73.

in explaining the factuality of particulars. The Greeks, in their logic, sought to escape the limits of particulars by hiding them under the shadow of the sheltering wing of universals. Theirs was, as Dewey has said, a logic of "subsumption."[21] But whatever the status of universals, particular facts seem to possess a finish that is peculiarly their own; their stability and continuity are the emergents of lockages and dynamic balances of processes, and their form or factual character must be renewed moment by moment even as it is brought into being and passes away. A fact, therefore, is a stabilized stage in process, a spatial consummation of temporal movement. When we complete a task, we declare, "That's it." When we are confronted by an unchangeable situation, we say, in resignation, "That's that." Such expressions (tautologies) signify the finished character, the irreversibility, the necessity that marks the realm of fact. A fact is what it is; it is uncompounded with its opposite; it is the precipitate of a process in decision: to be or not to be, and to be just this rather than those other things. Tautologies are prized by logicians because they possess the unequivocal, non-contradictory character that fact also has. Like fact, they are impermeable to impairment; there is a quality of eternity about them. Similarly, the conclusions of deductive reasoning are impermeable to alteration; they explicate what meanings must be, given other meanings, and what facts must be, given other facts. Deduction strictly does not forecast what will come; it merely states what is or must be the case if something else is the case. It does not project what might be the future case as based on observed past cases; it merely asserts what a reasonable man must discover to be the case. It does not describe what happens or will happen in time; it prescribes that whatsoever does happen must conform to its necessities. For deductive reasonings to be sound and their conclusions to be true, their facts must first be fixed and purged of mixture and contradiction. Inductive reasonings cannot yield certain conclusions because their inferences pertain to the future, i.e., to what is not yet formed or factual. Their necessity is qualified because it pertains to what is not yet definite, decisive, and fixed. Thus it has been said that the only empirical necessity is the necessity of particularity.[22] But the necessity of valid deduction is certain, because it pertains to what is created, past, and already fixed, namely, facts. The principle of decision (excluded middle) is modeled after the decisiveness of achieved fact.

This principle of thought has already been treated in passing in the discussion of the other two principles. Two examples may illustrate the limits of its application. Was Jean Valjean guilty or not guilty when he stole

21. *Essays in Experimental Logic*. New York: Dover, 1953, p. 207.
22. Hugh Miller, *The Community of Man*. New York: Macmillan 1949, ch. 2.

the loaf of bread?[23] Must he be one or the other? The answer to that depends on whether we wish to be decisive in our judgment. And whether our decisiveness can be justified is not just "a question of fact" – i.e., of what has been done by Jean Valjean – but is also a question of the realities of the total situation. The accused may be in part guilty, in part not guilty (for society must have been in part responsible). That is to say, "extenuating circumstances" must be taken into account. Not only is it true that Jean Valjean as well as the circumstances are complex; but he has a certain history (as do the circumstances) and a certain direction of life (for character has a vector quality), indicating the future. So we must consider motives and the consequences of our possible punishments and rewards. Thus, to gain the "whole truth" and to do justice to the total situation, we must resist the option forced on us by the principle of the excluded middle. As the situation is complex, so our judgment must be complex, cognizant of its own partialities and limitations. The refusal to make black-and-white judgments, the approaches of tentativity, moderation, and reconciliation, have characterized Oriental thought in moral and legal matters for many years, and continue, as Northrop has pointed out, in the policies of contemporary India.[24] Modern psychology in the West tends to confirm the principles that creative learning proceeds *both* by punishment of behavior that must be extinguished *and*, at the same time, by rewarding of behavior that must be reinforced.

Let us consider another example. Must a man be either attached or non-attached to the world? Hindu philosophy, especially that expressed in the *Gītā*, as well as Chinese philosophy, holds that neither alternative is as effective as both together in bringing about fulfillment of life.[25] Not only, in that view, is the union of opposites possible; it is a categorial feature of the world. There is thus a metaphysical ground that excludes the static principle of exclusion; for the principle of the negation of the negation as found in Oriental thought means that while things are continuously separating from one another through differences they do so in virtue of their underlying identity, and are continuously emerging into a new state of tension. "Whatever belongs to the states of sattwa, rajas and tamas, proceeds from me," says Kṛṣṇa in

23. The form of the question gives away the kind of answer wanted. Dewey contrasts the procedure of the law court (which was the model for Greek logic) with the procedure in the laboratory (the logic of modern science). In the one, a proposition is given, to be accepted or rejected – i.e., to be *proved* by application of rules whereby a given case can be brought under its appropriate generality or "law." In the other, the connectedness of particular facts, known and unknown, is sought. It is interesting that courts of equity, whose procedures are more allied to scientific induction, sprang up in the West in England, which gave us also modern empiricism.
24. See his *The Taming of the Nations*. New York: Macmillan, 1952. These same approaches characterized the guerrilla and educational activities of the Chinese Communists.
25. For the psychological foundations for this attitude, see Charles Morris, *Paths of Life*. New York: Harper, 1942.

the *Gītā*.[26] "Where there is division there is something not divided," says the *Chuang Tzu*.[27] Eastern thought, recognizing differentiation and exclusion in things, has been dominated by the ideal of inclusion and not that of exclusion. Saṅkara, for instance, defines particularity or exclusion as the criterion of the unreal.[28] By contrast, the West has emphasized difference, exclusion, and strife, and this attitude has influenced, and has been influenced by, science.

III

Let us summarize some major distinctions and relations between Eastern and Western thought as implied in this discussion of the "laws" or principles of thought.

Western thought, in science, philosophy, and religion, has been strongly deductive. Many thinkers in these areas have proceeded from first principles, intuitively given, and have been guided by rigorous logical explication. While the greatest progress in science has issued from the dialectical mixture of theory and experimental observation, the large advances in knowledge have come through men like Archimedes, Newton, Faraday, Darwin, and Einstein – men adept at proposing hypotheses pregnant with implications. Similarly, philosophy has tended to pattern itself after the model of deduction, and many great Western philosophers have been mathematicians. In religion, Origen set the pace, and no one has ever matched the architectonic logic of St. Thomas' *Summae*. It is true that, as Whitehead has pointed out, the empirical temper of modern times has merged with and modified the deductive approach in science;[29] and the result has been great power. Empiricism has affected philosophy less, and theology only slightly; and the results in those fields have been accordingly less noteworthy.

Eastern thought has tended to be non-deductive – intuitive in a sense, mystical in a sense, experimental in a sense. As Burtt, Moore, and many others have pointed out, it has primarily aimed at the *practical* fulfillment of man; and if it soared into the heavens on the wings of speculation, it did so for the sake of seeking the problem and solution of human life more clearly and more comprehensively. Gandhi's autobiography is entitled, *The Story of My Experiments With Truth*. A strange title for a Westerner! For in the West one experiments with events to get truths for particular, con-

26. *Bhagavad-Gita*, trans. Swami Prabhavananda and Christopher Isherwood. Hollywood: Marcel Rodd, 1949, p. 91 (ch. 7).
27. Trans. Fung Yu-lan. Shanghai: Commercial, 1931, p. 57 (ch. 2).
28. Chatterjee and Datta, *op. cit.*, p. 387. The fatalism of such Oriental idealism has come under sharp criticism. See Joseph W. Cohen, "The Role of Philosophy in Culture," *Philosophy East and West*, vol. V, no. 2 (July, 1955), pp. 99–112.
29. *Science and the Modern World*, ch. 1.

tingent purposes often far removed from personal fulfilment, the religious quest, and God. While Gandhi, unlike many ancient Indians, was an activist effecting broad social changes, and was influenced by Western thought, he was essentially an Indian (much like Buddha and Mahāvīra) in his independence, his dissatisfaction with useless speculation and ritual, his humanism, and his adventurous and radical experimentalism. Similarly, the "naturalism" of the Chinese is an expression of the opposition to philosophizing carried on in independence of the practical affairs of man, whether it be other-worldly speculation or the sophistries of logic. Chinese philosophy reflects, as Fung says, "the aspirations and inspirations of the farmer," living close to nature: "the philosopher only tells us what he sees."[30]

Second, Western thought has tended to aim at an absoluteness in its method, while Eastern thought has been content with relativity and approximation. The excitement felt by the Greeks when they first discovered the glorious clarity and certainty of mathematics and logic was never really lost to the Western mind. For though during the Dark Ages mathematics and logic went into eclipse, the crescent of the invading Arabs, bringing with them the lost learning of classical times, began to shine and grow and illuminate the world more brightly than the medieval manuscripts; and progressively, as men became disillusioned with theology, they had need of the inspiration kindled in them by the eternal light of logic and mathematics. The obsession with the certainty of logico-mathematical techniques increased as men became more uncertain with their aims; and finally, in the highly developed sciences and in philosophies like positivism, men found a seemingly adequate substitute for religious absolutism. Absolute method replaced absolute end. Means became be-all and end-all. But in the East men could tolerate plurality in the realm of means because they were absolutely certain of the end. Common sense, oral tradition, the scriptures, intuition, conscience, mystical experience – all the natural enemies of a critical philosophy in the West (since the sophists) which prides itself on clarity and system – became in the East the handmaidens of the thought that attempts to see life steadily and as a whole. Diversity of perspectives is an immediate and inescapable datum of our common experience; it is impressed upon us as we interact with the world and with one another. Hume, reflecting the physical science of his day, and the social intercourse of the 18th century coffee house and salon, saw that; Descartes, alone in his study, did not. Discounting the mysticism and asceticism of the East, we can see how Easterners are in the same case with Hume: if you begin with three men with three different viewpoints having a dialogue concerning religion, or with six men, all blind, perceiving an elephant from different aspects, then you predetermine the

30. Fung Yu-lan, *A Short History of Chinese Philosophy*, pp. 19, 25.

problems and solutions in ontology, epistemology, and ethics, in a direction quite different from that taken when you consider a piece of wax or introspect on your own states of thought or inquire into the mathematical relations of the notions of Newtonian apples and moons. In the first case, methods vary, and one is apt to say there are several methods to the same end. In the second case, one is apt to absolutize method itself.

Social conditions have underlain this difference in outlook. In the agrarian, "tradition-directed" cultures of the Orient philosophers have generally been more dependent upon and integrated with their cultures than have philosophers in the West. Though science and technology in China were far advanced over Europe in ancient and medieval times,[31] the Chinese never became obsessed by them as methods. The imperial order and a certain respect for nature seemed to keep both speculation and experiment in bounds. Moreover, the West for the last 1000 years has had a turbulent social history in its transitions from feudalism to capitalism and through the various stages of capitalism. Science and technology advanced as they rode the fleets of advancing capitalism. In both cases the stable harbor of feudal religious faith was left behind in favor of the open sea, the uncharted continent, and the unexploited market. The method of conquest became the one certainty, a self-fulfilling process as it scored success after success. But in both China and India men believed in a final, absolute unity inclusive of differences between people, perspectives, and empirical relativities. Enthusiasm for method never supplanted this inclusive belief.

Such belief is not a mere verbal convention, passed down by tradition. It survives as it is nourished and sustained by the reinforcing day-to-day contacts of people with one another and with the things and processes of nature – by the interactions within family life and work, and by the assured recurrence of these interactions. As cultures develop science, technology, urban life, classes, and division of labor, they tend to become estranged from these sources and lose this belief. All of the advanced capitalist countries are illustrations of this loss. As an alternative communism maintains that the loss of belief and the alienation of science can be overcome if the conditions for cooperative communal life and work are provided. It claims, in short, to combine man's belief in the unity of man and man and man and nature with the methods of science and technology. The success of the socialist countries is a measure of the truth of this claim.

Experimentalism as a method – in East or West – always yields probabilities. This has been plain, in the West, from Hume to Einstein, and has been taken as axiomatic in Eastern thought. Even the supreme experience – carry-

31. See Joseph Needham, *Science and Civilisation in China*, vol. I. Cambridge: Cambridge University, 1954.

ing with it the human, practical, saving knowledge of ultimate reality and value – is, while always objective, always relative. Deduction, then, becomes practically dispensable. Deductive certainty is useless if it does not begin at a point of certainty, for the conclusion can be no truer than the premises, and that beginning point must be empirical if the conclusion is to have content; and if, on the other hand, deductive reasoning does begin with a certain premise, empirically arrived at, the Easterner is inclined to feel that such reasoning is likewise useless, for deduction cannot increase certainty and is, moreover, no substitute for what is given directly in experience. In the Eastern view, if we had a genuine experience of ultimate reality and value, we would feel no need to impose our particular (or relative) version of it upon someone else (as has been done in Western holy wars), if indeed we could give articulation to its full concreteness; nor would we be compelled to "prove" it deductively to someone else (as has been done in the numerous "proofs" for God, the soul, reality, etc. in the West). Tradition and communal living give a silent and tacit certainty which no "inner-directed" culture, for all its anxious "proofs," with its desire to overcome its isolation and estrangement, can match. We speak because we do not know, because we are seeking to find what we think and to explicate what our meanings intend, because we search for escape from the "labyrinthine ways" of our own minds. But, as the Chinese have said, when we renounce such efforts at knowledge, and forget, and become empty, then we may be filled with a wisdom which logic cannot supply; and, like Confucius, having "forgotten to forget," we may proceed to let the living process control thought rather than *vice versa*.

Modern thought in the West, through the development engendered by its own internal contradictions, has moved in the direction of the East in its emphasis on empirical probability. Hugh Miller has pointed out that the dethronement of classical thought came with three discoveries: the disestablishment of absolute geometry and the proof that geometry is physical hypothesis, the uncertainty principle in physics, and Goedel's proof of the incompletability of number-theory.[32] (There were other factors.) The shift in viewpoint is summed up in Einstein's classical expression demolishing classicism: "physical concept are free creations of the human mind."[33] What are the necessities for modern scientific thought? Such thought appears to have no need of such hypotheses.

Logic in the West has suffered from the same blows. It has never fully recovered the balance which defined its serenity and certainty in the days

32. Hugh Miller, "The Science of Creation," *Proceedings and Addresses of the American Philosophical Association*, 1950–1951, vol. XXIV (September, 1951), p. 31.
33. Albert Einstein and Leopold Infeld, *The Evolution of Physics*. New York: Simon and Schuster, 1951, p. 33.

before disturbing questions like those of "existential import" were raised. The rules of inference applicable to existents, as in the traditional syllogism, square of opposition, and immediate inference, cannot apply to conditionals. Because the attempt to deal with existents and conditionals (in this sense) in the same system leads to contradictions, the tendency has been to separate traditional logic from modern logic, which deals purely with conditionals. The task of the latter has been put as follows:

> The propositions of logic either are conditionals or are reducible to conditionals, and logic presupposes only to discover means of certifying conditionals to be necessarily true. Logic investigates what follows necessarily from the hypothesis of existence; it need not assert existence. . . a determination as to what does exist is not within the province of logic.[34]

A basic form of such reasoning is as follows:

> If A (antecedent), then C (consequent); namely, if (A) for every individual, if it is an S then it is a P, and there is an S, then (C) there is an S which is a P.

This form is an attempt to re-establish in logic the certainty or necessity which in Aristotelian and medieval logic was grounded on first principles reached through intuition and authority. The formulas of modern logic are algebraic: they aim to state an invariant structure for a certain range of contingent events or meanings. While classical logic sought to provide standards which could adjudicate disputes and regulate discourse,[35] modern logic arises in the setting of science which finds itself *in medias res* and seeks to move from one fact to another by way of reliable inferences. Whereas ancient logic fixed its conclusions by first fixing its major premises and its rules – the "laws of thought" being the presuppositions of this universe of discourse– the only fixity to which modern logic can give allegiance is the general structure of facts of a certain kind. Indeed, the modern mind (in the U. S. A.) rebels against any kind of *a priori* fixity or "fix," whether in the law courts or in business transactions. A "fix" suggests arbitrariness, subjectivity, and the imposition of prejudice upon reality. The facts should be allowed to speak for themselves. And the facts reveal the form.

But how certain is that form? The famous problem of the "justification of induction" remains to haunt modern logic. In the form given above, how do we know that the proposition "if A, then C" is true? It has been said in its defense that such a proposition – the law of implication – is a necessity of thought. But is not this law in part empirical, insofar as thought has

---

34. From an unpublished paper, "Logic and Existence," by Professor Leo Simons.
35. John Dewey, *Essays in Experimental Logic*, ch. 6.

67

empirical origins and termini? Do we not accept the proposition that a true conclusion must follow from true premises because we have discovered specific instances of its being the case? And if the law of implication is existential and inductive, then how can reasoning based on it be perfectly certain? Again, the proposition, "If it is an S, then it is a P," by similar reasoning, must be inductive, for the reference to the connection between S and P would be of no effect if particular S's not exist. But the argument fails deductively unless said proposition can be asserted with certainty. Of course, in this argument, as in all kindred ones, one may disregard existence and adhere strictly to formal meanings; but then the argument becomes useless if no term whatsoever refers to existence (as it does in the above).

Hugh Miller has argued that inductive inference is necessary and certain, and that induction is a type of deduction. "It is the conclusion, not the inference, which is probable."[36] Thus the following argument would be deductively valid:

> If 50% of the rabbits we have *observed* are male, then *probably* 50%, *approximately*, of all rabbits are male. 50% of the rabbits we have observed are male. Therefore, probably 50% approximately, of all rabbits are male.

That is, on the basis of our observations, we are *compelled* to make a statement of *probability*. But it may be asked what the nature of this inferential compulsion or necessity is. To the extent that the generalization is true that all samples are representative of their classes, and, further, that the rabbits we have observed are a sample, then the consequent follows. But while it may be true that all of the samples so far observed are representative of their classes, we have not observed *all* samples and *all* classes. But this objection may be sophistical. The main point is that the compulsion that asserts what *might* be is different from the compulsion that asserts what *is* or *must* be. The inductive leap from observations concerning past instances of a group to an assertion as to what might be observed concerning future instances is a *predictive* necessity. If one is not desirous of predicting one need not feel such a necessity. The meaning of our past observations becomes *prescriptive*: they signify the requiredness of a certain expectation and act, which is unqualifiedly aroused but which has a certain *probability* of being fulfilled. But in the case of deductive necessity the meaning is purely formal, the necessity arises out of the application of prescribed rules, and the results are absolute, that is, are not probable but certain.

Finally, the probable conclusion (resulting from the necessary inference) that 50% of all rabbits are male applies to the class and not to the individual

36. *The Community of Man*, p. 14.

rabbits. Particular individuals cannot be lifted up (without loss) into the realm of abstraction: a particular S is not the same S which is a member of a class. Thus the modern stricture against traditional logic, that we cannot validly infer particular propositions from universal, hypothetical propositions, must hold also for modern logic; for conditional propositions cannot yield existential propositions. If the reasoning of a logic that employs generalizations in the form of conditional and not existential propositions is to be useful, it must draw those generalizations from existence. But as existence is not perfectly necessary but is probable, those generalizations must be probabilities (with the predictive necessity indicated), and the conclusions must be probable. And if the generalizations are definitional or logical (or empty), then they can lead only to empty conclusions, useless with respect to existence. Since probability in our reasoning results from its infection with fact, the only escape from this result is the arbitrary decision – made in the common usage of words, or by logical fiat – to abandon the examination of individual men for characteristics of, say, animality and to decisively *define* them as animals. Our reasoning must proceed so that it cannot be contradicted by fact; yet at the same time it must, to be useful, begin with fact and end there. All reasoning moves between these two poles: our postulations determine what is given, and the given determines our postulations. And a too tenacious adherence to either pole, in neglect of the other, leads to an incomplete interpretation of experience and an inadequate way of moving through it and realizing its values.

A third difference between the thought in West and East has to do with modes of language and meaning.

On the face of it, Western science and scientific philosophy look positive and affirmative. But are they? How positive is a conclusion derived by one of many mathematics, or one of many logics? How determinate is a conclusion in a system of reasoning which itself is contingent and has limited application in space and time? On the other side, Eastern thought looks negative: Indian philosophy is chastened by the everpresent voice, "Neti, neti," and Chinese philosophy is forever negative in approach[37] and conscious of the pervasive *Tao* which does and undoes all things. Negative in passing and minor matters, the Orient aims to be positive in abiding and final values. In excluding the principle of exclusion, it aims to be totally inclusive. In transcending what is superficially immanent, it aims to be more deeply immanent. In negating negations, it aims to affirm the principle which cannot be negated. Thus the longest way around is, for the Orient, the shortest way home. To be able to say something one may have to be willing to say nothing; and to be able to know anything, one may have to renounce all knowledge.

---

37. Fung Yu-lan, *A Short History of Chinese Philosophy*, p. 341.

To understand the flower in the crannied wall one may have to acknowledge the limits of one's understanding and (as some Western idealists would say) one's grasp of the total system of things which constitutes the sufficient reason for its being; and when one has reached the realization that each is in all and all is each, mere experience, unutterable and mystical, may have to suffice. As Fung Yulan says, "One must speak very much before one keeps silent."[38] Thus the silence, the near-silence, or the sometimes paradoxical and contradictory language used in the Orient is not just childishness or foolishness, as we in the West might say; or it is foolishness which, in the language of Taoism, is wisdom. It arises from an awareness of the limitations in our perceptions, our conceptions, and our symbols in representing our experiences and thoughts. Negation is a way of stating that we do *not* know all that is to be known, about one thing or everything, and it may release us into a more accurate, qualified knowledge of each individual thing (since each thing is in the world) as well as a cognitive reverence for the whole of things. Negation thereby may make us more positive, in both our knowledge of the world and our achievement of value.

We have already seen that Western logic, with its so-called "laws" of thought, attempts to be definite in its assignment of constant values to terms and its fixing of meanings in its universe of discourse. When it speaks and reasons, it severely limits its objects and their relations one to another. The shifting of identities, the contradicting of terms and propositions, cannot be permitted: the logic of language cannot allow it. But where Western thought tends to speak of the limited, the East tends to speak of the unlimited. The language of the West aims at specification and control, in both thought and action; the language of the East is designed to express what has been received, or to relate the speaker to what cannot be expressed or controlled. In the West the language of logical response is discrete, sharp, and incisive, reflecting a world that is through and through atomic. It deals with the irrational by Aristotelian laws, or (in mathematics) by an arbitrary Dedekind cut or (following Kronecker) by the denial that the irrational exists at all.[39] Such a viewpoint comes into clearest focus in the skeletal scheme of the 18th century philosophy and mathematics. Mumford remarks:

> Clarity at the expense of life. But what clarity! Read Galileo, Descartes, Spinoza, Newton, Locke: it is like taking a bath in crystal-clear water. Their universe is clean, neat, orderly, without smells, without flavors, without the rank odors of growth, impregnation, or decomposition; above all, without the complications of real life.[40]

38. *Ibid.*, p. 342.
39. E. T. Bell, *Men of Mathematics*. New York: Harcourt, Brace, 1944, p. 260.
40. Lewis Mumford, *The Condition of Man*. New York: Harcourt, Brace, 1944, p. 260.

By contrast, Eastern thought paints a more complex picture of the world – in either the terse and suggestive language of the Chinese, or in the subtle distinctions of Indian thought, especially when directed to the phases and ranges of intensely personal experience. Oriental thought catches the qualitative flavor, the dialectical movements, the multifarious facets and complexities, the many-levelled hierarchies and progressive inclusions of the world. It portrays what the Western picture omits: "the soil, the bacteria, the mat of vegetation, the animal life... the dense atmosphere of actual experience,"[41] and not just the barren outline of the human and natural landscape, rarefied and abstracted.

"Ideal" language, for some Western philosophy today, consists in tautologies – "empty" language which fully explicates the meaning intended. To know what you mean is the first requisite for a logician; the second is to follow the rules whereby meanings are validly combined. But in the East a thinker may not know what he means, in the sense that he can fully and exactly express what he experiences. He may possess certainty in his qualitative contact with individual things, and certainty as these contacts are multiplied and diversified and felt as a unit. But certainty of this kind is different from logical clarity, which is certainty of another kind. To feel the qualitative and multiple world as one, does not mean muddiness or the undoing of the categories of objective identity and objective diversity.

Moreover, the Easterner, not living within a scientific or deductive tradition, has not felt the need to express his insights rigorously and to elaborate them in a systematic way. Eastern thought is not always explicit in its definitions and strictly logical in its procedures; it is suggestive, adumbrative, and sometimes jagged, and its method of exposition follows more the pattern of the proverb, the poem, the narrative, the informal essay. Because it portrays its objects in their depth, it is not always completely in focus, and there are gradations and shadows; there is a vagueness to objects in the background. In the case of Zen, Oriental thought is downright sacrilegious toward the categories of logic, for it boldly and roguishly invokes contradictions in signifying what is ultimate. In the case of mysticisms, which have been in the main mothered in the East, the language is always contradictory. Why must this be? A preponderating impulse in the East has been to identify oneself with that quality or structure, that principle or experience, which lies within and around the mottled and ever moving world immediately presented to us – to merge one's own being with that Being variously called *Brahman*, the Higher Self, *Puruṣa*, *Nirvāṇa*, *Li*, *Ch'i*, *Tao*, *Satori*. Easterners have been interested not only in one particular quality or relation which a given subject might have; they have sought to know it in its manifold quali-

41. *Ibid.*

ties and relations. Whether the sage's "emotion follows the nature of things," as with the Neo-Confucians;[42] whether he "responds to things, yet is not ensnared by them," as in sentimental Neo-Taoism;[43] whether he must be "empty and without bias;"[44] or whether, as in Ch'an Buddhism, the sage's mind is either a "bright mirror" or no mirror at all[45] – the problem in China is not merely to dwell in the world, but to let the world dwell in one: the One should become one. In opening oneself to the myriad and indefinite number of entities in the world, one must not be narrowly restrictive, over-simple, preferentially partial, and statically exclusive; one must "entertain" the world, as at a party, come what may, with no stern host standing guard at the doorway of the senses and feelings. This means that S involves not merely S; it involves also the whole realm of what is not S. And p is not the only predicate of S; q, r, s, *ad infinitum* (i.e., non-p) are also. As Charles Morris[46] has observed, the mystic, by responding to diverse symbolic objects, may develop simultaneously contradictory dispositions or incipient roles: one may be "both the fish that swims and the gull that dives," or like Ch'eng Hao have emotions that accord with the nature of things, yet of himself have no emotions.[47] But in a deeper sense the mystic acquires a contradictory experience, which is reflected in his "primary" language. By exposing himself to the full concreteness of an event (or subject), in such wise that he can increasingly appreciate its own intrinsic qualities and the qualities displayed in its relations to its neighbors, in space and time, and in such wise that he can increasingly understand its internal relations and its relations to other subjects, he comes to feel and to know that S is more than S. And if by the act of empathy or *Einfühlung* he feels a progressively heightened identification with all the events of his experience, much as he has discovered that S to be involved with all that is −S, then he can truly say that the universe is in him and he in the universe. The mystical experience is an experience of enhanced unity; it is a momentary balancing of conflicts and resolving of struggle. In the words of the *Gītā*, it is the (temporary) conquest of the oppositional *gunas*: the mystic is "free from the pairs of opposites."[48] For in that dialectic identity of differences which is the basic cause of the development in things[49] there is a continuous shifting, first to the side of

42. Fung Yu-lan, *A Short History of Chinese Philosophy*, p. 287.
43. *Ibid.*, p. 238.
44. *Ibid.*, p. 224.
45. *Ibid.*, p. 256.
46. "Comments on Mysticism and Its Language," *Etc.*, vol. IX, no. 1 (Autumn, 1951), pp. 3–8.
47. Fung Yu-lan, *A History of Chinese Philosophy*, vol. II, trans. Derk Bodde. Princeton: Princeton University, 1953, p. 524.
48. pp. 45–46 (ch. 2).
49. Mao Tse-tung, *On Contradiction*. New York: International, 1953, p. 12. This view is anticipated in Chinese philosophy.

unity, then to the side of opposition; and the mystic experiences the eternal oscillation as it moves toward maximum unity. At that point differences tend to fade into the background, and the qualitative unity may become so intense that feelings of denial, negation, and renunciation come to dominate the experience or its subsequent interpretation.

The primitive transmission of energy from one event to another provides the basis for mystical experience; on top of that comes the identification given in kinesthesis, through the specialized senses; and on top of that comes the symbolic role-taking described by Morris. And as one becomes more and more receptive to things, directly or symbolically, one becomes full (and yet never satiated) in a way that bursts the bounds of logic. The mystical experience is so resistant to limits, so all-inclusive, so rich, that it leads either to the alogical attempt to talk about everything at once ("talking in tongues" or speaking in contradictions, like "dark light") – or to silence. It is so complete, in its identification of experiencer with what is experienced, that the two merge into one. And it is so full, in its perception of the concrete things making up the experience, that one must call it a "void."

A logician may be flabbergasted with such freedom with words. Is all the slow, modest, and painful labor, by which man has achieved an understanding and control of his world, to be swept aside or disregarded by reckless mystics? Logic has already made a worthy start in setting its house in order, sweeping away the cobwebs of superstition, casting out the "idols," clarifying the "laws" and rules of sound thought, and resolving certain "paradoxes" through inventions like the theory of types. Formal logic, for example, tells us that any and every proposition follows from a contradiction. What can be concluded from the language of a mystic? Everything? Yet that is just what is aimed at: to have an experience (and to communicate that experience) of the source of all things, actual and possible. A logician cannot bear the burden of all things. To try to grasp all things at once, not to mention the attempt to express them, is an overwhelming task and an impossibility. So he deliberately selects some few things upon which to fasten his attention, and some few meanings which he can more or less understand, and proceeds to trace out some few connection between those things and other things by tracing out the connections between his meanings. Concentrating on a few trees, he cuts a small path into the woods of the world. The world as such would engulf him, and his reason. But the man of the Orient wants to know whether the logician can see the woods for the trees, and whether he knows the direction which his path is taking.

To live in the world, to pursue one's own good, to get what one wants, to have one's way with the world – this has been the purpose of Western man. To allow the world to live in one, to permit it to pursue its purposes in one and have its way with one[50] – this has been man's orientation in the East. Limitation, convergence, logic have marked the one; infinitude, divergence, mysticism, the other. In the West, man goes out and conquers the objects of the world, one by one. In the East, he is conquered by them, in all their plurality and all-embracing oneness.

We are thus led to a final distinction. Because Western thought deals with what is and with the general relations that hold for all things that exist, it does not by the same token deal with individualities, contingencies, and growth as such. It may define *laws* or general tendencies that pertain to individuals, probabilities, and growth, but such laws do not predict that behavior of individuals as such. In the realm of logic, the notion of necessity or causality is a strict one: as there cannot be more in the effect than in the cause, so there cannot be more in the conclusion that is implied in the premises. Logic aims at balance, at equation, at tautology. Hume's revision of the Scholastic concept of cause – changing "impartation" to equivalence of cause and effect[51] – was perfectly adapted to the necessities of an incipient science; for in his view nothing more can be attributed to an unobserved cause than is observed in its effects. In logic, this means that a conclusion cannot be derived from anything more than its premises, and that a conclusion, to be fully adequate, must be implicit in its premises. The law of implication ($p \supset q$), as applied to events, means that if the event p as cause is given, then it *must* be followed by the effect q.

Among the several reasons why this kind of logic was not developed in the Orient was the consideration that empirical prediction of effect from cause, especially in human matters, is not always possible. *More* may be displayed in the effect than in the cause. Thus both Indian and Chinese philosophy, implicitly and explicitly, anticipate the Maxwellian doctrine of "singulars," the Marxist transformation of quantity into quality, and the theory of emergent evolution. Transformation – growth within or toward the ultimate – is a basic religious principle in the East. The Buddhist and Nyāya-Vaiśeṣika philosophies teach that the effect does not exist in the cause antecedent to its production.[52] The Confucian *ho* or harmony signifies the emergent quality when differences are brought together in a certain way.[53] The science and the scientific philosophy of the West have thus been concerned with the basic relations of formal logic as applied to the understanding and control of nature, while the Orient has been attentive to the creative concrescences of nature which elude and transcend those relations. It is true

50. The expression belongs to Charles Morris.
51. Edwin A. Burtt, *Types of Religious Philosophy*, rev. ed. New York: Harper, 1951, p. 226.
52. Chatterjee and Datta, *op. cit.*, p. 259.
53. Fung Yu-lan, *A Short History of Chinese Philosophy*, p. 174.

that in recent decades Western thought, in reaction against the abstract atomism of mechanical materialism, has developed an organic, ecological point of view, while the East, especially India, has had its share of dissociated supernaturalism. However, we are here speaking of broad and long-range contrasts.

S. K. Maitra has expressed the difference between the approaches to fact and value in an arresting way:

> If A is the cause of B, and if A and B are both existents, then A must be greater than B. But if A and B are values, then a very small value A may produce a very great value B. In fact, the logic of Value, or as we may call it, the logic of the Real, is very different from the logic of Concept. Here the causal law is transformed into the law of end and means. The principle of this law is just the reverse of that of the causal law. Here a finite means produces an infinite value.[54]

We may think of exceptions: the fission of one atom may cause a multi-megaton explosion, and a great Shakespearean play greatly performed may produce minuscule results in an insensitive spectator. But the distinction between reality conceived as effete and reality conceived as growing is important. Some in the West, notably Whitehead, have argued that the concrete processes of value (concrescences) are more basic to the world than the abstract structures of fact. This is a large claim, and we do not propose to examine the issue here. But in the case of man, the search for values as things, processes, or situations conducive to the fulfillment of needs appears prior to and determinative of the search for knowledge of facts as means to such fulfillment. If, moreover, no organism or species is structured or functions to serve another exclusively,[55] and if an evolutionary continuity and a general network of interdependence characterizes the ecological community of our planet, then it would appear, contrary to most Western philosophy, that no strict line can be drawn separating man from nature and values from facts. Carbon and oxygen in air, earth, and water are facts, but as indispensable means for sustaining the life of plants and animals they are also values.[56] Man is a value-seeking process interacting with other processes. He is successful insofar as he finds out the general forms or laws that characterize those processes in space and time and thereby can foresee, control, and fashion them for his own fulfillment. The mechanistic equations of the sciences have proved useful for controlling

54. *The Spirit of Indian Philosophy*. Benares: S. K. Maitra, 1947, p. 192.
55. This is Garrett Hardin's formulation of "Paley's Principle" in *Nature and Man's Fate*. New York: New American Library of World Literature, 1961, pp. 58, 72.
56. For an exposition of the view that values pervade nature, see S. Alexander, *Beauty and Other Forms of Value*. London: Macmillan, 1933. Also C. Judson Herrick, *The Evolution of Human Nature*. Dallas: University of Texas, 1956.

processes, applicable because their equivalences describe a kind of necessity. Yet they are sometimes inadequate to the complex transformations occuring. The biologist C. Judson Herrick has written:

> The formula written by the earlier chemists, $2H+O=H_2O$, is now outmoded. The equality sign is replaced by an arrow, an energy factor is included, and also a factor of pattern of organization. The revised formula expresses, not a balance but a process, and this process is directive, not random.[57]

Is the world (in its whole or in its parts) a story or a syllogism, a development or an equation, a work of art or a work of science? The East has viewed it as a process, unfolding itself; the West has seen it as endowed with order, in space and time. The reconciliation of these two views can be discerned in the biological formula given above, which unites both viewpoints. If we distill out the order of our experience and discard the process, we are left with pure form, such as the tautologies of logic and mathematics; if we expel the order and concentrate on the quality, we are left with pure quality and a substratum of change that, for want of a standpoint and structure, appears as mystic changelessness. But the primary datum of our experience is qualitative movement, interaction, and transformation characterized by dynamic order. There is a logic in events, but it is not perfect, as Plato saw, because events change, interact, unite, and are created and destroyed; there is a movement toward symmetry, never completely fulfilled; there is an activity which, apart from order, would be wild and chaotic, but which, because of that order, has its energy transformed into the direction of development and plot. Thus the determinism of Western mechanism, true to the degree that the past determines the present ("whatever is determinable is determined"[58]) must be supplemented with the doctrine of emergent evolution. Similarly, the Buddhist and Nyāya-Vaiśeṣika doctrine of *asathkārya-vāda* (the non-existence of the effect before its production) must be qualified by the Sāṃkhya and Vedānta view that the effect is in some sense pre-existent in the cause[59] and that necessity is genuine.

The empiricism and logical rationalism of Western science have told us a great deal about the world. But as practised they have produced social and ecological consequences from which increasing numbers recoil. On the other side, Eastern intuition and mysticism, while they have opened our sensitivities to the world, have turned away from the material foundations for the good life. Is there a way through this dilemma, a route for man which will unite the best in each method and view in the service of man's fulfillment?

57. "A Biological Survey of Integrative Levels," in *Philosophy for the Future*, ed. Roy Wood Sellars, V. J. McGill, and Marvin Farber. New York: Macmillan, 1949, p. 224.
58. A. N. Whitehead, *Process and Reality*, p. 41.
59. Chatterjee and Datta, *op. cit.*, p. 259.

IV

The evidence of the lives of Paleolithic peoples indicates that with their "totemic cohesion in space and time" organic naturalism was a world view natural to them, though it was mixed with superstition and the mistakes of rich metaphor.[60] In spite of the divisions and alienations of the class societies of the first great urban civilizations, this world view persisted as a common outlook among the masses of people. While it was exploited by tyrants and priests, who distorted it for their own power and profit, it can be discovered intertwined with the authoritarian politics and cosmic imperialism of ancient Sumer and Egypt.[61] In the West the Jews created in their theology perhaps the most consistent and influential transcendental break with this old naturalistic tradition. For while the ancient Greeks enjoyed nature, as their mythology shows, and while the Ionians and others produced the first self-conscious philosophies independent of religion and naturalistic in substance – it was both Jewish and Neo-Platonic spiritualism which provided the other-worldly ideologies through the long centuries of Greco-Roman disintegration and the dark ages that followed. A thousand years after Christ the revival of the cities was accompanied by a revival of the naturalistic outlook. As Lovejoy has pointed out, the idea of "the great chain of being" was present, ambiguously, in both Plato and Plotinus, was taken up by Augustine and Dionysius the Areopagite, was accepted though repressed by Thomas Aquinas and the other Schoolmen, was presupposed in the Platonic views of the new astronomers, reached a "conspicuous" and "determinative" expression in the philosophy of Leibniz, entered into the rationalism and optimism of the 18th century, was "temporalized" in ideas of progress and evolution, and was turned away from rationalism by the idolatry of diversity among the Romantics.[62]

In this tradition of the great chain of being Hegel inherited the Platonic notion of plenitude, "that no genuine potentiality of being can remain unfulfilled,"[63] and fused it with the Christian notion of an overruling Spirituality, the Enlightenment notion of Progress, and the Greek notion of dialectics. Thus, like Leibniz before him, he conceived the idea of bringing into the scope of reason all the processes of nature and history. Marx, a student of Hegel, was gripped by a similar vision. But under the influence of Feuerbach – in turn influenced by the French materialists, inspired by the Greek and Roman naturalists – Marx saw the root flaw in the Platonic Hegelian

---

60. Gertrude Rachel Levy, *The Gate of Horn*. London: Faber and Faber, 1963, part I.
61. H. and H. A. Frankfort, John A. Wilson, and Thorkild Jacobsen, *Before Philosophy*. Harmondsworth: Penguin, 1949.
62. Arthur O. Lovejoy, *The Great Chain of Being*. New York: Harper, 1960.
63. *Ibid.*, p. 52.

system: the development of real historical and natural processes begins not in abstract Ideas or Spirit but in actual material bodies and forces. God is not the source of movement, conflict, continuity, and growth, but rather, that source is in material nature, in molecules, species, and environmental forces, and in society in forces of production and social classes. Marx saw the implications of both the methods and findings of the sciences for an understanding of social and historical processes. (Hence Engels could compare him to Darwin.) The great chain of being was for him not a state of society and nature already guaranteed or accomplished but a state *possible* within the existing social order and *realizable* by men under appropriate conditions of collective understanding and action.

Thus Marx rejected both the Indian view that the universe is a succession of processes and appearances devoid of any ultimate order or outcome, and the Western Platonic-Christian view that the universe is completely predetermined in all details by an almighty Providence, as well as the Western scientific view of mechanical materialism elevating reason over the real world. Marx proposed the rudiments of a science holding that there is a general order of development in history. He denied that the rising and dying social orders of history cannot be known, that man can take no hand in determining events, and that reason in a contemplative, abstract sense rules or can rule the world. The Oriental dimension in Marx's thought is the emphasis on the priority of natural and social processes: they precede man's reasons and actions, determine what he must know and do, and contain qualities and forms which his reason does not exhaust. The Occidental dimension is Marx's conviction that the world of processes is knowable and will respond within limits to man's descriptions and actions.

Marx's view of the world was a view of orderly processes, dialectically understood. It was arrived at by an analysis of "practical-critical" activity. In this analysis Marx criticized mechanical materialism for wanting sensuous objects quite abstracted from purposeful human activity.[64] (We may add that such a search, evident in the "science" and positivism of much modern thought, is the counterpart of individuals who are themselves alienated from one another and the world and who, being "things in themselves," are looking for their confirmation in the world – isolated individuals seeking and finding isolated individuals.) At the same time Marx criticized the abstractness of idealism – though he paid tribute to its development of the role of man's action in knowledge.[65] Concentrating on social practice, Marx sought to change, preserve, and surpass the objective emphasis of materialism and the subjective emphasis of idealism.

64. Karl Marx. *Theses on Feuerbach*, I.
65. *Ibid.*

Pure sensuous objectivism, empiricism combined with rationalism, forgets the human and creative element which ought to be at the origin and center and at the end, as goal and test, of all knowledge. Here Marx levels a criticism at most of Western science and technology, prostituted in their "neutrality" for the uses of the ruling groups. At the same time, idealism, while it strives to stress the creative and human element in knowledge, fails to make connection with the sensuous, material world which is the other side of all practical knowledge and of all being.

It is along such lines that the traditional separation between Western and Eastern thought, a separation that cuts across geographical areas, may be overcome. It should be noted that this synthesis is not abstract and theoretical alone but concrete and practical. It pertains to knowing-as-being, to thinking-as-doing. It begins with the primary fact that man as "the ensemble of the social relations"[66] is in the world and must interact with it in order to live and to live well. Knowledge as a problem arises only within that context, and as a practical and theoretical problem can be resolved only within that context. That means that the reconciliation of East and West ultimately rests on joint action of peoples in attaining the common human goods of food, shelter, and clothing, and peace, equality, and freedom.

Indian thinkers like Aurobindo, Bhattacharyya, and Radhakrishnan have developed the notion of "integration," which tries to incorporate the scientific and evolutionary emphases of the West with the intuitive and esthetic approach of traditional India. Such efforts, however, seem to me limited by the idealistic premises from which they begin, cutting them off from the great struggles of the masses for survival and material welfare. The work of D. D. Kosambi and Debiprasad Chattopadhyaya, who call for a socialized India, is directly relevant to such struggles; the philosophy they offer is directed not to the salvation of the individual soul but to the feeding of hungry bodies and the lifting of the level of "the ensemble of the social relations."

For a century before Marxism became the dominant philosophy in China, thinkers there were strongly influenced by Western science and scientific philosophy. Given the background of organic naturalism in Chinese thought,

---

66. *Ibid.*, VI. The full original passage reads as follows: "Aber das menschliche Wesen ist kein dem einzelnen Individuum inwohnendes Abstraktum. In seiner Wirklichkeit ist es das ensemble der gesellschaftlichen Verhältnisse." In English: "But human nature is no abstraction dwelling in each separate individual. In its actuality it is the total unity of his primary interpersonal relations." (my translation) Here Marx quite clearly rejects the awkwardness of the floating Platonic universal to which atomism must resort in order to arrive at a "human nature," and he does so in favor of an organic, dynamic view that avoids the Hegelian obliteration of the individual and locates the human "nature" or "essence" in social, objective processes. Cf. George Herbert Mead's definition of mind as social process via significant symbols.

one should not be surprised by the adoption of Marxism – a way of thinking which in Joseph Needham's words, is "in extraordinary congruity with the ideas of dialectical materialism, descended from Leibniz through Hegel."[67] Every philosophy is modified by the cultural traditions and institutions of the society in which it is disseminated and applied, and within the past 25 years we have seen the modification of Marxism within China. What is important to observe is how this Western philosophy, which arose in reaction against much of Western philosophy, is being adapted to the largest national society in the world and one of the oldest in the Orient.

Marxism is a potent philosophy, directly touching the lives of one-third of the world's three billion people. It has been taken up by 15 nation-states because of its practical relevance to the urgent problems of individuals and societies. At the same time, it represents a state of thought and practice in the history of man. It is limited by the material and intellectual conditions of its origin and its career. It will be modified and will be superseded by other philosophies. But during this period, in the last part of the 20th century, the paramount human question is how this philosophy, or indeed any other, can be used and improved to facilitate in an optimal way the fulfillment of all people throughout the planet.

67. In a review of *Chinese Thought from Confucius to Mao Tse-tung*, in *Science and Society*, vol. XVIII, no. 4 (Fall, 1954), p. 375.

Chapter IV

THE UNITY OF MAN AND NATURE IN EAST AND WEST

Man's habitat is nature. There he is created, both as species and as individual, the very atoms of nature's atoms, a compact body and society of bodies that breathe nature's air, drink nature's fluids, feed on nature's foods, and contend with its adversities. There, in and with nature, man strives to survive. He acts upon nature, not only to gather his sustenance, like other animals, but to produce it. He creates tools and industry, transforming nature and himself, and exchanging his labor for its products.

Man's home is nature. There he is born, struggles and grows estranged, takes delight and knows despair. There he doubts and dreams, sings and grieves, suffers and dies. Out of the countless eons of nature's gestations, man rises, a weak wet thing upborne on the foam of time, unbinding his eyes and flexing his strength like all of his many father suns and mother earths before him: an ancient force brought to fresh focus, a creative power recapitulating in new ways the old drama. Many of nature's past experiments are epitomized in him: cells akin to the first living things, the hunger of the Infusoria, the gill of the fish, the tail of the land vertebrate, the sociality of the mammal, the lust of the primate. But in his symbolizing life man celebrates and prophesies a new world emerging, like him, out of the body of the old, a new world of awareness, knowledge, and power. So man's history is nature symbolized, guided and given a voice. And in his creative conservation of nature, man reciprocates the nurture of nature.[1]

Thus man's unity with nature is his identity of substance and process with nature's, his exchanges with it, and his recapitulation and epitomization[2] of nature's own evolution. Man is also affined to nature through the qualities[3] and forms of his perspectives in thought, feeling, and action. The only world he knows is the world (nature) of his experience, immediate or mediate, and the only experience he has is an experience in and of that world.

Toward the matrix (mater, matter) of nature man is dependent and independent. Man receives, but the also gives; he is puppet and puppeteer,

---

1. Hugh Miller, *The Community of Man*. New York: The Macmillan Co., 1949. See also the publications of the Foundation for Integrated Education.
2. George Conger, *A World of Epitomizations*. Princeton: Princeton University Press, 1931.
3. See F. S. C. Northrop's work.

role-player and playwright, natured and naturing being. As man is mothered by Nature, looking backward in gratitude for her gifts, so he is parent himself, mothering and fathering the children of the future. So man, as individuation, serves mankind; so man's physical and spiritual identification with nature, rising to rational consciousness and the vision of not-yet, orders the present and controls the future. As creature man slowly emerges out of the primeval, opaque waters of nature, bearing always distinctive birthmarks – the eyes of wisdom and the undoubling fist of many-dimensioned power – some say the guerdon, others the stolen secret, of the gods. With that talent "which is death to hide," rising to consciousness that turns itself upon self, mankind, history, and nature, man then transforms nature. The primeval waters are released, locked, damned, and turbined into the stream and current of history, and this industrial process in turn transmutes the structured banks of nature. Mountains are brought low, valleys are exalted, rough places are made plain, and deserts are made to blossom like the rose.

Man is nature's child; he is also her parent. She must play the mother to him, and he must lie back upon her bosom; but apart from man, how would her children of time, the offspring of Chronos, the humanity in history, be cared for? Moreover, man needs not only a mother and a child; he needs a lover. Love is the mediation between past and present, between source and outcome; it is the creative flow that binds all together in time. The love that transmits past to future mates itself with a kindred but contrasting nature. It leaves home and mother so as to woo and wed a novel nature. It detaches itself from the withering tie so as to initiate a new attachment and a new line. But wooing is a dialectic of give-and-take, a dance of approach and retreat. It is an act of creation that combines supine mystic absorption and upright aggressive differentiation. It unites the soft receptivity of the child and the devoted detachment of the parent, the passivity of the female and the activity of the male.

Thus say the ancient scriptures of the world: the child of nature springs from the union of Sky-Father and Earth-Mother – Izanagi and Izanami, Yang and Yin, Nut and Geb, Ouranos and Gaea, Zeus and Demeter, Dyaus Pitar and Prithivi Matar, Odin and Hertha, Sky and Earth, and so on through the innumerable names given to this immortal pair. Strong bones and tender flesh, firm order and sensitive plasticity, active thought and receptive feeling – these primal elements are poured and mixed and stirred, and the temper is man, heir alike of heaven and earth.

Yet today such a union is a dream of what has been, far away and long ago, or a hope of what might be. What nature has joined together, nature's journeyman has put asunder. Men are divided from one another and from nature, in varying degrees, throughout the world. This is a fact. Yet a survey

82

of the major religions and philosophies of some major cultures of the world shows a significant difference in what they assert about man and his relation to nature. In general the West, as Northrop[4] and others have pointed out, is theoretical, determinate, scientific, and male in emphasis, separated from and opposed to nature, while the East is intuitive, indeterminate, mystical, and female in emphasis, identified with nature in some way. Our task in this chapter is to trace the origins of these views regarding the unity and division in man's relations to man and to nature, as well as his unity and division in actual social life.

In the prehistoric, food-producing stage of his existence, man had a feeling of an immediate unity with an all-enfolding, at times terrifying nature. His orientation was totemic and magical; it aimed at uniting man's animal needs and those unknown, mysterious powers of nature upon which man depended for his life. Man felt a kinship with the flora, fauna, fish, and fowl of his earth, and sought to maintain or enhance this kinship through rites of sympathy and identification. His viewpoint was primitively naturalistic; it was primarily material and maternal; it aimed to preserve and increase the sources of his food, the plants and animals, in nature. Later, when men became agricultural, cultivating their own cereals, fertility rites emerged, including the ceremonial marriage and the symbolic, sacrificial death of the "corn-king." It was out of the matrix of this agricultural economy that great fertility cults of the dawn of history – Osiris, Tammuz, Attis, Demeter, Dionysus, Odin, Indian śakti and Śiva, and Chinese earth-worship – sprang. These cults of the Great Earth Mother arose in those regions of the Mediterranean, the Near East, India, and China where the vital grains of mankind were first developed, probably by women, and where the givers of life were the goddesses of the soil and waters – settled, constant, rhythmical, conservative, maternal. Ishtar of Sumer, Isis of Egypt, and the Maize-Mother of central America were archetypical goddesses. With apparent independence, cults of fertility have arisen among still more primitive (though not necessarily older) peoples. In *The Sexual and Religious Symbolism of the Tukano Indians*, Gerardo Reichel-Dolmatoff has given an account of Amazonian cosmology still more elementary than these: everything in the cosmos exemplifies the sexual principle of reciprocity – the male energizing, the female being energized, both locked in eternal copulation, while persons are involved in unending exchanges with others and with non-human nature.

There is little doubt that the geography and climate of the great alluvial river valleys of the world shaped those cults and that the original matriarchal economy that grew up around them further influenced their character. There is less evidence concerning the character and religion of northern peoples.

4. *The Meeting of East and West*. New York: The Macmillan Co., 1946.

Yet several thousand years ago there seems to have been some differentiation. The origin of this separation is not clear. We know that the naked human species originated in the tropics, as the work of L. S. B. Leakey and others has confirmed. During the interglacial periods some of the peoples in the settled tropics must have been beckoned by the warming climes and the wandering game to move into northern regions. This very process of migration, if it endured over a long time, must have had some effect in selecting out a more active physical type, nervous and zealous for the hunt. Environmental pressures in turn must have supplemented this selection. At any rate, as recently as a few millennia ago the differentiation appears definite, symbolized by the militant gods of the sky and the fertile goddesses of the earth. The gods of the sky, huntsmen with their star-chained hounds and comet-feathered arrows, nomads in their restless cycles, warriors with their sun-gold shields, their rapier rain, their thunder-salvos, their lightning-lances, their dawn-spears, their eagle-sentinels, their cloud-battalions – these gods, descending from the north, heaven-descended, were born of colder climes and more rigorous terrains. They appeared in ancient North America (as contrasted with the goddesses of Central America)[5] and in the Indo-Aryan peoples of the second millenium B. C. as in search of pastures for their cattle they moved vigorously to invade the warm, fecund southlands lying soft, receptive, and ripe under the sun.

But the Aryan invasions came relatively late, and expressed the antagonism of a nomadic, pastoral people to both peasant and urban communities. An older and deeper antagonism prevailed, of which two stages can be discerned. The first had its beginning at that point in pre-historic "barbarism" or Neolithic times when food-production through cultivation of cereals commenced to supersede the hunting, fishing, fowling, and collecting of fruits, etc., which marked the food-gathering stage. The economy of early food-production, while it entailed some division of labor, and exploitable surplus, was predominantly communal. So man began to plant, cultivate, and selectively improve nature's grasses, roots, and trees.[6] By 3,000 B. C. this food-producing revolution in the cultivation of certain natural resources – characterized by self-sufficiency and absence of specialization[7] – was well established in many places. Then came the first major antagonism in man's social organization. As man undertook the domestication of animals[8] a marked division of labor occurred, as well as a surplus of commodities,

5. Hartley Burr Alexander, *The World's Rim*. Lincoln: University of Nebraska Press, 1953, p. 88.
6. Gordon Childe, *Man Makes Himself*. N. Y.: New American Library of World Literature, 1951, p. 59.
7. Gordon Childe, *What Happened in History*, N. Y.: Penguin Books, Inc., 1946, pp. 52–53.
8. Childe discusses the climatic origins of this in *Man Makes Himself*, pp. 67–69.

and a patriarchal form of society which, taking its place at first alongside the older, agrarian, matriarchal economy, gradually came to dominate it.[9] Thus "mother-right", the concomitant of an agrarian economy, was overthrown and the principles of blood-ties, soil, equality, universality, harmony, and peace were replaced by man-made law, rational thought, distinctions, hierarchical order, conflict, and war. The older sense of unity of man with man and of man with nature was ruptured.

Out of this first antagonism grew a second, brought on by the "urban revolution" for which the Neolithic revolution had prepared the ground. Urbanism was marked by the increasing production of surplus commodities (and hence exchange), growth in population, specialized craftsmen (including intellectuals, priests, and government officials), merchants, money, foreign trade, wars of exploitation, concentration of wealth in the hands of a ruling clique, widespread slavery, and progressive crises in the distribution of commodities. Urbanism thus came into conflict with agrarianism, insofar as the latter was still small and democratic, and this conflict was expressed in the traditional antagonism of city and country, of civilization and nature.

These two antagonisms were kindred: pastoral patriarchy provided a pattern for urban patriarchy, and the beneficent shepherd became the divine king who herded his horde with shepherd-crook, now called a scepter. Religious ideology reflected this change: it elaborated dualisms and supernaturalisms. Throughout the civilized world this clash between patriarchy and matriarchy, under the democratizing pressures of the Iron Age (which began before the first millenium B. C. in Asia Minor), reached a climax in the 6th century B. C. Laymen arose to denounce outmoded religion, priesthoods, and the *ipse dixits* of their day. "Prophets dared to receive direct revelations from the deity – that collective soul substance of barbarians that had comprehended and transcended all the members of a tribe."[10]

It was the century of Heraclitus, Zarathustra, Mahāvīra, Gautama, Laotzu, Confucius, and some of the great Jewish prophets, including Jeremiah and Second Isaiah. Most of these teachers and systems, while contradictions within themselves, urged men to conquer or transcend the contradictions in their societies. Faced with social crises, they sought, like all innovative and revolutionary thinkers, to lay hold of a pattern of living that would organize human living, individual or social, in a new way. They focussed intently on human character and human relations and tried to distil out their essence. It was a time for the assertion of humanistic principles in the face of the dehumanizations of the new Iron Age. At times they concentrated on man and human society (Gautama, Mahāvīra). At other times they visualized

9. See the research of J. J. Bachofen, Lewis H. Morgan, Frederick Engels, and Robert Briffault.
10. *What Happened in History*, p. 204.

man in a restored relation to a non-human nature from which he had become alienated (Lao-tzu). But in all cases the social conflicts of this period meant that that part of nature that was *human* nature now captured the interest of thinkers though non-human nature was always evident in the background of thought.

Thus in the class conflicts of his time Zarathustra championed the struggle of the new Iranian farming class (probably created by new iron tools) against the old, corrupt, magic-wielding priests – a struggle that took the ideological form of naturalism vs. supernaturalism, of the orderly, ethical forces of nature and society (the "Immortal Holy Ones" and other missionaries of Ahura Mazda) vs. the capricious deities of the old Aryan religion, invoked to sanction the nomadic cattle-rustlers of the north. The disruption and waste of the Aryan animal sacrifices and intoxicating rituals became intolerable in the developing agrarian economy. What was required was a single belief in a force of Good against Evil, uniting the individual farmers in a war against the Turanian nomads and their diverse, destructive daevas. Moreover, Zarathustra did not leave his cause to nature, chance, or the gods: He located this life-and-death struggle within the bosoms of men. Responsibility for the course of human affairs was lifted from the priests and the old Aryan gods and put squarely upon the farmer's conscience and action. (Compare Jeremiah's: "I will put my law in their inward parts, and write it in their hearts.") Zarathustra's religion was an ideological response to the economic demand in Iran for the protection of private property in land, crops, and animals. Hence his religion called for a new relation of man toward nature: cultivating the soil with its grains and fruits, weeding and irrigating the crops, reclaiming wasteland, and protecting animals like cows useful to farmers. Against the nomadic depredations on settled communities, his religion prescribed order among men as they worked and traded: truth-speaking and the recognition that a stable ethical order will outlast the disorder of lies and theft. Good deeds have good consequences; evil deeds, evil consequences – such conviction was felt so keenly that it was projected into the very nature of the cosmos. The idea of a last judgment is comforting to every class in the ascendancy.

In India the clash between the invading Aryans and the native population took a different form. The Aryans came out of what is now Uzbekistan looking for pasture. Equipped with their own food on the hoof (cattle), horse chariots for making war, and ox carts for transport, they rapaciously swept through the old tribal settlements, peasant communities, and Indus cities. They mingled with local populations, imposing their language; they disseminated techniques; and they formed new communities.[11] Their gods,

11. D. D. Kosambi, *Ancient India: A History of Its Culture and Civilization.* Cleveland: World, 1969, pp. 76–77.

like their blood, mixed with native Indian counterparts. But the antagonism between the nomadic Vedic gods and the gods and goddesses of the Indian land and the river valleys was never overcome.

With advances in metal-making, agriculture, the use of metal money, and commodity exchange, Indian society of the 6th century B. C. reached a new crisis. Several classes appeared: free peasants and farmers; wealthy traders; financiers and bankers; and wealthy patriarchs of households. Lest such an economy be riddled and destroyed by constant warfare and relapse to a primitive, barbarian level, protection and social unity for all these classes were required. Only an absolute monarch could supply the protection and unity. The new religions of the 6th century India – those of the Upaniṣads, the Ājīvikas, Mahāvīra, and Gautama Buddha – were ideological responses to this social problem. The repudiation of ritual, especially Vedic cattle-sacrifice, by all the new religions was a protest against the extravagant use of food by a single privileged caste.[12] It was during this same period too, as D. D. Kosambi has pointed out, that Kṛṣna, as the representative of the new agrarian economy and the protector of cattle, began to displace the Vedic and the Aryan pastoral war-sacrifice of cattle. More sweepingly, these protestant religions rejected the utility of the traditional scriptures and priesthood. Their claim in behalf of the power of the individual person – any person – to achieve his own salvation was an ideological reflection of the new economy based on widespread private ownership. As the trader, farmer, or manufacturer might by hard work accumulate physical wealth and save himself from physical poverty and death, so the individual person might by proper discipline accumulate spiritual wealth and save himself from spiritual poverty and death. Though at a lower level, this Indian economy can be compared to the bourgeois economy of western Europe which gave rise to the Protestant revolt against traditional religion and its ritual of monopolizing and wasting wealth in money (instead of animals). The new economic classes in India and the founders of the new religions both felt the need for transcending the old tribal organization, and the philosophy of *Realpolitik* – recorded in the *Arthaśāstra* – arose to answer this need in the political sphere. It was a ruthless "universalism," put into force by the tyrants of Kosala and Magadha. Not until the remarkable rule of Aśoka, in the 3rd century B. C., was it demonstrated that humanism in the form of public works – hospitals for people and animals, free medical care, groves, wells, orchards, conservation of natural resources – is both good politics and efficient economics. Gautama argued and Aśoka proved that the conditions of human living then required selfless detachment and benevolence toward sentient things. The antagonism of the old Vedic rituals and the new classes was finally removed.

12. *Ibid.*, pp. 100–102.

The creators of the Upaniṣad philosophy worked within the Vedic-Brāhmanic tradition but imparted to it the spirit of individual insurgent independence being asserted in the economy. The *brahman* present in the Vedic sacrifice and evoked by the precise prayer-formula of the priest was a creative power, the very secret of the gods and the key to all good things. These brash young students who set down the Upaniṣads dared to ask: Might not that divine secret, held to be hidden in the recesses of the universe, but responsive to human chant, be hidden in very man himself? If the priest brings the secret out of the fire of the sacrifice, can he not also bring it out of the fire of his own soul? For if the creative power arises in the soul as the result of the sacrifice, is it not smoldering there in the first place? The Upaniṣad philosophers were spiritual Prometheans who stole the fire of *brahman* from the gods. As for Luther, every man might become his own priest.

It was a time of ideological confusion and search. Many wandered about looking for a way of life that would yield significance and would transform their sense of alienation from self, others, and the world. The mystics of the Upaniṣads claimed to solve the problem by declaring the unity of the apparently isolated self with the whole of the universe: "Ātman is Brahman." Rather than going out to the world, they brought the world into themselves. They overcame the hiatus between themselves, the priest, and *brahman* not by ritual subservience but by becoming priest and sacrifice and *brahman* in one. They did not slay the priest or quench the fire. They seized the formerly exclusive property of the priests. They swallowed up and internalized the formerly forbidding and alienated divine principle. Caste and ritual are of no account. Every man's soul becomes, indeed is, divine. The doleful effects of time, karma, and reincarnation can thus be literally outwitted – for it is wit that triumphs over the divisions of our natural existence.

Who would deny that such an idealist solution is humanistic, displacing the gods and the priests from their thrones and placing each man at the center of things? Yet in seeming to supersede man's separation from other men and from nature this solution glosses over the distinctions and oppositions between men and men and between men and non-human nature. It is an easy intellectual solution, a solution born of solitude and meditation, which a family man and a working man, who must struggle with others and with the physical world day by day, cannot accept. While it expresses in idealized form a fulfillment of man's longing for recovery of his lost unity, it could not practically serve the purposes of any but a leisure class, whether wealthy or mendicant.

The religions of 6th century India inherited two ideas that were axiomatic for them at the time – *karma* and rebirth. The idea of transmigration was originally the primitive idea that the soul of the deceased person returns to his totem in some bodily form; ancestor worship stems from the idea. *Karma*, as a crude law of cause and effect, was no doubt developed from the agrarian observation that what a man sows he will reap, and the idea of rebirth is confirmed in the regeneration of plants from seeds. The invading Aryans found this idea among the native tribal population and their priests turned it to their own account. Since merit for good deeds and punishment for bad deeds do not appear until the next incarnation of the soul, *karma* provided a powerful reinforcement for the division of castes. Moreover, by the 6th century B. C. *karma* as a law of accumulating or diminishing merit reflected the commodity and money economy based on accumulation. It meant not only the fruit of the seed and the storehouse of harvested grain; it meant a pile of accumulating money and the maturing of a loan. This commercialization of *karma* was significant, for it provided a transition from the agrarian-rooted and brahmin-exploited *karma* to the psychological and hence conquerable *karma* of the heretics of the 6th century B. C.

The brahmin priests were reactionary. They stood atop a social trap which fixed each man in his place because of presumed past deeds and misdeeds and doomed him from an escape in this life. Human living was construed as constructed of dark corridors leading out of the remote past and into the remote future, with all doors of exit locked. It was a system adapted to generate dumb obedience and despair in the masses and smug confidence in the ruling classes.

The recognition of *karma* is a quasi-naturalistic attitude, even if the subject of the law of cause and effect is a living but non-natural soul. The Ājīvikas of this period inherited a system of evolutionary natural science in which bodies are graded in ascending levels of complexity from the simple, sensitive atoms through the vegetables and animals and up to man in his various stage of purity. In the process of reincarnation each living soul begins at the lowest level and passes, after 8,400,000 kalpas, to the end of the final stage and release. This process of spiritual evolution through physical forms is strictly determined and is subject to neither chance, the intervention of the gods, nor human will. There is a certain liberating breadth in this grand vision of the cosmos and man's place in it, comparable to the vision of the Stoics or of modern scientific evolutionary thought. No petty human wishes or illusory hopes stain its clean detachment and calm objectivity. Yet, while this philosophy has absorbed the hard-headed realism of the new classes, its velleity and passivity make common cause with the old oppressive brahmin class. Apparently some of the Ājīvikas did not permit this view of life to depress them, if we are to believe the report that Gosāla drank and participated in sexual orgies. This dionysian indifference to the course of things probably derived originally from the fertility cults, and the idea of spiritual escape seems to have been only half-heartedly overlaid upon that.

Western supernaturalism and predestinarianism has been similarly ineffective in controlling the daily appetites of most people.

But just as the new agricultural and commercial classes were breaking out of the old pastoral economy, so new ideologies arose to escape from the dark oppression of *karma* and the endless rebirth into misery, and to open the doors to a bright and free future.

The earliest of these heresies was Jainism, which may predate the 6th century B. C. by as much as two centuries. It was a religion of heroic resistance to fate. Jainism as a pre-Aryan philosophy began with the naturalistic notion that the physical world consists of indestructible atoms whirled round in an everlasting process of combination and dissolution. The problem of human living is that sentient, eternal souls are caught up in various bodies of this matter and, undergoing the endless suffering that is consequent on bodily involvement, are struggling to break free from the law of *karma* and rebirth. Jainism provides the following analysis of the cause and corrective for the soul's suffering. Being ignorant about the way things and souls are and the way they are implicated in each other, the soul, influenced by previous karma, gives way to anger, pride, infatuation, and greed. As modes (though inessential) of the soul, these qualities in their stickiness attract the finest particles or karmic matter. This accumulation of matter in sheaths around the soul produces the bondage of the soul to embodiment, rebirth, and suffering. The solution is to prevent the influx of new karmic matter into the soul and to purge the soul of already accumulated matter. The method of liberation is knowledge of the problem, respect for truth, and practice of the five great vows: ahimsā, truthfulness, non-stealing, non-self-indulgence, and non-attachment.

Although the specific social conditions accompanying the rise of Jainism are not now known, it is probable that this heroic effort of the human spirit signified a widespread struggle throughout society. The overpowering force of the physical world and the idea of *karma* rule the imagination of peoples at a tribal level. But the advent of agriculture and the rise of cities inevitably creates a new outlook: man labors to create a new world with his mind and hands, and when he rests and observes, he finds that his creation is good and that he has risen above the limitations of blind physical nature. The Jainas had a similar insight in the moral domain. Their injunctions against killing, deceit, and selfishness in general suggest a response to the challenges of new and complex social organization. In the 6th century B. C. such moral standards, running directly opposite the Vedic way of life, facilitated the advance of an economy built increasingly on transactions rather than on brute force and authority. While Jainism is an ultimate dualism, eventually separating all souls from all bodies, for practical purposes it brings man closer to nature by atuning him to the sentient plants and animals all around him. It sensitizes him to a cosmos in which all creatures are struggling to secure surcease from the blind and painful lust for life. And in this sensitivity it does not resign itself to fate or rely irresponsibly on the gods or priests. It nobly calls on man to take up the titanic task of liberation from bondage: "Man," said Mahāvīra, "you are your own friend. Why do you wish for a friend beyond yourself?"

A contemporary of Mahāvīra, Gautama also started from the presuppositions of *karma* and rebirth. Like him also he showed that the responsibility for suffering lies with man himself, who must work out his own salvation with diligence. The elaborate chain of causation between ignorance, craving, clinging, and continuity of personality is as subtle as any modern psychological analysis. What was of great import was Gautama's *naturalizing* and *humanizing* of an otherwise blind and impenetrable process operating out of the reach of man. Gautama had the insight and courage to focus on this process of ego-enslavement going on in man and to propose how it might be understood and conquered. He showed that suffering comes from selfishness, which in turn springs from the illusion of self. The "middle way" between asceticism and indulgence was a recognition that desire cannot be totally extinguished through withdrawal or sublimated in mystical absorption in the universe, and that the incessant pursuit of desire is equally fatuous. Unlike the Jainas, his quest for selflessness carried him back into the world instead of away from it. Being in reality a temporal composite of processes and qualities, what passes for the body-associated self is only one of many such clusters of processes in a nexus of similar clusters.

This is a more unitary and social view of man than that of Jainism. Jainism like Epicurean atomism isolates and substantivizes souls. For it each soul is a monadic individual, eternally lonely. The sympathetic regard that it is asked to exercise for every other individual soul can only be arbitrary, since even after it breaks free of the karmic bondage here below and ascends like a bubble into the heavens, past the ethereal spheres of the radiant gods and up to the very dome of the universe itself, resting there eternally in motionless bliss and perfect knowledge – how can it have need for or be affected by its neighbors? In spite of Hīnayāna, which seems to follow Jainism at this point, Gautama had a social view of man which avoids both pure mystical monism and atomism, physical as well as spiritual. (It later broke into dualism; but Mahāyāna carried forwarded the social view.) Hence the Buddha's ethics follows consistently from that view: right views about the nature, cause (selfish desire), and removal of suffering; right resolution to renounce attachments, ill-will, and harmful acts; right speech, which cements and makes happy social relations; right conduct – preserving life, not stealing, not indulging the self; right livelihood, which means harmonizing one's way of working by harming neither animals nor men;

right effort to eradicate evil thoughts; right mindfulness, or the vigilant awareness that the various states of the body and mind are not permanent and are not the self; and right meditation, or discipline in mental training.

All of these are severe internalized controls over individual desire, and their ultimate intent is to bring the individual person into harmonious and happy relations with other persons and with the rest of nature. This philosophy reveals a deep concern with the state of society. Its preoccupation with the suffering that flows from uncontrolled desire indicates a period of social breakdown and of conscienceless activity on the part of many. Gautama and his followers, sensitive to the horrors of killing and greed, of the heedless exploitation of both man and nature, turned away from them and sought earnestly to establish a new social order on the foundations of self-abnegation rather than self-assertion. The measure of the truth and applicability of this new vision of individual and social life has been evident in the success of Aśoka's reforms and in the great growth of Buddhism throughout the world for 2500 years.

Living at a higher stage of Iron Age development, Jewish prophets found themselves confronting a ruling class who "grind the faces of the poor"[13] and "buy the poor for silver, and the needy for a pair of shoes,"[14] and on whose hands is found "the blood of the innocent poor."[15] Here the commercialism of their own people, the greed and cruelty of the big empires, hypocrisy of official religion, and the indulgence of the fertility cults are all excoriated. The Iron Age disseminated iron weapons and tools but also ideas about justice. And the antagonism of the demands for justice and mercy among men, over against the anti-humanism of trade and empire, were obvious to those who had eyes to see. The Jewish prophets exhorted men to return to an earlier communal pattern of humanizing relations with one another. But the economy of the Near East was too advanced into class divisions and war among rival empires for any Aśoka or religious Messiah to change matters and to resolve the contradiction. Five hundred years later the utopian insurrection of Jesus and his comrades was crushed by the Romans. Yet even that victory did not eliminate the antagonism between the urban powers and the later followers of a crucified leader who likened his people to tender lambs, fallen sparrows, and the lilies of the field. For Jesus, who viewed himself in the line of these prophets, the sense of each man's unity with every other man and with nature, and the sense of class exploitation, had reached a peak of new intensity in history. The crises of the Iron Age with its slave empires were deepening. Although the imperial power prevailed, it was already beginning to crumble, unable to organize man's society or man's

13. Isaiah 3: 15.
14. Amos 8: 6.
15. Jeremiah 2: 34.

92

relation to nature in ways that could sustain the large population that it was undertaking to rule and to tax.

In China the class conflicts that gave rise to early philosophies were unique. During the Ch'un-Ch'iu period (722–481 B. C.) the society dominated by the patriarchal, aristocratic, racial, slave-master rulers disintegrated. The primary economic cause for this disintegration was the use of iron plows. This change in the mode of production was accompanied by the growth of individual owners of lands, handicrafts, and trading enterprises, by commodity exchange and the use of metal money, and by increasing antagonism between the new private economy and the old patriarchal, communal economy based on blood ties. Some nobles became wealthy; others were thrown down into the class of plebeians or slaves. New landlords competed for hegemony with each other and with ruling slave-masters. Slaves broke away from rural communes, and commercial cities became the new political unit. It was a time of turbulent class conflict and struggle.

Philosophies arose in response to this conflict. The ideology of the old patriarchal slave system included ancestor worship, filial devotion, blood kinship ties, ritual, and political rule by aristocracy.[16] Roughly speaking, the philosophers sided with either the dying class or the rising class, urging the conserving or improving of the old ways and the old ideology or else proposing new ways adapted to new conditions.

In this struggle Confucius took the position of a humanistic, moderate conservative, rational and skeptical of the mythology of the old order (e.g., the beliefs in the gods and in the afterlife) but zealous in his preachment for upholding the *li* in familial and political relations. With the widespread dissolution of patriarchal relations, philosophers began to inquire into the meaning and foundation of human relations, and Confucius' concept of *jen* (man-to-manness) was a striking insight, though it was confined within the *li* of traditional proprietary relations. While Confucius came from a poor family, he was descended from nobles, developed an interest in the classics at an early age, and aspired to become a scholar in the traditional sense of serving and advising a political leader. Yet as an unattached, wandering, and often unemployed teacher whose ideas were never acceptable to the patriarchal rulers, he was aware of the limits of prevailing politics. And he was open to the humanizing influences of the age – in religion, for example, he asked whether the belief in the supernatural or the rites for the dead served any useful human purpose.

In the thought of Lao-tzu we can detect a similar though different un-

16. The foregoing account on China follows Kuan Feng and Lin Lü-shih, "Characteristics of Social Change and Philosophical Thought During the Ch'un-Ch'iu Period," *Chinese Studies in Philosophy*, vol. II, no. 1–2 (Fall-Winter, 1970–71), pp. 80–112. This is a translation, from the Chinese, of a portion of *Essays in Ch'un-ch'iu Philosophy*, Peking, 1963.

resolved antagonism. There is in the *Tao Te Ching* an unprecedented grasp of the dialectical way (*Tao*) of things, of the way in which things are implicated in their opposites and subtly pass over into those opposites. During this period in China's history, Lao-tzu had the opportunity to observe the mutual transformation of things, their appearance, dissolution, and reappearance, and to speculate on the ultimate law that governs such changes. There is nothing like his work with its succinct formulations of the way things change. Yet it is quite general and is not applied to historical change. The *Tao*, as the model for man's imitation, is detached, and passive; and while it is a dynamic way – "The Way that may truly be regarded as the Way is other than a permanent way" (1)[17] – the expositor of it recoils before the conflicts of actual history. Politics in the traditional mold is scored – but disowned. The ruler rules by not ruling. (57) He follows the Way (59) and behaves like a steward rather than an authority. (51)

One criticism of Lao-tzu's work is that it is idealistic and reactionary, that it sides with the patriarchal rulers against the rising landlord class.[18] Yet he is critical of all government that tries to manipulate and force people against their needs and will. He reproaches state coercion for producing poverty. (57) He recognizes the role of force in past societies and realizes that another way must be found for eradicating destructive antagonisms among people. The good leader will serve and not dominate the people. (66) Neither patriarchs nor landlords are willing to render such service. Thus Lao-tzu's ultimate position separates itself from both of these warring classes. He discerns that neither class, with its fixed and partial interests, can lead the whole society and speak from a universal perspective. Yet this discernment is couched in metaphysical terms which are cryptically political. The criticism of both classes as pretended carriers of a universal order overtly leads to a position of passive detachment and retreat. Implicitly, however, it appears to aim at transcending all classes.

Lao-tzu's book was an effort to reach toward communism at a time and place when a universal class and the conditions conducive for ushering in a classless society did not exist. Yet a society in which the state has withered away is almost described in chapter 57 of the *Tao Te Ching*. Simple, rural, utopian communism is depicted (80), with a bucolic felicity somewhat like that of Thomas More's *Utopia*. A prevision of international harmony is set down in Chapter 61. Lao-tzu was groping toward a society beyond the realizable possibilities of his own day. In this sense he may be called idealistic. But while he could not solve the real antagonisms of his time, he foresaw a time when all antagonisms of man with man and man with nature might be

17. *Tao Te Ching*, trans. J. J. L. Duyvendak. London: John Murray, 1954. Numbers in parentheses in the following pages refer to chapter numbers in this translation.
18. Kuan Feng and Lin Lü-shih, *op. cit.*, pp. 95, 101.

resolved if man would understand and follow the dialectics of his unity with nature.

Moreover, this work consistently manifests a sympathy for the common man and the lowly station. The "uncarved block" is the state of integrity in the individual and the state of communal solidarity[19] among men in society before cities and the divisions of labor of "civilized" society fractured that into "vessels" or specialists. (28) Like the Jewish prophets Lao-tzu bitterly decries that gluttonous luxury and ostentatious display of the ruling classes:

> When the Court is well purified, but the fields are full of weeds and the granaries are empty, (the rulers) wear decorated and embroidered robes, gird themselves with sharp swords, glut themselves with food, and have superfluous possessions; – this I call robbing and bragging.[53]

And again: "If the people starve, it is because of the quantity of taxes consumed by their superiors." (75) Thus while the metaphysics, though an organic naturalism, tends to be abstract and does not develop Shih Po's idea that "things are produced when matter combines," strains of materialism emerge when Lao-tzu makes comments like those above. The wise political leader, he says, does not exalt ability or hold out rewards that turn people into robbers. He "empties their hearts and fills their bellies" (3; cf. also 12) – a way of contrasting the chaos of a society based on private property and private desire with a society in which every person receives according to his basic needs. This latter precept looks like vulgar communism – though Lao-tzu did not intend to exclude the cultivation of the right attitude – but it is put forward in deliberately jolting contrast to the social-climbing "culture" of the newly wealthy classes of landlords, farmers, and merchants. Lao-tzu is scornful of the Confucianists who believe that a permanent government can be established, tidy and lawful, based on moral principles found in nature. (Compare the 18th century Western European bourgeois religion of natural reason.) Nature treats everything "like straw dogs." (5) Therefore, he seems to say, it is foolish to try to arrest the transformations of history, which is a part of nature. Yet Lao-tzu does not draw the conclusion that history has a direction which man can know and facilitate. Rather, he concludes that since all things change, man should seek the tranquil source of change and there abide.

Finally, the idea of revolution, though it seems to be implied by the recognition of class exploitation and the material basis for successful government, is not openly expressed. Yet in one place it is alluded to. The know-

---

19. Joseph Needham, *Science and Civilisation in China*. Vol. II, *History of Scientific Thought*. Cambridge: Cambridge University, 1956, p. 114.

ledge that one cannot rule through mere cleverness, through isolation from the needs of the people, is virtue. This "is profound, is far-reaching, and operates contrariwise to things, till in the end it attains the Grand Conformity." (65) The term *fan* ("operates contrariwise") means both "to reverse" and "to rebel,"[20] just as "revolt" in English (from Latin) means to turn round or turn back: all revolution is a turning back toward a condition previously overturned. The reversal requisite for the achievement of social harmony is a movement of revolution against the social order that Lao-tzu criticizes. But clearly the leader cannot alone effect a revolution, since "he makes the mind of the people his own" (49); he must be the leader of a people's revolution; he must follow where the people lead.

The juxtaposition of these revolutionary ideas alongside the metaphysics leads one to suspect that the *Tao Te Ching* is a compilation of at least two works and that the form in which we have it is the product of emendations which have expunged the boldly radical parts – in the same way that the Gospels of Christianity are a mosaic of the slabs of orthodoxy and the chips of the original radical cornerstone.[21] Confucian scholars and ruling groups preserving the manuscripts of antiquity might tolerate pictures of utopia but they could not tolerate too much talk of revolution. (Even so the revolutionary tradition persisted: Mencius asserted the right of revolution, and the peasants' revolts of the Ch'un-Ch'iu period left their mark in the people's culture.)

The *Tao Te Ching* likens the *Tao* to "the valley" and "the dark female" (6) and beckons people back to the "root" from which they sprang. (16) Such images, along with other evidence, confirm the impression that this philosophy had ancient roots in agrarian society nourished in a river valley, and that the final compiling of the book sometime after 300 B. C.[22] represented an adulteration of the early contents. Nevertheless, the naturalism remains intact. The *Tao* of sky, earth, and man unites to make all things interact in a constantly changing and organically integrated pattern. "The mother" is the source of all things. (1, 52) It is that on which the wise man feeds. (20) In a remarkable passage Lao-tzu speaks of "surrendering one's trust" and returning to the source. (16) His recurrent image of the infant comes to mind, the simple and dependent infant who "feeds" on the mother and who through surrender to her grows and flourishes. Against an urbanized society of separations and estrangements among men, Lao-tzu was groping back toward the creative origins of human living – and found the key in the suckling, trusting infant, a symbol of adult man's childlike relation to nature. The antithesis of this sustaining relation is the disintegration of distrustful city

20. See the footnote of Duyvendak, *ibid.*, pp. 139–140.
21. S. G. F. Brandon, *Jesus and the Zealots*. New York: Charles Schribner's 1967.
22. Duyvendak, *op. cit.*, his Introduction, p. 7.

life. The antagonism between the agrarian, feminine Way and the way of the male-dominated, class-based cities is clear and explicit.

Taoism is one of many orientations in the East that began and remained maternal. Of course Confucianism was determinate, hierarchical, and autocratic, and we have already observed that the Aryan outlook in India – which left its influence in the code of Manu – was highly determinate. On the whole, however, the Eastern philosophies and religions have been more sympathetic to "the dark female" that have their Western counterparts, which have inclined to the paternal and male viewpoint. Why has the East been more friendly to naturalism, whereas in the West supernaturalism has flourished as nowhere else?[23] Why has the East stayed closer to the southern, agrarian orientation, while the West seems to have favored an orientation opposite to that? Is there a significant differentiation between culture along a north-south axis?[24]

Some answers suggest themselves in geography, economics, and biology. If we look at a map of the world showing the originating places of the leading religions of man, we find them located in an area stretching from the Yellow Sea in the east to the Red Sea and the Mediterranean Sea in the west, and lying between the 40th and the 20th parallels north. This is a temperate and sub-tropical zone. The religions sprang from non-mountainous regions in relatively populous centers of civilization supported by extensive agriculture. China, India, and the eastern coast of the Mediterranean still rank among the most populous areas in the world. The societies in these regions were agrarian, and it is natural that the world view and the view of man associated with that way of life would be reflected in the religions and philosophies there. (Where the world view shows little or no maternal influence, as in parts of Judaism, Zoroastrianism, and Islam, specific conditions other than geography must be considered.)

23. Idealism, which Conger identifies with Indian philosophy of religion, I regard as a kind of attenuated naturalism which assimilates material nature to ideal nature. Historically naturalism, which is associated with materialism, has been opposed to idealism. Yet both tend to be monistic in metaphysics (recall how Marx and then Dewey transmuted Hegel), and both tend to be opposed to the dualism of supernaturalism, which is the archenemy of naturalism. As for China, I think it is generally agreed by scholars that, alongside the proliferation of popular superstitions, she has tended to be monistic and naturalistic in outlook.
24. This division is suggested only in passing in Charles Morris' *The Open Self*. N. Y.: Prentice-Hall, Inc., 1948, pp. 40–42. It is, I think, confirmed in Northrop's analysis of northern Protestantism and southern Catholicism in both Europe and the Americas. See *The Meeting of East and West*. New York: The Macmillan Co., 1946. The cultural differences between the more promethean northern Europe and the more sensuous, esthetic Mediterranean Europe were transplanted to the western hemisphere, differentiating North America from Latin America. In 1900 José Enrique Rodó brought out a similar distinction in his *Ariel*, and the buoyancy of socialist Cuba's *humanismo* illustrates how a Latin American culture can give its own unique flavor to the social prometheanism of Marxism.

India and China are both more or less autonomous geographical units cut off from the outside by natural barriers of mountains, seas, and deserts. While invaded periodically, they have evolved in their river valleys and plains stable and conservative cultures, living at a relatively simple agrarian level. Such conditions have probably been conducive to the selection of well adapted physical types in these regions over a period of several thousand years.

By contrast the cultures of western Europe and North America, incomparably younger and more dispersed, have developed in and spread out from islands or land masses with easy access to rivers and seas. Such bodies of water invited and indeed commanded exploration and trade. Westerners have thereby organized and given technical force to the restless mobility of nomadism. The freedom of movement allowed them by the slow tempering of Europe's climate, with the consequent accelerated interaction of peoples and ideas, was a prime mover in the West's crusades, navigations, wars, and sciences. It abetted the expansive force of an urban and autocratic economy, which had to seek new markets or die. Westward the course of empire took its way. This three-thousand year struggle has perhaps selected out and preserved a mesomorphic physical type.[25] For such a type life is regarded as a quest and a struggle, and the natural myth springing from the conditions of struggle was the Zoroastrian, Jewish, Christian, and Muslim dualism depicting a cosmic battle between the forces of good and the forces of evil.[26] Ahura Mazda commanded his believers to rectify the unrighteous with the sword; this god of flaming light became the symbol and model providing sanction for Xerxes in his Western expansion. Similarly, the waves of Christian and Mohammedan advance which swept over Europe were expressions of a deity who wrestled with principalities and powers and who marched in the vanguard of the legions of light against the rulers of the darkness of this world. Persian, Roman (Mithraic), and Mohammedan armies rolled over Europe like the crescendo movement of breakers on a beach, eventually spending their forces in that westward expansion. And the myths of all expressed the urgency of the struggle between good and evil. Charles Morris, following Huntington, maintains that "the power-inventive,

25. Mesomorphy is the degree of muscle, bone, and connective tissue in a human physique. The evidence for this is common sense and conjecture. I know of no thorough comparative study of Eastern (and Western) physiques. Ashley Montagu says that the Chinese type tends toward the childlike and feminoid. *The Natural Superiority of Women*. New York: The Macmillan Co., 1953, pp. 71, ff.
26. The social and economic roots (the "kinship system" and the "occupational system") of the aggression of Western society are dealt with in some detail by Talcott Parsons in "Certain Primary Sources and Patterns of Aggression in the Social Structure of the Western World", in *A Study of Interpersonal Relations*, ed. Patrick Mullahy, New York: Hermitage Press, Inc., 1949, pp. 269–296.

98

power-accumulative, power-driven, and power-explosive West" is "a great northward thrust of mesomorphy...."[27]

But the Orient, unaware of the grim rigors and uncertainties of the frontier, built a different account of the cosmos: good and evil, forever turning and interchanging places, are white and black phases in a circling, the day and night of *Brahman* or *Tao*. The "path of life" does not move onward and upward toward the pinnacle of the pole: it is rather a turning, a bending back on itself until the self comes full circle and knows at the uncircumscribed center of things that the self is the All and that the soul is God. Persistent progress poleward or westward will only lead a man home through the mysterious East – the longest way around, perhaps, but the shortest way home. If the Westerner answers that this great circle that girdles the little globe of man's experience must be a spiral, then the Easterner will reply, That too turns on itself. And so we are lost between East and West, circles within spirals within circles.

The practical dualism of the Western pioneer, whether on the frontier of Gaul or Massachussetts, has converted itself into a horizontal supernaturalism; and the catalyst for this conversion has come from those who retreated from the struggles of life and lost themselves in an other-wordly mysticism.[28] Moreover, Promethean man, as Mumford points out, making an enemy out of whatever appears to stand in the way of his purposes, felt the threat of anabolic woman, and to make terms with her reduced her to a plaything.[29] In this supernaturalist view man, the wanderer out of heaven and the warrior star-crowned, felt himself fatally magnetized by the attraction of mother earth. So he fell from heaven into her garden of paradise, and descended to her bed to enjoy the fruits and transact the pleasures of that playground; he was the Roman imperial eagle, weary of wars, coming to rest in the lap of Cleopatra's burnished barge. Disobeying his nomadic instincts, man was lured into the toils of domestication: woman, aided by the serpent of the fields, her bosom-companion and co-conspirator, successfully tempted man off the straight and narrow heavenly highways and into the hearth-fires and seductive flowering fields of her home. The winged feet of Mercury were shorn; the golden locks of the Samson-Sun were fleeced; Attis was slain; Osiris was buried. Man, who once in undistracted bliss tasted of the ambrosia and nectar of the gods and hoped for the eternal houri of heaven, must till the fields by the sweat of his brow and eat of the common bread baked in the maternal oven. Like the oxen whom he followed, man was yoked into

27. Morris, *op. cit.*, p. 41.
28. Thus W. H. Sheldon says that "as species we may have been more or less caught in the monkey trap of leakage of mysticisms from hebephrenic minds over into somatotonic bodies." *Varieties of Delinquent Youth.* New York: Harper and Bros., 1949, p. 847.
29. Lewis Mumford, *The Conduct of Life.* New York: Harcourt, Brace and Co., 1951, p. 203.

docile, domiciled domesticity. But every man who called himself by the manly name of male yearned to be free from this fall into the stickiness of the feminine. The aristocratic philosophies of India taught him refined and esoteric techniques for obtaining his release. These came to us in the West by the mediation of the Greeks, who received them from the Pythagoreans and passed them on to the Christian theologians. The classical Aryan potencies of light and justice were transformed in the West into the abstractions of philosophy. Thus the popular gods were consigned to the incessant dance of Śiva and his consort Kālī, and to the perennial rising and dying of nature's sons and daughters – Dionysus, Orpheus, Persephone. The ruling class, invariably male, might find its salvation above and beyond the popular pastimes of bread and wine and circuses, and the mortal frailties whose name is woman.

Yet the victory of the male over the female in the supernaturalist West has never been complete. There is no victory in retreat, even if the retreat is heaven. Conquest comes through the assimilation of the enemy, as every battle issues in a transformation in the antagonists. Opposition means unity, and because the opposition is dialectical, victory and defeat will always be temporary forms assumed in an unceasing process. So the triumph for which the male has yearned would have meant the kingdom of heaven: annihilation of sex, mystery, fertility, time, and history. Where male is isolated conclusively, eternally, from female, how on earth can there be creation or re-creation of this life? How can there be redemption, a second opportunity, a new life, a child? But the Westward way is withdrawal, abstraction, escape, annihilation; it is not the way of immersion, concretion, action, and fulfillment. Not surrender to what labors and suffers below, but refuge in what rules and contemplates above. We have lost the faith of our fathers (nay, our mothers) that that incarnate god who was reviled by evil and crushed by death rose again from the grave to abide with men wherever they are gathered together, and that he lives and suffers and dies and rises again and again in time, for in time there are the almighty father and the holy mother who never fail their children and are with us until the end of the earth.

In the sub-tropical cultures of ancient civilizations, the maternal has maintained its hold over peoples; through the millennia of violent conquest and half-conscious torpor, her hand has rocked the cradle of civilization. The masses in Greek and Roman times continued to celebrate in their mystery religions the creative and redemptive powers of Mother Nature even after the principles of urbanism and autocracy had come to dominate a large portion of their lives. In time a division of labor was worked out permitting the male element to pass on and express his restlessness in the expansive power of imperial armies and the sublimated Faustian search of science while the women remained at home to tend the grains which they had rescued and fostered from the beginning, and to cultivate the arts of childrearing, of domestication, and of peace.

So for the several thousand years of human history men have striven to cope with the disharmonies and alienations of an urban existence, wrestling with the tensions of unity and variety, emotion and intellect, the ploughshare and the sword, as Jacob wrestled with the angel, or as the earth-bound Anteus wrestled with the heaven-born Hercules. Man's life is a crux and a crossroads; his religions have blazed two trails, one the upward supernatural path paved with mother-of-pearl and lined with ghostly primroses bleached of all chlorophyll, the other the downward simple regression into animal nature. Both in the end fail; one abandons the body, the other the mind. Heavenly harpists gowned in Milky Way shrouds and playing each under his bloodless-grapevine and star-blossomed fig tree, are no more possible to man now than the simple communism of Taoism and of early Christianity. But these latter, as historical facts ingredient in our living heritage, may give us a clue as to where we go from here. The butterfly comes from a pupa, and not from an abstract possibility.

Supernaturalism has a natural history. It is the myth that naturally facilitates the functions of a society divided against itself: ruler against country, intellectual against artisan, reason against emotion, heaven against earth, God against nature. The convenient ideology of many a ruling class, supernaturalism is one of the asthenic fruits of asceticism; it was borrowed and transformed into a marketable commodity by the professional hirelings of autocracy. We may presume that this asceticism was fed by many sources – the constitutions and temperaments of certain men, divided economies, and straitened conditions of living. Perhaps it was in part an attempt on the part of urban rulers at controlling sex in the interest of maintaining the stability and security of a patriarchal society. Engineered by the agencies of propaganda, supernaturalism provides, in addition, a specious appeal to man's need for unity: city-dwellers and inhabitants of empire, fragmented and anonymous, seek some principle that appears, at least, to be over-arching, invisible, infallible, and unifying. The picture of a single, otherworldly father, a shepherd who rules the herd with a rod of anger and whose Word is law, benign but severely just to his earthly flock, is concrete and personalized. It is the highest ideal that people living under patriarchy can conceive. It has dominated Western religious thought. Yet alongside this theme, blown with such baroque fanfare from imperial thrones, has run the softer, more modest, more mellow flute-notes of a simple naturalism. This latter lacks the spectacular, charismatic, spellbinding power of supernaturalism, and does not lend itself to authoritarian social structure, as the history of the Anabaptist movement shows. It appeals primarily to folk who live on the land, or to those laborers in the city who experience directly the joys and sorrows of common striving and suffering, or to those of the city only recently removed from the rememberable rural unities and progressions – the growth of the grain, the glory of the flowers and the grandeur of the hills, the unanxious life of the birds, the bucolic pleasantries of a Cotter's Saturday night, parental and filial love, and the short and simple annals of the poor. Natural piety in man is hard to kill, for man is a creature, an autochthon, of nature: transplant him to a city and this tough grass still springs up on the sunlit side of a factory where men eat their lunches and share the crusts and hopes of their lives.

Naturalism is the natural enemy of autocracy. It tolerates no potentates in heaven, nature, or society. It does not adapt itself easily to the hierarchical principle of urbanism, or to its highly analytical, abstractive, and overspecialized character. It is agglutinative: it proclaims an immanent principle of unity, here and now. It is antagonistic to rigid compartments and arbitrary impositions. It is inimical to fixed ultimates. It repudiates privileged permanencies, and despises radical discontinuities. It is a philosophy of flux; as all men are born of nature, so all die in nature, and so all are equalized in the democracy of life and death, and, if they live and die nobly, are saved unto a life beyond life in the invisible but living stream of history. Naturalism can believe in a communion of saints, past and present; the great souls of the past through their deeds and thoughts become incarnate in the throbbing body of present creative time.

The Western world has had its own submerged but forever re-emerging, resurrectable heroes: Dionysus, Persephone, the Suffering Servant and Messiah of Judaism, and Christ. How different these dark, blood-stained gods of earth from those leisure-loving gods of Olympus and the Celestial City, reigning from on high with authoritarian caprice, knowing nothing but eternal light and the harmonious music of the spheres, philosophically unperturbed in the empyrean! Brahmā and Zeus may be done with their labors, retired to their suburban estates far from the madding crowd; but these gods and goddesses, driven forever by the lash of time, the gonads of the flesh, and the lures of the spirit, must be always active, restless, sportive, creative, suffering, dying, and rising again. And they will always be dear and undying to the masses of men and women because they are the tragic but redemptive embodiments of the people, the unfailing holy comforters and fellow-sufferers who understand and inspire man in his eternal labors of love. Western theologians, in the service of the leisured class, have sought to etherize Christ upon a heavenly table, to evaporate his earthly potency into a kind of spiritual essence faintly smelling of formaldehyde and Levantine spices and dwelling in ivory palaces not built with horny hands, and to transmogrify his broken body and shed blood, into mere symbols – devitamin ized bread crumbs and watered-down grape juice. But every man who has been crucified with the Christ of thorns and nails knows that his redeemer lives and rescues life from death through the blood of the everlasting covenant.

In the East, near and middle and far, this unity of man and nature is fully as old and as deeply rooted as in the West. Presumably the settlements if not the civilizations on the Yellow River go back to c. 3000 B. C., the time of the first Egyptian, Sumerian, and Indian civilizations. And the sacrificial principle is there in China, no less than in India. The notion of the *Tao*, which is victorious in defeat and eternal through all destructions, is a refined form of the principle; the Chinese P'an Ku, creator of the world, fashions it with hammer and chisel until at last, lying down in the midst of his labors, his body disintegrates that it might give motion and life to his work. So he put his heart in his work until, ceasing to beat in him, it beat in his creation. He is like that fluid Chinese Dragon of infinite incarnations. And who is Śiva, but that pre-Aryan, pre-rational energy of earth and of flesh, that elusive fire who loses his life in the act of creation, only to find it again? And are not the forms of his coming and going, his passing away and his coming again, partial facts, behind which or within which stands the central fact of creation itself? In spite of the imperial structure that came to rule in India and China, Aryanism, and later, Vedānta, were forced to assimilate Śiva as later Confucianism assimilated the concept of the *Tao* and the masses of the agrarian Chinese assimilated to good advantage the Mongol male nomadic hordes that periodically came down like a wolf on the fold. Chinese feudalism, at least until modern times, does not display the anguished tensions of our own Western feudalism; the Chinese scholar, it has been said, was a Confucianist in office and a Taoist when out of office. In neither India nor China did the extremities of urbanism overtake the culture;[30] and the opportunities for a supernatural deity were in the case of India circumscribed by sea and mountains, monsoons and dry seasons, and in the case of China by sea and "a complex network of high mountain ranges separating a number of flatter areas."[31]

What now is the picture of the world which Indian and Chinese thought has painted after pondering its convolutions and evolutions, its appearances and disappearances, these many years?

---

30. Perhaps because, as Childe says, rice-growing in the Orient did not permit leisure; perhaps because as Needham says the imperial supervision of irrigation in China prevented the rise of an independent middle class and hence of science; perhaps because the pastoral (and extreme patriarchal) economy never took strong hold in the Orient, it being, in its originally settled portions, lowland and plain; perhaps because monotonous climatic conditions throughout much of the Orient, as Huntington suggests, "arrested" those cultures.
31. Joseph Needham, *Science and Civilisation in China*, Vol. I. Cambridge: Cambridge University Press, 1954, p. 66.

(1) It is a world of ascents and descents, of attainments and dissolutions, of intensities diluted into indefinitenesses and of crystalline particularities thawing and resolving themselves into universal waters and vapors. When the Oriental eye gazes into the crystal ball of the universe, it sees not a solidity but a flux, not the posture of speculation but the motion of sport, not the late-Greek fixity of the statue or statute but the agitation of the dance.

> The cosmos wheels and whirls and spins,
> Never stops, never begins,
> Undulates on roller-coasters,
> And palpitates like holy-ghosters.

> Frenzied are her jumps for joy,
> Like a capering coltish boy;
> Quivering are her nostrils wide,
> And throbbing her red heart inside.

> All the sand grains dance a jig,
> All the stars are whirligig,
> All live things shout as if to say,
> "Come, join us in our dance today!"

Fire is the cosmos, all flames and flickering, fleeing and returning, fleet images, swiftly alive on subtly leaving feet, dancing in and out of herself like a life self-wreathing, teasing us to attraction and distraction. She is all image, all raiment, all apparel and appearance – a succession of bodies, or realizations – or phenomena, as we are apt to call them, tempted to postulate some noumenon or presiding spirit that binds them together as an actor binds together certain acts on stage. We follow after the dancing, transfixed into motion by the eternally moving vision, swept along by the incantation of its rhythm, seeking the Dancer and doing the dance itself and always asking in the secret chambers of our hearts who pulls the strings and calls the tune. That unresting wonderment in the Upaniṣads echoes again, across the canyons of the ages, in the silent recesses of our spirits. Like a will-o'-the-wisp that naked unbodied world-soul eludes our grasp; chased over the vast curved roof of the universe, she tosses this or that piece of livery to appease her pursuers, only to slip into a new one. So, by dispensing an image of beauty here, a patch of knowledge there, a frame for contemplation, or a relevant lure to some practical action or passion, she keeps her devotees at a distance and occupied in properly mortal pursuits. Thus she keeps up appearances and always reveals, always conceals, herself:

> She dips and leaps,
> Dims and brightens,
> Laughs and weeps,
> Lolls and tightens.

Her charming surfaces veil her deep,
Her soft limbs yield lest her strong body break,
And her icy thoughts in her warm bosom keep,
She shakes all her lovers, whom the gods can't shake.

Ever decomposing, she must always compose herself, since she is as much chaos as cosmos, disarranging and rearranging, discharging and charging again, diminishing and increasing. So the divine masquerade, like a cloud, diffuses and drifts and gathers into the driving piston stroke of a storm only to explode and shatter again and disperse into myriad motes aimlessly moving in space. The world is the condensible and dispersible *Ch'i* of the Neo-Confucianists; it is the kinetic dance and courtship of Śiva and his consorts; it is the Heraclitean fire forever going up and down.

(2) It is a world of creation. This second proposition is perhaps less explicit in the religions than the first; but it is complementary to it. The image of the world as pervasive and continuous change is in general accepted in the great religions as a final fact. But theologians have attempted to penetrate beyond it to something firm and changeless. Sometimes they accept the play of change as sheer mystery and as an inescapable cycle or wheel (as in both India and China). Sometimes they hold it to be *māyā*, the delusion of the outward mind washing against the shore of the fixed and interior soul (as in India). Sometimes they strive to rise above it, as in Western supernaturalism.

But in all religions, and particularly at the popular levels, and at those momentous points in their development when an innovation of insight pierces established habit and custom, the idea is expressed that if the divine has any meaning, that meaning is to be found in the events and qualities and structures, the changes and transformations, of our present experience; that the divine is a process of continuous creation in time; that men are participant in this process, progressively incarnating it, understanding it, and facilitating it by their actions in human history; that not only is man the supreme expression of nature's divine creativity, to whom it reveals itself through the transformation of man's responses, but also man is now the principal agent through whom that creativity must advance itself in the reconstruction of nature and in spiritual progress; and that only in creative union with his fellow-man – in creative communication and cooperation – and with the rest of nature can man serve this supreme directive of nature and history and contribute to its triumph. The unique mental and spiritual achievement of our time is the dawning realization of the presence of the divine among us and in times past of human history; and therefore the unique challenge and obligation of our time is so to feel, think, aspire, act, and sacrifice that the divine in ourselves and our posterity may be fulfilled.

Chapter V

SOURCES AND SOLUTIONS OF HUMAN CONFLICTS

In this chapter we shall try to identify some of the basic conflicts among men in early civilizations, to investigate some of their causes in the dispositions and environments of men, to consider their consequences in the philosophical and religious ideologies of those civilizations, to indicate the presence of similar conflicts in contemporary societies, and to suggest some lines of solutions.

For perhaps a million years Paleolithic man roamed over the continental land masses in small bands, hunting and fishing and gathering his food as he could. His principal conflict had to do not with his fellow man but with the conditions and forces of nature against which he was forced to struggle and on which he depended in order to satisfy his elemental needs of food, clothing, shelter, and safety. The totemic religions and cave paintings in which Paleolithic man depicted mammoth, bison, reindeer, horse, and fish, in a magical effort to control them, reflect his sense of dependence on, and his conflict with, these powers of raw nature.

Then, sometime after the last glacial sheets lying over northern Europe began to melt and recede – perhaps 15,000 years ago – a dramatic change occurred, opening the way in time for the development of civilization. Normally, the Atlantic-borne showers, deflected southward by the icy mountains of Europe, had moved across the Mediterranean Sea and northern Africa, through Mesopotamia, Arabia, Persia, and finally India. The result had been a temperate, fertile climate, producing parklands and savannas teeming with the richness of tropical life. But with the melting of the glaciers, the high pressures of the anticyclones over the ice sheets contracted, causing a northerly shift in the normal path of the rain-bearing, low-pressure air masses. The regions once lush there were thus robbed of their year-round watering. Desiccation and desert slowly ensued where life once flourished. But the change was a gradual one. And during this gradual change Paleolithic man, roaming the land in small bands, moved first into the settled and agrarian communities of Neolithic life and finally into the first civilizations – the Egyptian, the Sumerian, the Indian,[1] and later the Chinese.

Faced with the challenge of a dwindling food supply obtainable through

1. Arnold J. Toynbee, *A Study of History*. Abridgment of Volumes I–VI by D. C. Somervel. New York: Oxford University, 1946, pp. 68–69. He is quoting from V. Gordon Childe, *The Most Ancient East*, chs. 2–3.

hunting and fishing and gathering, some Paleolithic men rejected the solutions of migration or of habitual food-gathering and in time hit upon methods of developing a new food-supply – they began to cultivate plants and to domesticate animals. Women collected the seeds of primitive wild grasses (ancestors of our wheat and barley), roots, and trees, and cultivated them in favorable places, such as river valleys where they were afforded natural irrigation.[2] At the same time men began to capture and domesticate and breed wild animals. The consequent surplus food supply made possible settlements, pottery, weaving, metallurgy, and other domestic arts and sciences. This change of life – the Neolithic revolution – proceeded slowly for millennia. And it provided the economic base for a no less profound transformation in human life, the urban revolution. For it was in the fertile river valleys of the Nile, the Tigris-Euphrates, and the Indus where the great urban civilizations developed about 3000 B. C.[3] (The Yellow River Valley civilization appeared somewhat late.)

The problems and conflicts of Paleolithic man, as we have said, were centered primarily in men's direct relations to nature. Given their primitive tools and weapons, such men in order to survive were forced to gather and own and enjoy their food in common.[4] In the later stages of Neolithic barbarism men continued to cooperate for collective tasks, as in the building of public ways and stockades. At the same time, however, various forms of private production developed – the division of labor based on sex, the specialized production and consumption of food, the making of pots, clothes, tools, and other necessaries by individual families, the self-sufficiency of individual communities, the rudiments of intercommunal specialization.[5] Also it is quite possible that the "corn king," who originally impersonated the dying and rising grain of nature and was slain in a magical rite, became a secular king, particularly if he were a war chief.[6] All these changes brought with them conflicts now internal to the human community. As they developed, moreover, these changing Neolithic communities with their increasing populations were forced to expand in their search for land and were thus thrown into conflict with other communities. The ensuing wars between clans claiming specific territories were sure to accelerate the process by which the chiefs came to dominate land and other property. Neolithic society developed its own forms of class conflict centered around the ownership and control of land and water and the tools and techniques by which men made their living in relation to land and water. By the time the great

2. Gordon Childe, *What Happened in History*. New York: Penguin, 1946, p. 41.
3. *Ibid.* See also V. Gordon Childe, *Man Makes Himself*. New York: New American Library of World Literature, 1951, p. 115.
4. *What Happened in History*, p. 39.
5. *Ibid.*, pp. 52–54.
6. *Ibid.*, p. 58.

alluvial-based civilizations arose, a class structure of a master-slave economy was well established.

Man's alienation from his fellow man has always involved his alienation from nature. In early Paleolithic society man lived in a primitive harmony with his fellow man and nature, and his totemic religion was an expression of this harmony of individual man, clan, plants, and animals. The ruling powers of the Neolithic, agrarian communities were those of seed, soil, water, and sun. In the minds of men these became spirits and gods pervasive throughout nature, imbuing it with the throb and thrust of growing, ripening vegetation. But the developed fertility cults appear most forcefully and influentially during the early urban period of human history. And this fact seems to indicate a universal nostalgia, a longing on the part of men for a simpler and unitary society in the face of the fragmentation of urban life, and a desire of the ruling classes to unify and pacify the masses of peasants and workers, i.e., the slaves. Thus a basic conflict of classes in early civilizations was reinforced by this conflict between men's primitive sense and memory of their unity with one another and with nature, dating from Paleolithic and Neolithic times, and their division and exploitation in urban civilization. In broad terms, this latter conflict was the conflict between man's old, magical and religious dependence on nature and the new attitudes generated by the application of sciences to the control of nature.

For the masses, however, this conflict was not clearly focussed. Most men, as late as Lucretius' time in the first century B. C., remained sunk in the attitudes of submission to the powers of their environment, both natural and social. Though gathered into cities, men were aware that they still depended on the land, water, sun, and grains, as evidenced in the myths and rituals of the cults of ancient Egypt. Such a feeling of dependence on nature through the centuries had gradually projected itself onto the corn king (the representative of nature), the chief of the tribe or clan, and then the dominant person – king or priest – of the new urban society. So deep was the sense of dependence on nature, and so gradual and obscure was this transfer of feeling to social leaders, that men did not – until the Jewish prophets and the Greek philosophers – draw a distinction between nature and society and their relations to each. In actual fact, urban society was possible precisely because of the new attitudes induced by new techniques and tools of knowledge and control by society over nature. But these techniques and tools were ruled by such a small groups using the masses to their own advantage that the masses were not awakened to their own potentials for knowledge and control. Thus the masses were carried into urban society retaining a religion of nature; they were brought from a world of dependence on nature to a world of dependence on a ruling class of men; and it would require a new "industrial revolution" before large numbers of them realized that it was not necessary for them to remain dependent on nature and the ruling groups of society, and that they might themselves become owners and controllers of both nature and society.

The story of the first urban civilizations is the story of applied sciences. In preparation for it, between 6000 and 3000 B. C., men harnessed oxen and winds, invented the plow, wheeled cart, and sailboat, discovered the processes of smelting copper ores and the physical properties of metals, and worked out a solar calendar.[7] They developed canals and ditches for irrigation, the plow, orchard-husbandry, fermentation, bricks, the arch, glazing, the seal, writing, numerical notation, and bronze.[8] "In no period of history till the days of Galileo was progress in knowledge so rapid or far-reaching discoveries so frequent."[9] The result of this scientific revolution was a qualitative change in the mode of production, the structure of society, and human relations. Dominant classes appropriated and monopolized the wealth that these discoveries made possible – wealth that increased alike from the instruments and techniques that facilitated the cultivation of the land, the industry of artisans, and the processing, transporting, and selling and buying of products. A whole new apparatus of professions and classes, made possible by this economic foundation and required by it, came into being. Large numbers of men, released from food-production, took their places in a society stressing division of labor: workers, specialized craftsmen, overseers, administrators and officials of the state, princes, priests, scribes, trained soldiers. A ruling class sprang into being, the copestone of this whole structure – a class with the power to move and command, a class which because of the unprecedented economic power under its control could lift human exploitation to an unprecedented level. The results were the mass slavery and war of Empire. Was it any wonder that the masses of men sought and found comfort in those religions which, in reminding them of their origins in and dependence on Mother Nature, gave them a sense of order and purpose in the urban chaos? And was it any wonder that the State, seeing the power of such religion to secure social compliance, fostered and encouraged them, developing an elaborate apparatus to this end? For the State, as the arm of the ruling class, existed to suppress the slaves whose labor supported that class and to moderate and order the conflict between the rulers and the ruled. This conflict was interlaced with the conflict between "the communistic traditions of the gentile order"[10] and the new economy of division of labor and private property.

7. *Man Makes Himself*, p. 87.
8. *Ibid.*, p. 180.
9. *Ibid.*, p. 87.
10. F. Engels, *The Origin of the Family, Private Property and the State*. Moscow: Foreign Languages Publishing House, 1952, p. 178.

This "communistic tradition," as we have seen, dated from prehistoric Paleolithic times and continued into Neolithic society and the settled, agrarian communities which were the precursors of early civilization. Commodities, private ownership of property, the division of labor, and antagonistic classes emerged within these communities over a long period of time, so that when the first great civilizations appear these new features are full-blown, existing side by side and in conflict with the older tradition.

This conflict was accelerated by the invasions of Bronze Age Neolithic barbarians into the centers of civilization in the second millenium B. C. At that time the people speaking the root Indo-European tongue broke out of the steppes of southeastern Europe and central Asia and moved southward through the mountain barrier separating them from the river valley societies. Perhaps one of the impelling reasons for this movement was the climatic change we have mentioned, so that, in search of water and grass for their cattle and horses, they came out into the Iranian plateau and through the Hindu Kush mountain passes into the Punjab. Perhaps the pressures of Mongoloid tribes farther north and east, or new bronze equipment in the form of improved ploughshares and broadswords, or, as Toynbee says, the weakening outpost of Hammurabi's empire and its eventual breakdown,[11] accounted for the vast migrations. At any rate, these Indo-European invaders succeeded in leaving the imprint of their language and their gods upon the cultures whom they conquered, building upon and coordinating what they found. Their triumph seems to have been especially marked in the Indus valley, where the determinate dualism between aristocrat and slave, language and nature, soul and body, had already been established.

For three millennia prior to these invasions, the trade economy of the Bronze Age, rising out of class divisions, specialization of labor, and the improved methods of transportation like the sailboat and wheeled vehicles, had all moved men in the direction of universal forms of thought. Interaction of cultures tended to be accompanied by economic, military, and philosophical and religious unity. Consequently the Aryan Dyaus Pitar, or Jupiter, migrated into favorable environments and came, in Greece, to dominate the other Greek gods, as in India he assumed ascendancy over the indigeneous fertility deities and as the *vedas*, or words of wisdom, and the *brahman*, or sacred mystical power of knowledge, came to triumph over the pre-Aryan *śakti*. It is easier to universalize a principle of order, a concept of the mind, than a nat ural potency, particularly when that principle is male and when the authoritative principle in the social structure is embodied in a male warrior-king. For the gods brought by the Aryans to India, Iran, the Aegean, and other parts were predominantly male in character – gods of the sky,

11. *A Study of History*, p. 28.

of the sun and rain, of light, of power, of physical order and social justice, of loyalty and faith-keeping, of storms and wars. While it is true that the agrarian cultures provided a male consort for the earth-mother (Tammuz, Attis, Adonis, etc.) and while also the male element became dominant as the myth moves southwestward,[12] still these cults were primarily female, while those of the conquering groups were male.

The Aryans were a clear-eyed, realistic, aggressive people with an earthy religion and a philosophy that interpreted the determinate things of this world according to determinate laws. Northrop identifies them with the West and, though he does not say so, we may assume that they constitute one important starting point of the determinate outlook of the West. They had a relatively well developed class structure, with institutions of caste, power politics, legal codes; and they had a syntactical language,[13] as contrasted with older pictographic or hieroglyphic languages (such as appear in Eastern cultures). They had the principle of fixed and definite duties and obligations – *dharma* – and the principle of cosmic order as expressed in India's Varuṇa, ṛta, and Mitra. As they came to dominate conquered peoples, so their ideas came to prevail. They are the ideas of an active, assertive, muscular, manual, dominating culture whose point of view bears the stamp of severity and order frequently found in nomadic peoples.[14] Their notions of caste and legal codes do not so much signify a philosophical dualism as the hard-headed, practical arrangements of a self-consciously "noble" strain of people in conflict with the easy-going animisms and materialisms of the native populations. That is to say, the dualism of the Aryans was economic and moral rather than metaphysical. Their main god was a god of valor and force: an ideal projection of their cherished virtue: Indra. He was also "protector of the Aryan color" and "destroyer of the dark skin."[15] That division of souls into good and bad, and that division of hereafters into "white light" and "abysmal darkness,"[16] founded in class divisions, was the dim precursor of subsequent dualisms found in the West and of Magian religious struggles. The Aryans were pastoral, and, as such, patriarchal, even after their social organization became agricultural.[17] Their society was a class society based on the ownership of flocks and herds. The ideological struggle between the Aryans and the non-Aryans can be seen in India, but the conflict is still obscured to scholarship. What Sir John Marshall referred to as

12. *Ibid.*, p. 392.
13. F. S. C. Northrop, *The Taming of the Nations*, New York: Macmillan, 1952, pp. 56, 88, 142.
14. Toynbee, *op. cit.*, pp. 166–171.
15. M. Hiriyanna, *The Essentials of Indian Philosophy*. London: George Allen & Unwin, 1949, p. 11.
16. *Ibid.*, p. 13.
17. Robert Briffault, *The Mothers*. New York: Macmillan, 1931. p. 246.

the pre-Aryan "cults of Śiva and the Mother Goddess" does not seem to have been indigenous to the Aryan Vedic religion.[18] Śiva's initial rejection by the Aryans, and his later acceptance as successor to the Vedic Rudra,[19] would indicate that the Aryans over a long period of time assimilated the figures and qualities of the native religions to their own uses. No doubt the endomorphic components in the Aryan people in India found it easier to make their peace with the dionysian deities of pre-Aryan India: Soma became their popular tutelary god. And the ectomorphic elements were in time smelted out as the pure priests and speculative philosophers of the *Rig-Veda*.

The gradual dominance of the Aryan thought-forms was not achieved without struggle, or without a price, or without a striking transformation. The struggle was sharply focussed on the steppes of Iran, where Zarathustra waged his battle against the priests of the old Aryan gods. Speaking for the farmers of that region, Zarathustra inveighed against the magical practices of the ruling priests, the animal-sacrifices of the old religion, and the cattle-rustling of the northern nomads. The virtues he proclaimed were life-conserving ones – tilling the soil, raising grains, growing fruits, reclaiming, irrigating, and cultivating the land, and preserving animal life. He presumably opposed Mithra, the prominent god of the Iranians, the god of wars and of light, though he appropriated for his own god some characteristics of the gods of his enemies. Originally the struggle seems to have been one of order against disorder, control against caprice, reason against magic, unity against plurality, conservation against destruction. Underlying the ideological conflict was the economic struggle of the new economy to assert itself. But the irony of the religious victory was that in time a thorough-going dualism became established in which the "right," instead of working creatively in this world of plants and animals and men, was, as in the ancient, dualistic, priestly religion, removed from it and rendered mysterious and approachable only by specialized techniques. The dualism of "magianism" was born. Zarathustra's new religion was a purified naturalism, an agrarian viscerotonia, urging man's unity with the creative powers of the Aryans, who were aristocrats and magicians. But eventually Zarathustra's religion became the prey and the instrument of aristocrats, too.

The late Aryans in India were in all likelihood lusty mesomorphs who enjoyed their feasts and their *soma* and who were able to make an easy peace with the practices of viscerotonic, female, fertility religions which they encountered in the warm countries that they invaded. In fact, they disappeared as a distinctive stock and their religion disappeared along with them. But during this period of cultural migrations and interactions, the dissociation

18. *The Legacy of India*, ed. G. T. Garratt. London: Oxford University, 1945, p. 258.
19. *Ibid*.

of detachment, of the disinterested mind, took its rise – a cerebrotonic tendency to jettison the hope of salvation in this world and progressively to withdraw into pure consciousness alone.[20] We can see this tendency in the youthful precocity of the Indian Upaniṣads, the Pythagoreans, and later Platonic philosophy. The Great Mother and Dionysus, on the one hand, competed with Prometheus on the other for the approval of the detached element in human nature and culture, i.e., thought. In this conflict thinkers pronounced a plague on both power and passion, on the machinations of rulers and the work at reforms and the needs of the masses.

Many like Sheldon have conceived this strategy of dualism to be a distinctively Christian device, but it arises whenever a culture has suffered severe frustration, disappointment, disintegration, and alienation – the results of malnutrition, the restraints of exile or captivity, the ruination of war, the breakup of a philosophy – and where there are widespread trends toward withdrawal, or what Sheldon calls viscerotonic-cerebrotonic attitudes. Or it may be that, in a relatively fluid society, the reaction of withdrawal and dualism sets in because the adventurous and heroic people, unable to endure the local frustrations, have migrated and have left behind the mentally and physically deficient and delinquent. Our philosophies reflect our condition. At any rate, the initial conflict between male, mesormoprhic north and female, endomorphic south was aggravated and perpetuated by the ideology of dualism.

The dualism developed by detached thinkers in India, the middle East, and the Mediterranean was thus propagated by primarily somatotonic ruling groups, conquerors, and missionaries and not by the cerebrotonic philosophers who fashioned it. The dominant classes unconsciously transformed and distorted it in applying it to their own advantage. The normal somatotonic mind is unaware of any cleavage between the life of his (or others') unconscious impulses and his own field of direct awareness and action. He is psychologically callous and oriented to external reality by motor and manipulatory aggressiveness. His extroversion is the extroversion of vigorous activity – it takes place on the good earth – and so, if he is to dichotomize people, he must dichotomize them as the economy dictates, i.e., as the rulers and the ruled.[21] But as he is primarily a man of action and not of ideation

20. William H. Sheldon, *Varieties of Delinquent Youth*. New York: Harper, 1949, p. 64 In Sheldon's terms, endomorphy is relative predominance of the digestive viscera, softness, and roundness; mesomorphy is relative predominance of muscle, bone, and connective tissue; ectomorphy is relative predominance of the skin, sensory-nervous system, and linear fragility. Viscerotonia, somatotonia, and cerebrotonia are these components of physique at the behavioral level, respectively: relaxation, extraversion of affect, love of food, sociality, etc.; bodily assertiveness and muscular activity; and hypersensitivity – or, in Charles Morris' terms, dependence, dominance, and detachment.
21. W. H. Sheldon, *The Varieties of Temperament*. New York: Harper, 1944, p. 53.

it is no trouble for him as chieftain or king or soldier to take over the ideological dissociation furnished him by his cerebrotonic clerks, scribes, priests, and philosophers. This appropriation occurred on a minor scale in the prehistoric or food-producing period prior to 3000 B. C. and then on a major scale during the urban period following.

The mesomorphic institutionalization of supernaturalism began in European history soon after the Christian (Platonic and neo-Platonic) theology came to dominate thought. While the monks and meditative philosophers could practice their hebephrenic delusion in privacy, the active rulers, knights, crusaders, inquisitors, and others interpreted this to mean a battle to the death between the strong and the weak, the saved and damned. What was meant to be a renunciation of the world was altered into the conquest of the world's temptations of passions. The inner and unconscious conflict of the somatotonic temperament – the conflict between the desires of the flesh and the demands of disciplined external action – was projected into the world, objectified, and handled in the typically somatotonic way. Impulses to eat, to sleep, to engage a sex partner, to be quiescent and relaxed – the whole array of comfort-loving, viscertonic impulses – could be attributed to others and in particular to women, witches, sorcerers, and the like, and could be managed by physical punishment or destruction of the evil objects. Salvation was thus not a matter of simple introspection and the renunciation of power; it was to be achieved by an unrelenting, uncompromisingly dualistic struggle of the rational male against the animal female.

The maternal mythologies of the pre-European and semi-tropical cultures symbolized a different mode of salvation. In them the death of the Sun or "corn-king" was redeemed by the faithful and periodic redemption of mother earth. The man must die in the womb of earth, that he might be reborn, and that the race of life might be perpetuated. But where the Aryan gods succeeded in subjugating and dispersing the appeal and power of the fertility cults, no such solution, so unflattering to the noble male, heaven-descended, could be accepted. Thus in India and Greece, while religion accommodated itself to demands of the populace by providing fertility gods and goddesses, India's Aryan gods grew pale, and the ultimate was viewed as subsisting absolutely separate from the fructifying and dying of jungle life and the extreme drouths and monsoons of the plains. In such a supernaturalism, resurrection of life is impotent, repeatedly postponed (at least for the mass of men), and impossible. Such was the conclusion frankly faced by those who assumed that the essence of humanity, the male element, is an alien wanderer in this world, "fallen" from his heavenly origins, mired in the stickiness of the feminine, which initiates its descent in the first place, needing to extricate itself from that in order to be saved.

The same determinate supernaturalism came to prevail in many parts of the West. It entered into the Christian tradition primarily through the Orphics, Plato, and other Greeks. In the *Timaeus*, God condescends to create the world through the intervention of the Demiurge; and the Forms of heaven fructify the Receptacle of the world, which lies passively in wait; but there is always some material (maternal) departure from the heavenly models of perfection. This Greek cosmogyny has its echo in the homosexual culture of the Greeks whose aristocracy subordinated women to the position of slaves.[22]

It may be asked why the Greeks perpetuated this point of view. The gods that the Greeks adopted were imposed by invaders from the north, and the result was a syncretism which, as in the far-flung commerce of the Greeks, stimulated synthesis and abstraction. The development of an Iron Age economy and a monetary system liberated certain individuals from the press of manual labor for the uses of speculation; and, as L. L. Whyte points out, in seeking abiding standards during a time of cultural interactions, men discovered the laws of logic and mathematics and set them over against the instincts,[23] identifying these latter with the *hoi polloi* and with women, since women, under the prevailing economy, displayed little more than the crude biological drives. The rise of cities, the differentiation of labor, the emergence of schools for specialized training, all tended to separate the male from female skills and to convince the male of his superiority of those traits which it was his cultural lot to practice.

Taking as their hero the handsome musician Apollo, father of Orpheus, the Pythagoreans, cerebrotonic philosophers, epitomized this separation and carried it to its highest pitch. They began by banning women, adopting celibacy, and practicing brotherhood. They interpreted the world as numbers; the female was associated with the even and with darkness, multiplicity, movement, and all that is evil, whereas one, light, rest, and the good were viewed as emblematic of the male in things. They were paralleled by the Brāhmanic order in India, which found mystery in words rather than in numbers. The Pythagoreans bequeathed to us a powerful heritage, passed down by Plato. But they were aristocrats, and in spite of their high level of thought they remained oblivious to the important roles of Dionysus and the maenads and the mothers in this world. Lacking the female perspective, they were, in Haldane's figure, like a man with only one eye, whose world, however clear, lacks depth.

The religion of Mithraism expressed in grosser and less disguised form this repudiation of the feminine earth. Originally, Mithra was the god of

22. See Simone de Beauvoir, *The Second Sex*, trans. and ed. H. M. Parshley. New York: Alfred A. Knopf, 1953.
23. *The Next Development in Man.* New York: New American Library of World Literature, 1950.

treaties or pacts, enforcing contracts and punishing bad faith. He was the god of light, the reward of truth-seekers, the support of those struggling against the powers of darkness and this world. In time, the god became transformed into a child of light, born of a virgin and thereby participant in the world of wet darkness but never dependent upon it. He grows to manhood and in the supreme contest of his life he slays the great bull with his sword – as the day overcomes the night and its nightmare (and Sleep and Death) by means of its shafts of light. Attending Mithra and assisting in what seems to be some form of parricide are the lion of power, the phallic torch, the dog, and the scorpion of rivalry. The dog licks the blood of the bull, which flows to the earth and fructifies it.

What is the significance of this drama? G. F. Moore says "it is thought by many to be a cosmogonic myth; it is the slaying of the primeval cow, from which the whole earth, plants and animals, spring."[24] The drama, on this theory, is a rejection of the female principle, and an assertion of man's triumph and transcendence over the principle by his totemic identification. The transmutation of "cow" into bull is a subtle way of attacking the father-rival who has identified himself with the mother and has thereby borrowed her fertility and power. The son defies the father, the more so because he is identified with him and must differentiate himself from him, though like many a son he merely re-enacts in his rebellion the narcissism, aggressiveness, and omniscience-complex of that parent whom he slays. Alexander, invincible and divine, "son" of Philip of Macedon, is the perfect Mithraic prototype.

The homosexual overtones of this myth and this religion are clear. Historically, the worship of Mithra was a religion of soldiers which flourished in the encampments of armies in the outer reaches of Roman civilization. It reflected the complexities of the superior-inferior struggle of homosexuality. It is for men only, with the secret and dramatic initiation rites of the taurobolium, the compact of loyalty, and the life-long brand of the brotherhood. Mithraism attracted the intelligentsia (male of course) and the philosophers refined and reconverted it into the religion of aloofness and light from which it originated, for it maintained the dualism of matter and spirit and the tension of animal and ideal which were inherent in the old Zarathustrian religion. In this new and purified form it betrayed the Jehovah complex of authoritarianism, the full-blown symptomatology of male chauvinism. Armies, with their structure of ascendancy-submission and their preoccupation with brute power, are bound to breed this kind of religion, a religion which has no use for the soft and feminine but which, in its weakness, secretly desires to escape the struggles of this world – a religion which

24. *History of Religions*, vol. I. New York: Charles Scribner's Sons, 1941, p. 599.

worships the sword and the arrow, the crown and the whip, the rigid and sacred rock out of which the god rises, but which in the end must surrender to the blood bath, oblivion, and its hope of an eternal and passive peace in heaven.

The dualism or "dissociation" of European man had its origins in what L. L. Whyte has described as the "Ancient Period" – roughly Gordon Childe's "food-producing" period, or the Neolithic Age, beginning about 8000 B. C. and lasting for several millennia. About 2000 B. C. the "individual" entered history for the first time, records prior to then telling mainly of mythical kings and founders of empires.[25] The growing consciousness of the individual's existence, and self-consciousness, were direct results of the new class economy, the accelerated travel and communication in the Near East, the ensuing uncertainty regarding the ancient standards of instinctive response, and the turning of the individual's attention to his own mental processes and to his own self.[26]

In consequence, the forces for coordinating diverse traditions were set in motion, and the nomadic Aryan tribes became the bearers and vanguard of those forces. The urban revolution, with its trade and commerce, had prepared the way for the conquering religious ideology of the Aryans. Whyte suggests that the three universalisms of empire, of monotheism, and of rationalism had a common origin – namely, the differentiations in individual thought and among cultures, which drove men to seek a unity. Since males filled the offices of kings, priests, and philosophers, it was only sensible that the males be identified with this new universalism, so imperatively called for, and that women, bound to the biological functions of child-bearing and child-rearing, should be relegated to the ancient and now outmoded life of instinctive response. Aristotle expressed this view quite explicitly. God was conceived of as an Egyptian solar monarch, a Jewish king, or a Greek philosopher; similarly, philosophers were idealized as kings and gods; and emperors like Alexander imagined themselves gods, or sons of gods, and undertook the study of philosophy.

Thus the abstractions of a monistic philosophy and of a monotheistic religion were effective agents of integration, but they simultaneously divided men against themselves by suppressing their impulsive life and creating an eternal sense of shame, guilt, inner conflict, and torment. "Man fell from innocence to sensuality and monotheism. . . . The fall of man represented the victory not of instinct, but of deliberate thought."[27] God, moreover, was conceived of as a stern, inflexible father, an imperious judge and an Olympian philosopher, a male master whose unrelenting superego and unitary power

25. *The Next Development in Man.*, p. 57.
26. *Ibid.*, p. 63.
27. *Ibid.*, p. 68–69.

118

have overcome the world of divisions and temptations. That is why Whyte can say that " 'Religion', in the European sense, is the operation of an incomplete substitute for complete organic integration."[28] The notion of the unity of mankind was, as Childe says, "an ideological counterpart of an international economy based on the interchange of commodities between all its parts."[29] But the principle of unification was an arbitrary, authoritarian, and external one, modeled on the pattern of the Oriental king-priest, rather than one immanent in the human situation.

On a social scale the impulsive life that was suppressed was in essence the life of the laboring masses who for centuries had derived their orientation from the cults of fertility. Urban society divided man against himself: not only did it divide one class against another, but, with its leisure and techniques, it made men conscious of their Neolithic heritage of sensuality in contrast to the new uses of practical and scientific reason. Urban man is called on in his work to check and postpone his desires, to delay his satisfactions; and this is particularly so if he lives in an economy of scarcity. At the same time he seeks outlets for those desires outside of his work – in entertainment and religion. Thus for the first time large groups of men became sharply conscious of their desires; the contradiction between desire and satisfaction grew increasingly apparent. For many, under the sway of official ideologies, the abandoned surrender to primitive desires appeared to degrade man toward the animals and to separate him from his "human" destiny. At the same time, the men locked into the oppressive system of slave society sought to satisfy those desires, while on the other hand the ruling groups strove to contain and control those desires which their system had helped to release and intensify. In Aristotle's philosophy one can see this ambiguity revealing itself: on the one hand he urges that the unique mark of all men is reason, while on the other hand he regards slaves, women, and children as sub-rational and hence subject to the control of their rational, male masters.

The Western world – western Europe and North America – owes its "progress" to the power of this class attitude, this masculine perspective, this Promethean mode imposing its dominance on the world, this conquest of successive economic classes. Marx and Engels described its peak phase in the *Manifesto*. For the dominant class in ancient classical civilization, the determinate *logos* was a convenient way of organizing personality and culture. It provided the base for law, philosophy, religion, science, and technology. It was the motif, banner, and guide for the spirit of Western expansion. As Dyaus Pitar lured the Aryans of old eastward toward the spring of day, so the Light and Order of Knowledge have drawn man, lusting for conquest, westward toward the unknown lands beyond the setting sun.

28. *Ibid.*, p. 78.
29. V. Gordon Childe, *What Happened in History*. New York: Penguin, 1946, p. 206.

The victory of the male over the female perspective in the West has never been a success; that would have meant the kingdom of heaven and the annihilation of time and history. In the subtropical cultures of ancient civilization, the maternal maintained her hold over peoples; through the millennia of violent conquest and half-conscious torpor, her hand has rocked the cradle of civilization. The masses in Greek and Roman times continued to celebrate in their mystery religions the creative powers of Mother Nature even after the principles of urban organization and oligarchic government had come to dominate a large portion of their lives. In time a division of labor was worked out which permitted the male element freedom to pass on and express his restlessness in the expansive power of imperial armies and the sublimated Faustian search of Science – while the women remained at home to tend the grains which they had rescued and fostered from the beginning, and to cultivate the arts of peace. While it is true that the Greeks and Romans developed for Western Christianity its determinate, philosophical, fatherly feature, and while the Persians gave to both Christianity and Mohammedanism its active counterpart, a military evangelism – still Judaic Christianity could not escape the birthmarks of its maternal origins, and it remained, as Nietzsche in his hyperbolic way would not let us forget, the main carrier of the feminine mode of life. Thus has arisen one of the principal tensions of Western culture – the tension between mathematics and emotion, between expansion and coordination, between the sword and the ploughshare, between science and religion.

Classical Judaism, in its literature, is a mixture and an accelerating dialectic between the male and female modes of life. The early chronicles of Abraham, Moses, and the Judges are predominantly formalistic in principle and uncompromisingly severe in punishment. The Lord God is a jealous God, chastening with his rod those whom he loves. This tradition began with prophets like Nathan, Ahijah, and Elijah, was carried to a high ethical level in Amos and Isaiah, and reached its climax in the fierce denunciations and prophecies of doom of the Exilic prophets. But in the midst of these terrible thunderings of Law, Justice, and Retribution, these lightnings of Threat and Wrath, one can hear the still small gentle rain of mercy and compassion, of tenderness and forgiveness, of kindness and love. Hosea, Isaiah, and Jeremiah conceived of Israel as a bride who has fallen into harlotry, and in whom there is no hope of a savior child. The highwater mark of this feminine spirit in the Old Testament was Second Isaiah. And in Jesus both traditions converged in dialectical opposition. But under the influence of Roman legalism and Greek philosophy, Christian theology lost the dynamic balance of its founder, a balance which was only partially restored by Protestant thinkers in the earthy romanticism of the Reformation tradition.

The popular historical religions, like the early philosophies, began at those points where the clash between the old, simple, agrarian ways and standards and the new complex, urban ways and standards, and between the new commercial towns and the old empires, became most acute. Throughout the civilized world this clash reached its climax in the 6th century B. C. – the century of Thales, Anaximander, Pythagoras, Anaximenes, Heraclitus, Zarathustra, Mahāvīra, Gautama, Lao-tzu, and Confucius – and contined as an attempted adjustment between two worlds. In its origins religion aimed at integration. In the pre-historic, food-producing stage, it was totemic and magical; it aimed at bridging the gap between man's animal needs and those unknown, mysterious powers of nature, upon which man depends for his life – the edible and otherwise useful plants and animals. Later, as man moved into settled agrarian communities, his attention turned to worship of the fertility forces on which he depended for life. This change was so great, in fact, that many authorities prefer not to apply the term "religion" to the totemic period, since it does not concern itself with a supernatural spiritual world.

With the coming of the urban revolution, religion underwent a radical change. Totemism, dominated by the notion of clan kinship, reflected a primitive, communal economy. Similarly, the religion of the urban period altered as the basic productive forces and social relations of men in this new period altered. Religion now re-expressed the strains between the simple, agrarian economy of the dimly remembered past, and the baffling complexities of urban society, with its specialized craftsmen, its division of labor, and its new antagonisms of owner and worker, farmer and city-dweller, professional intellectual (scribe, clerk, priest) and manual laborer, aristocracy and slaves, exploiter and exploited. The problems peculiar to urbanism thus generated new challenges to men, and new religious responses. The problems consisted in internal contradictions within the new urban order, and discrepancies between the old agrarian order and the new urban order. The story of the town of Babel, built on the plain of Sumar, expressed the writer's hostility to the big city. And a prophet like Amos not only inveighed against the greedy money-grubbers of a corrupt commercialism and the specialized priests who had prostituted their temples to popular demands; he also called men back to the simple dignity and justice of an earlier day. With a similar critique of the defections of men, Confucius urged men to return to the simpler life of the golden age of right relations with another, while the Taoists like Lao-tzu and Chuang-tzu directed them to the springtide of human life, where man remains forever in bud, proof against the perished, shivered petals that always follow a proud flowering. The Indian Upaniṣads pointed men to the pure bliss of sub-rational awareness, purged of the strains of senses and thought, a bliss wherein the multiple soul might be dissolved and blended into the unity of *nirvāna*. Jesus and Mohammed denounced the idols of the city and proclaimed the unified community of one simple God, the God of their fathers.

Thus the crises of the Iron Age gave birth to new orientations – some working within the framework of traditional religion, some disowning it. From those upholding the latter – in Greece called "lovers of wisdom" – came those bold and comprehensive speculations about the nature of the universe which offered to men secular, humanistic alternatives to supernatural, priest-dominated religions. These "philosophies," however, were not total breaks with the past. But as naturalistic orientations they served in the West as the crude beginnings of theoretical science. Perhaps because of slower economic development, the transition from religion to philosophy in China was not so abrupt. Taoism then, as in recent times, appears to have had both a religious and philosophical side. It probably derived from an ancient naturalism, but during the last half ot the first millenium B. C. it became a revolt against the artificiality, formalism, and divisions of urban class society, and directed men away from that society and to the sources of virtue in themselves and the rest of nature. It was also connected to magic, an effort to control the world rather than supplicating its unknown powers. Confucius likewise set forth a philosophy that turned away from superstition and called for rational moderation and humanistic conduct in institutional life. While these philosophies were not systematically investigative and experimental in the modern sense, they rejected the supernaturalism and mysticism of traditional religion. In India both Mahāvira and Gautama Buddha rejected the authority of supernatural revelation in the Vedas and urged men to work out their salvation for themselves. The philosophers of Cārvāka (Lokāyata) – a position which according to Chattopadhyaya is "probably as old as Indian philosophy itself" – described the authors of the Vedas as "buffoons, knaves, and thieves"[30] and proposed a primitive materialism of four elements. Like these other philosophers, they repudiated the authority of the gods, but they went farther by shedding all vestiges of spiritualism.

In Ionia the Greek philosophers arrived at a kindred critique of supernatural religion, advocating naturalism and eventually atomism. In seacoast cities like Miletus the spirit of commerce and practical inquiry produced independent and creative minds like Thales, who not only predicted an eclipse and hit upon a way to calculate the distance of ships at sea but also challenged the Olympian theology by suggesting that the world-stuff is water. The "nature of things," *physis*, in his view, is divine. Mysticism, however, is rejected. With Thales, as with Anaximander and Anaximenes,

30. Debiprasad Chattopadhyaya, *Indian Philosophy*. Delhi: People's Publishing House, 1964, pp. 185, 14.

the world-stuff is broken up into discrete parts moving according to a determinate order comparable to the order of the old *Moira*.[31] Such an order is rational, this-worldly, and subject to understanding and control. This point of view was a tremendous step away from unknowing religious acquiescence in the will of the gods and the destiny of fate. It laid the theoretical ground for science. It provided an alternative to the enslavement of the masses to both religious superstition and ruling classes. To this day, however, the full possibilities for the liberation of man through the methods of scientific inquiry have not been realized, either in religion or in politics. The naturalistic, humanistic vision of these early philosophers 2500 years ago remains to be worked out and rendered incarnate.

So men for 2500 years have sought to cope with the disharmonies and alienations of an urban existence rent by class divisions. The great spokesmen of religion have marked two paths for man in his distress: one way is the upward way, leading up and out and beyond this mortal world of life and time – the supernatural ladder of escape; the other way directs men backward and down to the simple life of natural needs. Both are inadequate; for the supernatural highway is an abandonment not only of man's problems and sufferings but also of his resources and opportunities, and today the ideal of the plain, natural communism of Taoism and early Christianity is but a nostalgic echo of the past and an unrealizable dream. The customary ideology of almost every ruling class, supernaturalism, is a habit worn by men originally ascetics, borrowed from them and embroidered upon by the ideologists of the ruling class. Originally reflecting the unnatural condition of the ascetics, partitioned off from sex and life and time, it then becomes a way of justifying the partitioning of ruler and ruled. Aided by the power of propaganda, it provides, moreover, a specious appeal to man's need for unity: city-dwellers and inhabitants of empire, fragmented and anonymous, seek some principle of unity that appears to be over-arching and invisible. The sentiment of natural piety is as tenacious as certain deeply rooted grasses which thrive underground and spring up perennially. But it has been possible for autocratic machinery to shear if off or plow it under for long periods, particularly in times of severe stress when man could find little ground for hope in his earthly situation and then looked beyond the stars. But never has propaganda been able to kill it entirely. To root it out would mean to root out man himself; for man is a creature and a native of nature, and every notion he fashions or receives bears the marks of its birth and its rearing.

Naturalism, moreover, is opposed to autocracy and divisive class structures. As there are no kings in nature, so, following the model of nature,

31. F. M. Cornford, *From Religion to Philosophy*. New York: Harper and Row, 1957, p. 143.

naturalism cannot tolerate kings in society. It does not easily accept the artificial division and distinctions of urban society. Naturalism is unifying, in method and goal. It resists special categories, privileges, and rule from a distance. It is skeptical of ultimates, absolutes, eternities, and radical breaks. *Natura non facit saltum.* It is a philosophy of transformation and process which sees no man or institution or society exempt from the changes of nature and history. The same writer who cried like the Taoists that "all flesh is grass" also rejoiced in the equality of all things in the universal flux:

> Every valley shall be exalted, and every mountain and hill shall be made low: and the crooked shall be made straight, and the rough places plain.[32]

Centuries later John the Baptist, that rugged insurrectionist of Jordan, quoted this passage in his preaching, including the verse, "And all flesh shall see the salvation of God"; and accordingly Herod, who, true to his class, believed in the divine right of kings, had him beheaded. John was a native of the Judean hills, a wanderer in the wilderness, at war with the corrupt hypocrisy in high places. And we cannot forget that Jesus, a humble carpenter from Galilee, was killed as a trespasser upon the sacred temples and courts of the big city; that he was accused of proposing that the wicked and corrupt temple of civilization be utterly torn down and rebuilt in three days; that his early followers were down-and-out, dispossessed proletarians who endeavored to translate his pastoral teaching into urban communism; and that in keeping with the urban and aristocratic organization of institutionalized Christianity, the Gospels were doctored and revolutionary energies were sublimated heavenward by a supernatural ideology.

For millennia religions have asked the question, Can man recover that unity of love, brotherhood, and peace which he enjoyed in days of his infancy? Can he re-experience that tender affection and family solidarity which he knew before the disruptive and evil forces of the city plagued him? Can he return to the garden of paradise, the benign state of nature, the primordial goodness of mother earth, abandoning the towers of Babel and the confusion of names which the crowded market place has burdened him with? Can he recover that freedom, equality, and fraternity which he once experienced in the bosom of the human family? Supernaturalism is an attempt to cope with this conflict of man's historical existence by organizing his living around the principle of arbitrary, patriarchal authority; it is the hierarchical, discontinuous, authoritarian, determinate, vertical principle of social organization. Naturalism is an attempt to cope with the same conflict by a principle that accents the continuous, democratic, horizontal relations

32. Isaiah 40: 4.

124

among men. In the early days of historical religion, when the conflict between agrarianism and urbanism was most intense, these two principles must have struggled bitterly for supremacy, for every religion today still bears the marks of the conflict and from time to time the wounds bleed afresh. Erich Fromm points out how the Oedipus tragedy, particularly as treated by Sophocles, and the Babylonian myth of Creation, reveal a struggle between the old matriarchal principle and the newer, authoritarian principle.[33] The myth of Dionysus' death reflected this struggle. Dionysus, the son of Persephone, goddess of the spring, is killed and eaten by the Titans, who are jealous of this heir-apparent to the throne of the universe. Yet the Titans are themselves destroyed by the fire of Zeus, and their ashes, containing the life-spirit of their victim and being spread over the world, impart that spirit to all animate things.[34] Similarly, the Dionysian power triumphed in the mysteries of Eleusis, Orpheus, Attis, Isis, Mithra, Tammuz, Śiva, Christ, and the rest. But the triumph was always a confined and partial one, and these mystery religions very early betrayed a hierarchy of levels of enlightenment. In the semitotemism of the early mysteries, men and women were content with the ecstatic eternity of momentary identification with their animal or plant gods, and the resurrection of the gods was credible because a new animal can be substituted for the one devoured.[35] But when the Orphic dualism between body and soul was introduced, man's sense of kinship with animal and plant nature was dissipated, and he became progressively concerned with what lies beyond nature. Likewise, the early nature-cults and mysticisms of India were modified and mastered by classical Brāhmanism, with its hierarchical principle in theology and politics. The Cārvākas, Upaniṣads, Buddhism, and, with some qualification, Jainism, were efforts to break free of this control and were democratic in emphasis, making the individual his own master and locating the principle of man's fulfillment in the nature of man. The same conflict occurred in China, organized around the poles of early Taoism and the official state cult of Confucianism.

Authoritarian organizations have never been able to kill completely the mystery-principle, and so have been forced to rest content with keeping it in bounds. The notion of an active, sportive, creative, suffering, dying, and rising god is a recurrent and undying idea among the masses because it is a direct reflection of their own existence. The leisure-loving gods on Mount Olympus, reigning from on high with authoritarian caprice, knowing nothing but eternal day and the harmonious music of the spheres; the god of pure philosophical calm resting unperturbed in the empyrean; the Brahmā or

33. *The Forgotten Language*. New York: Rinehart, 1951, pp. 195–235.
34. *History of Religions*, vol. I, p. 447.
35. Salomon Reinach, *Orpheus*, trans. Florence Simmonds. New York: G. P. Putnam's Sons, 1909, p. 85.

Zeus who is done with his labors: such may appeal to the common man as glamorous compensations in his moments of extremity, but they cannot have the continuing force of a god who directly incarnates their own struggles and defeats and victories, their own joys and sorrows and pains and triumphs. Edith Hamilton remarks that Dionysus and Demeter, the two divinities of earth, "knew heart-rending grief."[36] So it is that all the popular gods of the world's religions have lived close to the doings and tragedies of the people; but so it is that societies organized on the authoritarian, hierarchical, exploitative principle have turned this notion to their own ends by interpreting such gods under the myth of the descending, the condescending, the coming down of a superior king, a temporary benefaction on earth, and a return to the original throne, all men then having access to the divine king only through the special mediation of his civic or religious representatives here below. So rulers have undone the natural harmonies of humanity to "justify" their rule. So nature has been dichotomized into higher and lower to make "reasonable" the dichotomy in class society.

Down to our own day, the East has been dominated by routine and tradition. It has felt a simple affinity with the manifold of Being – a sympathy with all things which, like men, appear, endure, and perish in the great Procession. It has held, with a conviction born of cumulative cultural experience, that man's fate is the fate of cyclical repetition – relieved, if luck is with him, by the occasional, inchoate, shadowy shapes of some remote illumination – shapes like those appearing to Plato's chained slaves in the cave. Man is a mole, a winter groundhog, a subterranean creature who lifts up his head into the air and light for a few moments, and then returns to the destiny he shares with all things, hardly remembering his brief excursion in alien elements.

To recognize this brute fact, according to the East, this natural ignorance, this common routine which we share with all creatures and all things – that is the source of man's wisdom and freedom. (From this recognition, Chinese philosophy tended to go the way of organic naturalism, and Indian philosophy the way of idealism; but this divergence does not concern us here.) The historic, not yet urbanized East has thus emphasized the simple mysticism and natural piety of animal man within a nature which is fundamentally at one with man – the mysticism of immobility, of cyclical movement, of elemental bliss, of unspeakable, momentary, and eternal awareness.

The West, by contrast, has been a flight from organic stability. To live in the daylight of conscious awareness and analysis, Western man needed to repudiate the soft comforts and tribal securities of warmer climes. Europe and her American outposts are the advancing frontiers of analytical man:

36. *Mythology.* New York: New American Library of World Literature, 1953, p. 49.

the northward thrust of the Faustian spirit, characterized (as Spengler describes it) by the sense of unlimited space, of light, of dynamics, and of the infinite in time. By means of its simple mechanism or its anthropocentric idealism, Western thought has tended implicitly to separate man from nature and to neglect, until recently, the role and significance of man's participation in the physical and biological orders of nature.

But Western thought is now approaching the end of its tether. Indian thinkers have had no difficulty in accepting the Darwinian picture of the world: for millennia they have conceived of the divine energy of *śakti* as continuous change. Chinese thinkers have easily and smoothly assimilated the naturalistic organicism of Marx, Engels, and Lenin to their traditional mode of thought. In correcting its quantitative, analytical, dualistic methods, Western thought finds itself coming into closer congruity with the monism of the East. It finds that the organicism which it arrived at by the long and laborious circuit of natural science (a view not yet dominant in the psychology of the United States) is a perspective taken as axiomatic for centuries in many parts of the Orient, though the latter was mystical and lacking in predictive power.

So far as the differences between East and West spring out of physical differences and temperamental differences associated with those differences, they represent conflicts which are difficult to resolve and which may be radically and ultimately incompatible: burgeoning Dionysianism vs. asthenic hebephrenia; naturalistic immersion vs. supernaturalistic dissociation; present fleshly indulgence vs. futuristic spiritual abstention.[37] European civilization and the culture of the United States in particular exemplify the traits of somatotonia and viscerotonia carried to an extreme, and the traits defining these temperamental components[38] characterize our culture. While the traits defining the cerebrotonic personality characterize, in general, the cultures of the East, Western civilization might be conceived of as an explosive, capitalistic escape from the constrictions of the Near East and a tireless adventure which has not yet spent itself.[39] It produced the high middle ages,

37. *Varieties of Delinquent Youth*, p. 841.
38. *The Varieties of Temperament*, pp. 31–68.
39. The fullest economic critique of this escape and self-alienation of man has been offered by Karl Marx. At the present writing no western European nation has taken his critique seriously enough to apply the solution of socialism. The Soviet Union, which in both its geography and its pre-revolutionary economic history is European and Asian, took this Western solution and, under the comprehensive guidance of Lenin, applied it to its problems. It eradicated classes, exploitation of persons in their livelihoods, private production for profit, poverty, racism, mass ignorance, want of medical care, ethnic discrimination, economic discrimination against women, and illiteracy. It has coupled western science and industry with a communal spirit associated with pre-capitalist forms of production. By contrast, China, in becoming socialist, has remained primarily agrarian and as yet has taken upon itself neither the problems nor the opportunities of a highly developed

the Renaissance and Reformation, the French and nationalistic and industrial revolutions, the experiments in the New Wordl and the conquest of its two continents, European world hegemony, the scientific and technological revolutions, and nuclear power. World Wars I and II are signs that this capitalized Western somatotonia, for want of adequate outlets beyond the borders of Europe, has turned destructively on itself. In World War II the United States reaped the main advantages, being separated from the broils and blood of Europe and at the same time being free to expand westward into the Pacific and Asia, as many of her mesomorphic capitalists had attempted to do since the closing of the frontier in the late 19th century. But the restraining influences of an older (and more cerebrotonic) and disillusioned Europe, a rising somatotonic and communistic China, enlisting the sympathies of Asia, as well as the increasing dominance of selfish, Dionyisian appetites among the American population, prevented the United States from waging a holy war on a mass scale in Asia – though both the Korean and Vietnam wars were efforts in that direction. There is some evidence that the physiques of Indians and Chinese are relatively low in mesomorphy[40] and that Americans are relatively high in this component, though the conditions of unrest in China in the last century have probably initiated processes selecting out for political action a more mesomorphic type, while the relatively comfortable condition of the American economy has favored non-mesomorphic types. At any rate, the divergence in cultural and philosophical values is apparent. And in spite of the mitigation of the conflict by biological, geographical, economic, and cultural factors, the conflict is a real one between universal human tendencies – that of vigorous aggressions against the environment, and that of quiet awareness of the self.

The incompatibility between somatotonia and cerebrotonia "is more sharply defined than that between viscerotonia and either of the other two components."[41] History is the battle in which muscle and brain compete for viscera, either as an ally in the battle or as a companion or as a servant. In the Orient, the function of the viscera (viscerotonia) have been turned to family and religious uses, whereas in the West the somatotonia temperament has been transformed into Dionysian enthusiasm – gregarious celebrations, sports, businesses, and wars. This latter alliance has been more successful, since "endomorphy and mesomorphy tolerate one another in combina-

---

technological society. It still retains many of the virtues of an Asian agrarian way of life, freed of the oppressions of feudalism, colonialism, and imperialism. India, the second most populous Asian nation, is, alas, suffering from the worst of disorganized capitalism (including U. S. parasitic investments) and the customs and superstitions of a village culture.

40. *The Varieties of Temperament*, p. 432.
41. *Ibid.*, p. 507.

tion better than either tolerates ectomorphy."[42] Because young cultures tend to be somatotonic and older cultures cerebrotonic[43] (for several reasons), the present conflict between East and West may be seen as a conflict between two sets of traits or values emphasized at different periods of life. But this conflict rests back upon a biological one. The age of the Indian and Chinese civilizations and their relative stability through centuries of time probably have been significant factors in the production of ectomorphy – a luxury that "increases in aristocratic or protected and privileged stocks. . . . is killed off under hard (and probably urban) conditions. . . . [and] tends to advance or flourish when a stock is protected from the stern pressures of direct biological competition."[44] Thus, under the protection or sanction of emperors in India and China, a delicate type of priest and philosopher might be bred who would in his philosophy extol the cerebrotonic virtues, and, as in Mahāyāna Buddhism or the classical Hinduism expressed in the *Gītā*, tolerate the mild viscertonic living to which the great masses were committed. Once the ectomorphic type was established, it would tend to breed true[45] and its philosophy (cerebrotonia) would find receptive listeners and practitioners. In both the life of the individual and the human group, ectomorphy is a late flower; it requires a secure, protected environment, and its maturest fruit is a cerebrotonia which at the height of its glory ripens with a rare and other-worldly color, far removed from its natural roots. It needs to learn to fall to the ground and die, that it might be reborn; and this is what the great religious leaders, like Jesus and the Buddha, have taught. But frequently it cannot meet this challenge and make this sacrifice, and the consequence is a mesomorphic revolution, from within or without the culture, such as Europe experienced during the Renaissance and the 17th and 18th centuries and Russia and China and other societies in this century. Once such a revolution is set in motion, some scholarly ectomorphs may join in and play an important role in it; but they will ordinarily not be found on the firing line or at the barricades.

Probably much more of human conflict can be resolved creatively than we now imagine, for the poverty of our knowledge of reconciliation techniques is vast. Beyond and in addition to persuasion and education lie the possibilities of eugenics. If by random and short-sighted breeding we have produced an over-abundance of types who are proved to be constitutionally unable to live creatively with large segments of their fellow-man, then by planned and altruistic and intelligent breeding, we ought to be able to produce that kind of harmony among the members of the human species which will permit as

42. *Varieties of Delinquent Youth*, p. 18.
43. *The Varieties of Temperament*, p. 269.
44. *Varieties of Delinquent Youth*, p. 18.
45. *The Varieties of Temperament*, p. 303.

great a variety of types compatible with the creative development of all mankind. This means, initially, that those who have seen the vision of Man as diversity-in-unity must succeed in convincing or otherwise directing the somatotonic forces within the cultures of the world toward the ideal of a creative mankind.

In indicating the direction in which man should go, we have tried to trace, in sketchy and somewhat speculative outline, where man has come from and the forces impelling him to his present-day division and problems. We have tried to find the clue to man's future by analyzing his nature, and that broader Nature in which he lives and moves and has his being. Our thesis may be briefly restated as follows. "In a very broad sense," says W. H. Sheldon, "biological evolution may consist in three essential elements: an element of thrust, or bourgeoing advance; an element of retreat or inhibition; and an element of equilibration."[46] In human physiques these elements are identified as mesomorphy (muscle, bone, and connective tissue), ectomorphy (linear fragility and sensitivity) and endomorphy (soft visceral roundedness). Western civilizations are the outcome of a mesomorphic thrust northward impelled and reinforced by climatic changes and the dualisms of an urban economy with its ruling class science. Western sciences, philosophies, and religions have reflected this attitude of conquest and this practical, economic dualism, and have transmuted it in various ways. The element of equilibration, of biological balance and of animal impulse which keeps man close to the sources of his being, was carried along in this Western expansion, but was submerged. Eastern civilizations, because of climates more nearly tropical, confined geographies, and arrested and relatively simple economies, maintained a balance between the forces of ectomorphic retreat and those of endomorphic equilibration. In spite of the domination by philosophies of escape, the mass of Easterners living on the land stayed close to mother nature, and maintained in one form or another the attitudes of the ancient, endomorphic, maternal, life-nourishing, fertility religions of primitive civilizations. Extending Sheldon's analysis to hemispheres, we may say that the biological extreme of the West has been the explosive cancer of exploitation, imperialism, and scientific war, and the extreme of the hebephrenic East has been submission, retreat, and mystical simplicity. Both are tangential flights from the regular, sound orbit and spiral of life.

Man is in endless process of being controlled by the things and events of nature and of controlling those things and events. He receives from nature, and he takes from it; and there is no guarantee in nature or in his own nature that either side of this transaction will be infallibly good, for man or nature. In this process Eastern mysticism has tended to be blind,

46. *Varieties of Delinquent Youth*, p. 804.

and Western science destructive. But when such interaction becomes creative,[47] when it develops both man and nature in mutually fulfilling relations, when a dynamic balance is maintained between subject and object, emotion and perception, receptive detachment and dominance – then these extremes are transformed into values that reinforce one another. The feeling expressed in Eastern mysticism – the feeling of unity that man has with his fellow man and with nature – can thus avoid sentimental passivity and impotence and become an ally of the practical reason in its control of society and nature. It can sensitize and ground man's scientific action. At the same time man's science can avoid narrowness and rigidity, becoming flexible, progressively fruitful, humanized, and naturalized. Thus the traditional distortions of East and West – torpor and cupidity, inertness and violence, timidity and conceit, apathy and paranoia, softness and sharpness[48] – may meet, check one another, and be joined in a human, natural dialectical unity.

The new person must find completion in his unceasing creativity, the ripening of his latent constructive tendencies. His temperament – mixing, as the Greeks, conceived it – will be a vortex of variables, united by a human purpose and sensitivity. The new man must learn the art of "negative capability," the art of emptying himself and becoming a receptive vessel for the feelings of other creatures; while the new woman must acquire the skills of active manipulation and control over events. The complete person will realize, as Ch'eng Hao put it, that "the function of Heaven and Earth is our function," and that as Mencius said "all things are complete in us."[49] The principle of creative opposition and interdependence is inherent in all creatures. The complete person is fulfilled and empty; he actively strives for the improvement of himself and others, yet he knows that there is a naturalness about betterment which he cannot command or coerce. "He helps all things toward their natural development," says the *Tao Te Ching*, "but does not attempt to force their development."[50] Or in the words of Ch'eng Hao, following Mencius, "We must do something and never stop and never forget, yet never help to grow, doing it without the slightest effort."[51]

This full-orbed, creative relation of man with nature draws into itself all the fulfillments which man can ask for. The unitary principle of nature is its pluralizing. Man's devotion to or imitation of this principle would escape

47. The term "creative interaction" derives from H. N. Wieman, but he has used it mainly in connection with interpersonal relations. See *The Source of Human Good*. Chicago: University of Chicago, 1946.
48. See the work of the psychologist George Klein for the perceptual differentiae of some of these attitudes – e.g. in the *Menninger Clinic Bulletin*, May, 1953.
49. As quoted in Fung Yu-Lan, *A Short History of Chinese Philosophy*. New York: Macmillan, 1959, p. 282.
50. Ch. 64.
51. As quoted in Fung Yu-Lan, *op. cit.*

the extremes of monotonous mysticism and multiple, chaotic experiments. The result would be a balanced rhythm of closing and opening, of subjectivity and objectivity, of solitude and society, of centripetal and centrifugal forces. That balance is created in a dynamic dialectic of man and man with nature. Only in the unifying power of that interaction can dualities keep their identity and escape the skid into dualism; for the only monism is the monism of the many, cohering each to each by the common quality or creativity inhering in all.

> *Prajñā* is always trying to preserve its self-identity and yet subjects itself to infinite diversification.... thus to go on eternally in the work of creation – this is sunyātā, the *prajñā*-continuum.[52]

But man's identity is not a disembodied spirit. It is the functioning of an organism whose needs for survival and protection must be met before it can fully cooperate with others and create. The needs of endomorphy are primary. They anchor man to the earth. If man is to fulfill himself they must be brought into adjustive interaction with the real, concrete things of the world, the solids and liquids and air of the earth which nourish and comfort life. Here is the basis of man's biological balance – the solid, durable *tamas* of the *Gītā*. And here is the reason why the good life for people on our planet must begin with solving the interrelated problems of hunger, scarcity of food supply, and over-population.

Beginning with the Aryan migrations, the mesomorphic thrust through wilderness, over mountain, and by water has produced the Western civilizations of modern times. The ectomorphic retreat has come to fruition most fully in the older cultures of the East – in the classical Hindu philosophy, beginning with the Upaniṣads, in even the heresies of Hinduism, like classical Buddhism and Jainism, and in the speculative systems of Chinese thought. As pure tendencies, both mesomorphy and ectomorphy left behind them the ancient, endomorphic, maternal, life-nourishing, fertility religions of primitive civilizations. One may still find pure domination in certain militarism in the West and pure detachment in certain asceticism in the East. But generally the tendencies to thrust and retreat have carried along with them the elements of endomorphy, with the result of what Sheldon calls the explosive, burgeoning, outward indulgence of Dionysus and the contracting, asthenic, inward jettisonning or hoarding of Christus ("Brahmā" would be more accurate). Sheldon suggests that the biological extremes of cancer and hebephrenia "may be nothing more mysterious than an instance of the universal counterbalance between the second (somatotonic) and third (cerebrotonic) components," and that "the secret of continuance of the evolutionary

52. Daisetz Teitaro Suzuki, "Reason and Intuition in Buddhist Philosophy" *Essays in East-West Philosophy*, ed. Charles A. Moore. Honolulu: University of Hawaii, 1951, p. 45.

process in organic life may lie in a kind of symbiotic development of these two components in balance...."[53] We may therefore understand the West and the East as, respectively, thrust and retreat which make their peace with the forces of endomorphy: in the East this peace is a quietistic one; endomorphy is socialized into compassion or refined into selfless renunciation or mystical ecstasy; it has become the main emphasis in popular Hinduism, Buddhism, Taoism, and Confucianism. Faith and devotion are frequently the virtues of endomorphic persons guided by the ideals of unity and love, whether those ideals come from within the persons themselves or from the priests and philosophers without.

In the West the alliance between endomorphy and mesomorphy has been a dynamic one which transformed the selfish glutton into the warmhearted, extroverted entrepreneur, minister, executive, athlete. But in their extremes East and West show, as Sheldon's analysis suggests, a disequilibrium between action and thought. The conjunction of endomorphy with each of these two components has colored and qualified the conflict and has helped to soften and mediate it. Aside from this balancing factor on both sides – nearly all men, East and West, want the primary satisfactions of food, thermal comfort, sex, etc. – the inherent hostility which seems to exist between endomorphy-mesomorphy and ectomorphy[54] might have destroyed large numbers of men.

Life arises and flourishes in those warm, wet regions of the earth where food is easily obtainable and where the basic functions of digestion and assimilation can take place easily and efficiently. The functions of endomorphy – the realistic ingestions and conservation of environmental energies, and the easy expression of those energies – are indispensable to life. Endomorphy is close to mother earth and the springs of her life.

Both mesomorphy and ectomorphy represents biological departures or experiments from these central, vegetative functions. Mesomorphy is a movement outward and against the environment; it is simultaneously motor and protective: the development of dynamic power for aggressively acquiring food and for preying, rather than waiting for food or being preyed upon. Ectomorphy is a movement away from the environment; it is simultaneously inhibitory, hyper-attentional, associative and integrative of sensations: the development of the power of sensory feeling, imagining, and dreaming. Mesomorphy and ectomorphy are, in short, differentiations in two different directions: the mesomorph moves horizontally through space and time in conquest of the things and events of the earth; the ectomorph moves vertically beyond time into the fantastic world of eternity. When confronted

53. *Varieties of Delinquent Youth*, p. 804.
54. *Ibid.*, p. 794.

with a problem, the mesomorph's response will be fight, the ectomorph's, flight (into fantasy), and the endomorph's, a plight of dependence on others.

Men have wandered far from the organic center of their creative life. Man's Western experiment, in its restless and ruthless pilgrimage of power, expanding over the continents of Europe and the Americas in great waves of population, and later touching the fringes and hinterlands of other continents, aims at more and more power, and periodically explodes in the Dionysian orgasms of wars. Man's Eastern experiment has moved up and away from the needs and satisfactions of nature, relinquishing the grip on this life and retreating into the twilight brightness and then gathering dimness of detachment and death, a rejection of life, nature, reality. Wealth and poverty have thwarted man's fulfillment and distorted the direction and shape of his destiny. The soma and the brain were developed originally as appendages for the advance of life, as instruments in the service of living, but they have become values and ends pursued for their own sake and so, by action or inaction, destructive of life. Muscle and mind must serve life, or they will serve themselves, in defiance of life or in alienation from life. And life itself must serve new life, the life of future incarnation, which comes into being in time through the self-transcending effort and sacrifice of the present. The ultimate demand of life is not bigger tools or keener intellects; it is the demand of creation and re-creation, the demand of development, the demand of whole-hearted enthusiasm and heroic sacrifice, the demand of a creative future, the demand of detached-attachment and of humor.

There is a pattern of unity-in-variety in life which beckons as both lure and balm for East and West. For while the West has been lost in complexity, the East has been bogged in simplicity. Western man has gone astray in the Babel of tongues, the confusion of names, the word salad of unreason. A thousand voices have cried unto him, with a thousand panaceas. He has foundered in a net or words, caught in traps of his own making – tangled, torn, mangled in his own red tape and wandering alone in the mazes of his own Minotaur cities. And Eastern man, toiling wearisomely in his rice paddies or infertile earth, has hidden from his eyes the shining city of the new world, sinking down into the torpor of the simple life, or, if temperament and leisure permit, retreating into cold indifference. The way out of fragmentation and death for both East and West if a healthy, affirmative, integrative path of life that can enrich life without splintering it and unify it without falling into brutish simplicity or rigidity.

The demand on every member of life, be it an organ or a personality, is rightful subordination within the creative whole. Individual entities tend to insist on an importance out of proportion to reality. As Paul put it, the law of sin resides in our members, and wars against the law of the whole.[55]

Extremes in biological specialization, like the great saurians, may run rampant and rule for a time, a long time, but their excesses will be corrected by forms of life that are, as more balanced, more adjustive.

To advance, men and women must return, not to that torpid, mystical, hebephrenic annihilation of the East, but to those roots in nature that sustain the body of life in all its components and activities. They must go forward by going downward to the bodily sources of wisdom and constructive activity. They must go forward in that evolving harmony of opposites which develops nature on her creative and integrative side. In this men can learn from the intuitive capacity, tenderness, and helpfulness natural to woman. More endomorphic, more biologically conservative, more affined to the protective and healing powers of nature,[56] woman can be for human life in both East and West one of the new centers in our world culture. Too long she has been a mere plaything or slave in the Promethean West, and a dispensable appendage in the impoverished East. Males can learn from her the uselessness of extremes and the good of tensioned but harmonized opposites: past and future, old and young, male and female, activity and dream, as these are joined together in the service of a creative future for the children of mankind.

But in going back we must beware of the pit of primitive simplicity – satiated endomorphy – against which the warrior and the anchorite have warned us. We must renounce our present perversities of action and thought and return to the base of things, for, if we are building on the marginal swamps of life, our structures must fall. Only by first fulfilling the basic needs of man – the biological (or economic), the social (or political) – can we move on to express and fulfill that distinctively human need for creative development and self-transcendence in time. We must return to the center of things – not the dead center of vegetation but the productive center of spontaneity, the pregnant center, the center of the spiral of life that unwinds heavenward in time but always keeps its roots in the ground.

Every major religion and philosophy in the history of man has dwelt on the duality of man's experience: life-death, integration-differentiation, unity-plurality, intuition-analysis, permanence-change, love-wrath, righteousness-wickedness, good-evil, spirit-nature. Western religions (Zoroastrianism, Judaism, Christianity, Islam) reacted to this duality by postulating a dualism of irreconcilable and almost eternal conflict, to be resolved only at the last trump of time when good will rise triumphant over evil and, in the inscrutable dispensations of heaven, wipe away all tears. Eastern religions, particularly those of India, have postulated an ultimate metaphysical monism, beyond time but ever-present, such that the enlightened man sees the conflict as only

55. *Romans VII*: 23.
56. Ashley Montagu, *The Natural Superiority of Women*. New York: Macmillan, 1953.

apparent and transcends such phenomenal distinctions until he becomes one with the ultimate one. In both cases, the typical end evisaged is a static and transcendent unity obliterating process and hence conflict and suffering. But the Western way of extroversion and aggression and the Eastern way of inwardness and withdrawal are not the only ways of dealing with the tensions, dualities, and conflicts of the world. There is the way of transformation, involving simultaneous destruction and creation: the Jehovah of mercy and wrath, the Christ of transforming forgiveness, the Śiva who in the ecstasy of sexual union destroys lovers in order to bring forth a new being, the Dionysian intoxication and purification, the taurobolium of blood-drowning and rebirth, the Zen experience of contradictory order and fulfilled emptiness. The traditional religious views adumbrate the truth that life is conflict, and that man finds his way successfully through conflict only as he both acts and detaches himself. But they err in supposing that conflict, tension, and the duality of good and evil can be eliminated. The East, particularly India, has argued from the relativity of good and evil to a natural relativism and a supernatural absolutism. Yet while specific goods entail specific evils and such specific goods and evils change in time even into their opposites ("Reversal is the movement of the *Tao*"), there is a *natural* "good" which lies beyond such transformation, and that is Creative Transformation itself. As "*Tao* is a name which is not a name," this natural good of Transformation is a Good which is not a "good" – it is the necessary ground of all contingencies, the Process which makes possible all processes, the Law of all relativities. It defines the limits of death and of life; even the Taoists say that everything has its *Te*, or natural limits. It defines the limits of conflict and keeps relevant the alternative possibilities for the resolution of conflict.

What counts about conflict is its outcome. Traditionally, men have eschewed and deprecated conflict because so often it has reduced them to frustration, impotence, injury, and death – to states and processes from which full recovery and redemption seem, in the ways of this world at least, impossible. Literally, destruction of energy is not possible: "if the red slayer thinks he slays" he does not understand modern science. But the incapacitation of energy is possible: entropy and psychosis. And this is what man fears most of all; the reason why he has fastened his fear upon conflict (and his hope upon static "peace") is his false identification of conflict with the incapacitation of destruction.

What man truly wants in his wholeheartedness is not the predominance of pleasure over pain, or of satisfaction over dissatisfaction, or of security over insecurity, or some such simple preponderance of specific "goods" over specific "evils." Man is rather a Nietzschean bridge, an arrow shot from the bow, in the Heraclitean figure: a creature who seeks and cherishes for its own intrinsic sake the transformation of himself and his world, a creature who at root yearns for identification with the universal transformation – since man's transformation is a miniature, a contribution, and a stage in the evolution of the cosmos. What matters for man is not so much what is felt, thought, and achieved, as it is the general direction of achievement, the sense of unfolding movement; not the part but the evolving whole; not so much the content of his experiences as the way in which they mean and qualify one another, lead into one another in a coherent and mutually vivifying and progressive fashion, funding what is past with what is present and casting a focus of exploratory meaning into the future, fusing all that is felt and known in a significant whole that lights up and sanctifies each part – howsoever infected with triviality, futility, frustration, fatigue, or suffering these parts may be. The feeling of integral movement may be present from the beginning, selecting and guiding as man moves through concrete experiences; it may perdure through such experiences; and it may emerge toward the end as a kind of crown or unearned increment or "superabundance of grace" added unto nature. It is not the content of his experiences that contents man, for he cannot be contained, and requires discontent for true fulfillment. Man spills over boundaries, even those set by the gods; he is Prometheus unbound. It is not definite forms that man finally strives for, because he is in perpetual transformation. It is not some completed perfection toward which he tends, since he is of all creatures incomplete, and endlessly, inexhaustibly, perfectible. Man wants creative transformation; for that he lives, and moves, and dies, and rests, and is reborn, and lives again. Blessed is the man who finds his way fully and willingly into that destiny – in sickness or in health; in winning or in losing; in work or in play; in struggle or in torpor; in time or in the moment; in his conquests and his sufferings; in himself and in the gifts of nature. For in that destiny man may not only realize his true nature but may also, in the midst of what seems bewilderment and chaos, follow, Tao-wise, the great dialectic of the Universe, which is everlasting.

Chapter VI

MAN'S PROBLEM, NATURE, AND FULFILLMENT TODAY

Man's Problem

Ours is a time of great hopes and hazards. Most people on the planet today realize this. This widespread realization is unprecedented in world history. It is the point from which we must start if we are to fulfill our hopes and reduce the hazards. Why must we do so? Because people universally feel obligated to fulfill themselves.

The hopes and hazards are tied together. Both pertain to the future of man-kind, growing out of the present. Both are grounded in the increasing power of men over themselves and their world – in the promise and precariousness of that power. This increasing power takes many forms: atomic fission and fusion; the transformation of solar energy; the making of hydroelectric power; the conversion of the land's and sea's resources to human uses (energy, food, water, building materials, clothing, medicines); the determina-tion and control of cell division, of the mechanism of heredity, of biological deficiencies, and of diseases; the development of automation and computers to do physical labor and mental calculation; the control of weather; the sciences of learning and of social systems.

The greatest hazard is a thermonuclear, chemical, biological, or radi-ological war that will destroy or forever incapacitate the human race as a going concern.[1] Experts differ in estimating the probabilities of such a catastrophe; but even the lowest estimates are high enough to cause alarm. The next greatest hazard is the continuing or deepening of the poverty of two-thirds of the world's people. Such poverty is more than economic want; it is the deprivation of man's total being in its drive for fulfillment. Such deprivation has multiple causes: demographic, economic, social, political, educational, etc. Hence the hazard of human deprivation is widespread and persisting. Moreover, one of the solutions to this problem, the application of scientific techniques in the development of agriculture and industry, depends on a generous flow of capital from the richer countries to the poorer. But this flow is presently not forthcoming. "The gap between rich and poor is widen-ing."[2]

In addition, the hazards of war and deprivation are interlocked. The

1. For the relevant facts and judgments here, see Norman Cousins, *In Place of Folly*. New York: Washington Square, 1962.
2. C. P. Snow, *The Two Cultures and the Scientific Revolution*. New York: Cambridge University, 1961, p. 49.

world's governments now spend $200 billion each year on war preparations.[3] Expenditures for armaments deprive people of goods and services by which to satisfy their needs. They slow down economies, and, in the mutual acceleration of the arms race, drive nations toward genocide. Most significant, an economy of armaments prevents the flow of capital to poorer countries, a flow which is an indispensable transfusion for the revival of a moribund people and their healthy, autonomous life.

By the same token, the hope of people is their hope for world peace, for the end of deprivation, and for health and fulfillment. These hopes are interlocked. A world both wealthy and warring, or a world peaceful but poor, would be intolerable. Peace is a necessary condition and concomitant of a world economy whose interchange of goods, services, and ideas defines prosperity. And such interchange is the avenue to peace. What people yearn for, and find to be their deepest though dim object of obligation, is such prosperity. But prosperity is more than the absence of poverty. It is the negation of the conditions by which persons are de-prived, i.e., de-individualized. It is the presence of conditions that enrich the whole human being. "Prosperity" means fulfillment in the many-dimensioned individual – somatic, minded, spiritual – and in his relations to other persons and the rest of nature. "Prosperity" means that which is the ground and goal of man's hope (*sperare*). "Despair" means the loss of hope. And this is what we experience when we face or suffer the hazards of war and poverty.

Now what can philosophers say or do that is useful in this time of great hope and hazard for the human race?

Philosophers can clarify the generic concepts that are relevant to man's problem – which is the problem of his fulfillment. By "generic" I mean those concepts which define man as man, i.e., his concrete, invariant nature from situation to situation and culture to culture during our present era on this planet. (Here I reject the view held by some – e.g., some behaviorists and existentialists – that man has no generic nature.) By "concept" I mean an abstracted pattern of relations expressible in language. By "relevant" I mean concepts whose employment will make a difference to the problem in question. Philosophers have ordinarily maintained the general thesis that the clarification and employment of generic concepts can and do make a difference to man's problem. The reason for this is that people successfuly solve their problems by guiding conduct with concepts. Therefore problems of a generic kind – like, "What ought to be the goal of my life?" or, "How can human conflict be dealt with creatively?" – require generic concepts to be successfully solved.

I therefore propose here to clarify some generic concepts pertaining to

3. Cousins, *op. cit.*, p. 174.

man. These concepts, as well as my own attempted clarification of them, have been expressed by a variety of philosophers in the East and West. They are proposed in the conviction that for men to solve their present problem a necessary part of their knowledge is knowledge of themselves. This knowledge must be not only scientific. It must be philosophical, i.e., generic. It must pertain to the nature of man, his values, his methods of knowing these, his way of living.

Although the thinking out and the expressing of concepts concerning man are necessarily abstract (as is the thinking about chairs), the referents of such thinking are concrete. When we seek what is "generic" about man, we therefore seek what is most concrete in man's experience. Too often philosophers have occupied themselves with *mere* concepts. They have transmuted concepts into concrete realities. Thus they have implicitly urged that, since the real nature and value of men lies in concepts, then the right way of living for all men is to become philosophers. This error not only makes philosophy an idol, driving out all other human concerns. It confuses the abstract with the concrete. The proper function of the philosopher is, first, to use language to point to those generic, concrete elements of men's common experience. Such elements are definitive of men's reality as human beings, of the reality of their world, of the value and significance of these realities, and of men's ways of knowing and acting with respect to such realities and values. Second, the philosopher, through his concepts, should help to prepare men for action, action that realizes value. Only in such action can conceptual activity ultimately be justified. (For justification is a matter of the increase of value.) In its first function, then, philosophy is creative discovery; in its second, creative action. And these two functions are fused in the dialectic of thought and action. In this way philosophy becomes relevant to human life and values. For the one thing required of a philosophy is that it be viable. To be viable, it must facilitate the vital functioning of man.

Our ever-present, obtrusive realities are hunger, thirst, sex, nurturance, curiosity, productive and destructive activity, cooperation, individuation, rest, sleep, play, fright, and the rhythms of man's life running from birth through various stages to death.[4] These propulsive need-drives of the *gunas* – of gut, muscle, bone, nerve – have all too often been "overlooked" by the philosophers because they looked "up" and "over" instead of downward and inward and outward. Because philosophers have been led astray into the abstract, they have usually made only an esoteric appeal and have missed

4. Writers concerned with generic human needs, drives, or "instincts" are Michael Graham, Abram Kardiner, Otto Klineberg, Clyde Kluckhohn, Ralph Linton, Ashley Montagu, George P. Murdock, Henry A. Murray, E. C. Tolman. A graphic illustration of the human creature, in his sameness and variety, is *The Family of Man*, ed. Edward Steichen. New York: Maco Magazine, 1955. Corresponding to the data on human needs, there is a growing literature about common human values.

the common man, neither beginning with his realities nor communicating with him. They have usually come from the upper class or have served in its pay. Alienated from the daily struggles of men to live, they have indirectly and obscurely grasped the realities of human existence. And on the other side the masses of common men have ordinarily been so hungry, weak, sick, weary, or overworked in their efforts to survive that they have not had time to commit to writing their thoughts, save in folk songs and stories and other art. An implicit philosophy of, by, and for the people may be found in such art.

The realistic and effective philosopher is the thinker who works in living relations with common people. He endeavors to aid them in defining their identities as human beings and the realities around them.[5] He takes as his starting point the unrealized existential need-dispositions of individuals driving them toward fulfillment in the context of things and events yet hidden. To realize the self and the realities around it, it is necessary to act reflectively. The self of man and his world must be discovered through creative thought and action. Each self must perform this act of creative realization for himself. But while the philosopher cannot do this for any except for himself, he can through his special tools help others toward that fulfillment toward which they blindly strive.

> Now he may serve me only gropingly,
> Soon I shall lead him into the light.[6]

Man's Nature

1. *Exchanging.* We (our experiences and the identities holding our successive experiences together) are fundamentally defined by relations of exchange that occur within our bodies and between our bodies and other bodies.[7] The body is a locus and source of driving power.[8] It is energy, a vague vector

---

5. Some prime examples in this century have been Lenin, Gandhi, and Mao Tse-tung. Less influential but involved in political and social affairs have been S. Radhakrishnan, Bertrand Russell, Jean-Paul Sartre, and Albert Schweitzer.

6. *Goethe's Faust*, trans. Louis MacNeice. New York: Oxford University, 1951. Part I, Prologue in Heaven.

7. The materialists are correct in stressing the role of man's body and the idealists are correct in stressing his relations to others and his activities. Marx summed up the false dichotomy in his day between the two: "Hence it happened that the *active* side, in contradistinction to materialism, was developed by idealism – but only abstractly, since, of course, idealism does not know real, sensuous activity as such." *Theses on Feuerbach*, I.

8. *Brahman* means "energy, force, power, potency." Henrich Zimmer, *Philosophies of India*. New York: Meridan, 1956, p. 77. *Te* (in Taoism) has a similar connotation, like *vir*, in virtue. The category of power is common in the West, especially in modern times.

movement, in exchange with other energies. To be sure, we begin our existence inside the body of our mother, parasitically dependent on it. But we are still other than that body. And our existence is defined and sustained by the relations of exchange our body has with it. We move about in the uterus, respond to stimuli, suck our thumbs, kick and punch the walls that enclose us, absorb the oxygen, glucose, calcium, iron, fatty acids, etc., available through the umbilical cord, and eliminate waste products. On the other side, our mother reacts to us.

At birth, we dramatically move from an aquatic existence to the life of an aerific creature, with new relations to the manifold surrounding us. We breathe. We obtain our food through our mouths. We draw from our mother's breast milk, and in the process get oxygen and love.[9] We digest our food. Thus we evolve those exchanges necessary to our new mode of existence: respiration, digestion, and innovative adaptation to environment.

Still a new step is to be taken in this progression toward human individuality. At first the baby interacts with and adjusts to its mother's body. It kicks and pushes against its mother, crib, and other objects. It discovers the parts of its own body, sucking its thumb, fingering its fingers, touching its face, chewing its toes. Within the first year, in the intimacies of the touches, tastes, sounds, and sights developed in interaction with things and persons, the baby begins to acquire the skill of using symbols. This skill becomes the means by which it participates in the culture of its society. The meanings of symbols are truly the "means" of achieving our *human* nature. As the forms by which meanings are produced, carried, made objective, and communicated, symbols emerge in, and direct us toward, interactions with others and the world. These interactions are of a different order from biophysical interactions. Symbolic meanings are tools by which individuals exchange stimuli and responses and so progressively create – innovate, integrate, and control – a common world. The creative production and exchange of meanings via symbols is a defining characteristic of human beings.

Exchange means, first, duality. This duality is dynamic and moves from difference, to opposition, to negation. Each element in the exchange is changed by the other and eventually negated (by some opposite). Likewise, there is alternation in exchange: first one actor gives and the other receives, then the other gives and the first receives. Thus negation and alternation define exchange. They are the "primitive ideas" of exhange, as in logic. And from them can be derived implication (I $\supset$ the other), conjunction

---

9. Margaret A. Ribble, *The Rights of Infants*. New York: Columbia University, 1943. The mouth is also essential to speech, and in it we can see the linkage between physical love and thought. The large areas of the brain controlling the impulses from the pharynx, tongue, lips, etc. have now been demonstrated. See Wilder Penfield and Theodore Rasmussen, *The Cerebral Cortex in Man*. New York: Macmillan, 1950.

(I · the other), and equivalence (I = the other) or the unity of opposites. Exchange thus means the unity, interpenetration, and transformation of opposites.

Exchanging means mutuality or symmetry of relation. Exchanging between two persons requires giving and receiving on the part of each: aRb ≡ bRa. Now one person gives and the other receives; and then the roles are reversed. But perfect or static symmetry is impossible, because exchange takes time and time is asymmetrical. Exchange is, in a spatial world, necessary to change. It elicits and directs change, and gives definition to change. Thus the human person is a series of successive changes, cumulative and growing. He executes changes successfully as his relations of exchange contribute to his unitary direction and integral fulfillment.

A variety of features distinguishes the human species: internal fertilization, foetalization, prolonged dependency of the infant, acute sensitivity, absence of over-specialization, upright posture, brain, hand, the mechanism of language. But to understand the nature of man, we must see these characteristics in a functional whole. Together they represent a unique capacity of the individual and the group for effective, creative exchange with its human and non-human environments. Through that exchange man displays his capacity for variation and integration, i.e., for growth in experiences. Thus in his method of exchange with other persons and things, man shows a distinctive combination of variability and stability. His method of effecting viable exchanges (creative, symbolic intelligence) remains more or less constant. At the same time it enables him to cope with a wide variety of circumstances, to live in a wide variety of habitats, and to undergo and integrate a wide variety of experiences.[10] His abiding habit is his power to change and create new habits.

Man's exchanging, mediative power is rooted in a unique sensitivity and responsiveness. This originates in the infant's mammalian dependency on the parents and is reinforced by the long infantile period and the intense, linguistic sociality of the species. "Empathy"[11] (which is a highly developed and unitary functioning of the sensitivities) relates the infant directly and internally to its parents. It does so particularly as it reinforces the infant's primary

10. The generic characteristic of creative exchange is central to the Yang-Yin School, Taoism, and Confucianism (*jen*, or human-heartedness, is represented by a character that means both "man" and "two"). But Taoism tended to diffuse and make static the concept and Confucianism narrowed and restricted it to familial and imperial relations. In India the idea appears in the *Gītā*, the *gunas* of the Sāmkhya, the Brāhmanic unity of opposites in the Divine Being, Śiva and śakti (Tantra), and the Mahāyāna Mahāsukha or "great delight" of male-female union. The Jewish mishpat (justice), Greek dike (order), the Stoic politicon systema, and Christian love express a similar idea. For an explicit metaphysics of "espousal" see the work of Corinne Chisholm Frost.
11. More than any other ancient philosopher, Mencius saw the importance of this and built his philosophy upon it.

drives of survival and its sense of dependency. In turn the parents empathically respond to the infant, driven not only by a maternal or nurturing impulse but by the same sense of organic connectedness, developed in their own human career. Likewise the parents are sensitized and respond to one another as they are driven by the power of sex,[12] another form of human sociality.

This social view of man stands in contrast to the view that man's self at birth is fully antecedent, non-physical, discrete, fixed, and autonomous. It opposes too the view that man's relations to his world and other persons comprise a pre-ordained harmony. Man's personality emerges as his body interacts and exchanges meanings with other persons. Thus man's generic existence is best represented as a field of interacting forces emanating from and returning to creative centers defined by bodies existing in space and time. Normative society is neither an aggregation of isolated entities (bodies or souls) nor a unitary whole of which particular individual persons are mere appearances. Man's relations of exchange with things and persons are creative of his person and essential to it. Accordingly, the isolation of men in feudal or otherwise "underdeveloped" societies and the lonely anxiety of men in capitalistic, competitive societies, are deviations from the normal. They are forms of illness.

Thus the form of society and government best adapted to man's nature is democracy. In it men progressively correct and supplement one another's perspectives and collectively solve their collective problems. All individualistic views of human nature eventuate either in some form of anarchism, which throws individuals back on their internal control; or they end in some form of totalitarianism, which arbitrarily introduces control over the individual from the outside. Democracy rectifies the impoverishment of predatory individualism and the tyranny of totalitarianism by organizing individuals in relations of mutual creation and development. The tendencies to withdrawal and self-indulgence are modified by the love of others. And the tendencies to aggression and dominance are modified by the needs and demands of others. Nations and the planetary community can now ill afford the destructive pathologies of unloved, uncriticized individuals. Social democracy is their only preventive and cure. Democracy defines the institutional lines along which the primary human impulse of creative exchange may be

12. Sex as a fact of life has been by philosophers in the West ignored (Descartes, Kant, Leibniz); taken account of but discounted or subordinated (Plato, Aristotle, St. Thomas); acknowledged but considered evil (Gnostics, Manicheists, Augustine, Calvin, Schopenhauer); or viewed as central (Empedocles, Lucretius, Rousseau, and certain quasi-philosophers such as Whitman and Freud). Sex figures prominently in Tantra and Tāntric Mahāyāna (see Zimmer, *op. cit.*) and naturalistically in Taoism. See Joseph Needham, *Science and Civilisation in China*, vol. II, *History of Scientific Thought*. Cambridge: Cambridge University, 1956, pp. 146–152.

maximized.[13] It liberates equally the different powers of individuals through equal opportunity and the equal rights and duties of creative fraternity.

It has been said that the dependency of the child, or the permanent breast or mammalian nature of the female, or the sexuality of the human being, or the family, is the foundation of human life. There is a partial truth in all such theories. But the inclusive truth is the fact of exchange. The irreducible human unit consists of a man, a woman, and a child. Each is differentiated, each maintains a distinctive relation to each of the others, and each engages in active relations of exchange with the others and with the world.[14]

After birth the child begins to acquire the tools of humanity – speech, the symbols of his society (technology, art, religion, etc.), and the skills of production. Thus it participates in the collective life, the collective control of nature, the communication and communion called culture. It enters into and assumes a role in the network of relations of exchange of goods and services which define its society's economy. Finally, as the child becomes a mature adult, its empathic and sexual dispositions, deepening its sensitivities to others, drive it to associate with others in more intimate ways. In the usual case, there is sexual union, and the reproductive cycle is completed.

The concept of the autonomous individual – usually defined in Western philosophy as an isolated material body or an isolated empty body (i.e.,

13. Mencius, with his theory of the "four tender shoots" of morality innate in man – the feelings of empathy, shame, modesty, and right – consistently constructed his concepts of society on this popular, democratic, and non-coercive basis. He argued for the equal distribution of land and, though a sage-king was to lead, the sage was the least important element in the state, and it was the association of the people that determined the character of the state. Mo-tzu likewise conceived of a state constituted by mutual love among people. For a modern view connecting creative social relations and democracy, see Mary Parker Follett, *Creative Experience*. New York: Longmans, Green, 1924. And *The New State*. New York: Longmans, Green, 1920.

14. Indian philosophy (in the *Atharva-veda* and the philosophy of the Hindu householder) pays much attention to the family. In China, Confucianism stressed familial relations, and Taoism, man's relations of exchange with nature. Neo-Taoism developed the idea that everything, though in one sense independent, needs every other thing for its existence, and so in interaction "self-transformation" occurs. (See Fung Yu-lan, *A Short History of Chinese Philosophy*. New York: Macmillan, 1950, ch. 19.) Eventually the two traditions crossed and fused in Neo-Confucianism, in which man, identified with the creative Yang and Yin of the Ultimate, enters into unifying relations with all persons and all things (Fung, *op. cit.*, ch. 23). In Indian philosophies interaction or exchange of things occurs for the naturalists or seminaturalists (Ājīvikas, Cārvākas, Jainas, Hīnayāna Buddhists, Sāṃkhyas, and Vaiśeṣikas) – although exchange is, among atomists at least, not thought of as essential to the ultimate, partless realities. The schools that emphasized sexuality (Śivaism, Tantra) as well as Brāhmanism (in the "play" and threefold creativity of Iśvara) also held exchange in high esteem. In the West, Heraclitus, Anaxagoras, the atomists, and, in modern times, Hegel, Marx, Peirce, Dewey, Whitehead, Buber, Wieman, and Hartshorne have made exchange fundamental in their views of the universe. For two biological interpretations of the family, see Weston La Barre, *The Human Animal*. Chicago: University of Chicago, 1955; and N. J. Berrill, *Sex and the Nature of Things*. New York: Pocket Books, 1955.

146

soul) – is an abstraction. Every man's body is the consequence of the union of two gametes. That the body is not a be-all and end-all, separable from other bodies and processes – that it is relational, transitional, transitory – is evidenced in the process of meiosis. This sets aside the somatic, individualized body, or uses it as a convenient way station. By a process which *reduces* the number of chromosomes in the cell, it produces a sperm or egg, incomplete until it meets up with its opposite.

The individual body is the genes' bridge between generations – a bridge that is soon discarded (or can be) once the new generation has been built into a bridge. The act of sex – an exchange – is a major mechanism by which this bridge begins. Furthermore, the individual body collapses; the genes go on indefinitely. Thus the human being, at the biological level, may be defined as a linking relation between past bodies and future bodies. It is a knot in a moving strand, weaving itself into the evolving texture of the universe. An analogous function is filled by the psychosomatic personality,[15] as it becomes an inheritor and learner of culture and, later, a transmitter and teacher in the same culture.[16] All societies recognize and ritualize the fact that the individual person dies.[17] At the same time most religions and philosophies have affirmed that, though the individual may in some sense survive after death, certain realities and values outlast the individual: memories, ideals, principles, society, nature, gods. The individual is precious, but only as he incarnates or serves what transcends his passage.

Most persons are born and reared in a family; work (expend energy) in order to live; and become parents of children. Hence, as Freud has said, man has two needs, *lieben und arbeiten*. It is surprising not that men have proclaimed so many ideal ways to live but that sages have often missed the concrete nature of themselves and their fellow men in favor of some abstraction. An example is "brotherhood." This is a partial and derivative value – even if extended to its farthest equalitarian lengths, so as to ignore differences of sex, age, nationality, race, religion, condition, time, and place. The idea of brotherhood (or siblinghood) presupposes a more inclusive reality, namely,

15. To this extent absolute idealism, or pantheism, has been correct in viewing the individual person as an organic part or manifestation of a larger system (Śaṅkara, Spinoza, Hegel, Royce). (Materialism which allows for internal relations between ultimate particles appears to approach the same position. Here Spinoza may be taken either way.) At the same time the individual has a separate reality so far as it is an independent, free *relator* itself, adding, as James says, its fiat to the fiat of the creator (*Pragmatism*. New York: Longmans, Green, 1907, p. 291). Rāmānuja seems correct, Śaṅkara, incorrect, on this point. Particularity is real, as Vaiśeṣika holds, and is not, as Śaṅkara says, the criterion of the unreal. Here S. Radhakrishnan, in the tradition of Rāmānuja, is correct.
16. The importance of tradition in Indian and Chinese philosophies, as contrasted with its relative unimportance in Western philosophies, will be obvious to students.
17. A. L. Kroeber and Clyde Kluckhohn, *Culture, A Critical Review of Concepts and Definitions*. Papers of the Peabody Museum, vol. 47, no. 1. Cambridge: Harvard University, 1952, pp. 174–179.

a family.[18] And it is this that we are most *familiar* with – those relations of exchange in which we are cared for and care for others, either as children or parents. Siblinghood is important and for celibates takes on special significance. But it tends to flatten out into horizontal, contemporary relations. It undervalues the temporal processes of history by which we inherit the values of the past directly from our parents and pass them on, responsibly, to our children and unborn generations.

2. *Changing.* We are conceived, we develop as embryos, we are born, we grow as bodies, our bio-social selves emerge and grow, we pass from childhood to adolescence to maturity to senility; and we eventually die. So we are in continuous passage from one state to another.[19] Our present differs from our past. It is spread apart from it. This passage through and into states of being we call time. Our becoming, our concrete growing nature, is compounded out of such states of being. To this extent we are not entirely and forever fixed, decided, or certain. It is in fact a linguistic error to say "We grow." For in the beginning there is no substantial "I," though the self is latent and genetic. Always the concrete momentary "I" is the result of growth through exchange, an accumulation of experiences mnemonically bound together and unified by a genetic identity of form.[20] More accurately we should say: "There occurs an x (changing) such that if it has the characteristic f (creative exchange) it also has the characteristic g (identity through time)."

In conflicts of men and nations, the facts of change, uncertainty, and probability – in reality, value, and knowledge – are ignored at men's peril. Every living person, every social system, is continuously changing, sometimes slowly, sometimes rapidly. Of course not all change is good. A young person who changes into a destructive delinquent ought to be checked in such a change. But the corrective is not to check all or most change in him but to direct his changing nature into constructive activities of exchange. To

18. Compare Stoicism, Christianity, and the Neo-Confucianism of Chang Tsai, who said: "Heaven may be said to be my Father, and earth may be said to be my Mother.... All men are my brothers; all things are my kin. The ruler is the eldest son of my parents and the ministers are his stewards...." The figure of the Mother Goddess has been prominent in India since primitive times.

19. Some philosophers who have taken change seriously and viewed it as a basic category include Heraclitus, Gautama Buddha, the Taoists ("Reversal is the movement of the Tao"), the Yang-Yin School, Chu Hsi (Ch'i), Zen masters, Bacon, the British empiricists, the French materialists, Marx, Nietzsche, existentialists, and process philosophers. So far as Brāhmanism interpreted rebirth, the evolution of *prakṛti* (*māyā*), and the ceaseless play and alternation of the "day" and "night" of Brahmā as genuinely real, it correctly grasped the ultimacy of change. Often change has been either subordinated to some more basic category (as in Plato, Aristotle, Philo, Plotinus, matter-spirit dualism, supernaturalism, absolute idealism, or mechanistic materialism) or interpreted as illusory (nondualistic Vedānta and idealism generally).

20. Charles Hartshorne, *Reality as Social Process*. Glencoe, Illinois: Free Press, p. 102.

check his changing will result only in impoverishment of his capacities for good. For a capacity is a potential for action and hence for change. To this impoverishment he may react by apathetic acquiescence, indifferent detachment, or violent defiance – all of them normal reactions to an unhealthful condition. Similarly, the imposition of a pattern of fixity upon the individuals in a social system or upon a society as a whole will arrest change and hence development. It will produce the resentful unrest that, when physically expressed, results in individual violence or social revolution.

Hence it is that efforts to fix things and values in a changing human world, by the coercion of some final form, are doomed to tyranny, loss of value, tragedy, and death. Hence it is that efforts to absolutize some idea are doomed to bind and distort man's grasp of the world and his action toward it.[21] For the individual person is many, and lives in a world of many. The unity each person achieves is an outcome of interaction; his unity is successive and developmental, pursuing its own exploratory path. Hence the wisdom of Mencius, that the cultivation of the Great Morale requires constant effort but no forcing of growth.[22]

Why is it that men attempt to impose upon themselves, others, and whole social systems value patterns of fixity and certainty that are harmful? (The pattern of armaments expenditures is an example.) Why do men exalt one perspective and damn others? (Nationalism is an example.) Unfulfilled and hence anxious about their existence, men seek an apparent security in an ideal condition that lies opposite their own, namely, fixity.[23] If men possess the power to enforce a value pattern of fixity on others, then their anxiety is deepened by their personal identification with the pattern of oppression. If, on the other side, they are oppressed, they will cling to that same pattern for reasons of security, unless convinced that change is possible. So anxiety makes great demands on the system of oppression, particularly in the face of threats with respect to the system.[24] Thus in the conflicts of the great political powers we may observe how the mutually aggravating anxieties of the leaders increase rigidities in understanding and dealing with changes both at home and abroad. But the basic fact of human life is that change continues and that we must take and use change for advance – or decline and die.

---

21. An example of this is what the Jainas call "the fallacy of exclusive predication." Satischandra Chatterjee and Dhirendramohan Datta, *An Introduction to Indian Philosophy*, 4th ed. Calcutta: University of Calcutta, 1950, p. 184. Cf. Whitehead's "fallacy of misplaced concreteness," in *Science and the Modern World*. New York: New American Library of World Literature, 1948, p. 52.
22. *The Book of Mencius*, II.
23. One of the most profound analyses of this problem is that of Gautama Buddha.
24. Harry Stack Sullivan, *Conception of Modern Psychiatry*. Washington, D. C.: William Alanson White Psychiatric Foundation, 1947.

The great novelists show the truth of sociology: how character is wrought out of the interweaving of individual temperament and family, other persons, modes of work, physical surroundings, customs and cultural values. The bodies and processes of the world affect my body and its processes. And as an internal part of my "I" my body in turn initiates changes within that system of exchanges which I have with the external world. Thus as the world changes me I change it as I internalize it and as I externalize a response which forms a portion of the environs for the things in the world. This continuous commerce of things, this mutual creation, constitutes the rhythm of the universe. Hence to draw a sharp line between the "self" and the "non-self" is arbitrary.[25]

As reality is social, so is knowledge. The paradigm case of knowledge, which is science, shows the power of cooperative thought. Not only must knowledge be tested, refined, corroborated, and revised in the interaction of persons. It originates in that interaction.

> ...scientific ideas are usually born in a conversation, rather than in the mind of one man. The rigorous thinking needed to nurse a new-born idea into a useful hypothesis must almost always be done in private. But the fresh insights, the new associations between previously unrelated phenomena, often come from the interplay of two or three minds clashing in conversation[26].

The idea that knowledge can be spun out of the innards of the individual mind is untrue and pernicious. It afflicts many an expert and layman alike. It is the reflection of a static caste or class society, in which groups and individuals are divided off from one another and from the conditions of their common life. How can the philosopher learn the rough and multiple edges of reality when he retreats from the common people into his cloister? He might take a lesson from Gandhi, Mao Tse-tung, Lenin, and all thoughtful leaders who have linked their efforts successfully to the common people. The live-and-let-live policy of laissez-faire economies – alternating with the

25. The wisdom of the Upaniṣads and of the *Lao-tzu* is now evident in biology and ecology. "The species may be looked upon as an organism with literal protoplasmic continuity in the space-time of the physicist, through the continual union of lines of germ cells.... the evolution of each species is merely an aspect in the evolving pattern of life as a whole and indeed of the world as a whole." Sewall Wright, "Organic Evolution," *Encyclopedia Britannica*, vol. 8. Chicago, London, Toronto: Encyclopedia Britannica, 1959, p. 929. For the suggestions of a meta-galactic philosophy, see Harlow Shapley, *Of Stars and Men*. New York: Washington Square, 1959. No adequate philosophy can ignore the problem of planetary ecology – for purposes of man's economy, his esthetic needs, and his recreation, and the execution of man's obligation to nature.
26. Roger Revelle, "International Cooperation and the Two Faces of Science," *Cultural Affairs and Foreign Relations*. New York: American Assembly, Columbia University, 1962, pp. 5–6.

most ruthless kind of coercion in recent years, exercised through oligopolic control of the mass media – has produced a sense of self-sufficiency (alongside a sense of impotence) that is stifling to development. Men proclaim that they are "masters of their fate" in "the free world." The fact is that they more and more feel themselves as slaves and victims of fate. In the U. S. A., men shun debate on vital issues, are alternately polite and repressive, penalize spontaneity, unorthodox dissent, and freedom, and conspire to produce in one another a compliant timidity. Such an attitude is also cool toward international exchange (e.g., trade with China, the U. N., negotiation of international differences). But it impairs the very process of human growth and improvement, the cross-fertilization of perspectives.

What has always been true of associated individuals has now become true of societies. Societies, now interacting with one another increasingly, depend on one another for maintenance and improvement. Imperialism, colonialism, and the exploitation of one nation, class, race, or sex by another are fast disappearing. The advance of technology has been a great equalizer, for it has laid down avenues of exchange. The old insular attitudes resist the intercultural openness, the mutual respect for the rights of the individual person or society, required by a world economy built on exchange of material and spiritual goods and services. The critical problem is whether human attitudes can be transformed to support and guide the technological revolution now under way. Creative exchange is called for.

The fact that our lives are defined by change does not mean that we have no identity, knowledge, or value. The unity and direction of personality are developed in exchange – at first unconsciously, then deliberately. The ordering mechanisms that we inherit – the metabolic processes, the autonomic and central nervous systems and functioning, homeostatic mechanisms, perceptual *Gestalten*, and the unifying rhythms peculiar to the body's somatotype[27] – provide the aboriginal basis for an identical order persisting throughout changes and exchanges. To this degree the self is *a priori* and genetic, and the possibilities for all selves reside in part in the gene pool of the race.[28] To this degree the self, as the Upaniṣads say, is "unborn." To this degree, too, the first determinate act in the creation of the self is conception. And

27. W. H. Sheldon, *The Varieties of Human Physique*. New York: Harper, 1940.
28. All DNA Molecules in living organisms, though presumed to be the same, must be different in detail. For, according to Schroedinger, no two subatomic events are identical: it is only the temporal structure of the events that gives them "identity." (See *Science and Humanism*. Cambridge: Cambridge University, 1951.) The differences of species are due to the arrangements of the levels of the helices, and the differences of the individuals within the human species are of course due to the reduction division in the germ cells, the random association of genes in a daughter cell, the random union of egg and sperm, and the breaking and crossing over of the homologous filaments of chromosomes. See H. J. Muller, "Gene," *Encyclopedia Britannica*, vol. 10. Chicago, London, Toronto: Encyclopedia Britannica, Inc., 1959, pp. 100–101.

while every combination of genes is unique,[29] the Kantian "necessary" and "universal" character of the *a priori* judgments of persons is grounded in this common genetic makeup of all men. But the mature unity of the psychosomatic self is an emergent, specifically and symbolically formed in experience. Thus nature, culture, and the gene pool of the race provide the general and *a priori* potentials for selfhood.[30] These are actualized only via some particular natural environment and culture and some particular genetic combination carried in the individual body.[31] The self that emerges is the function of these three factors: it is bio-social-ecological.

Further, we acquire knowledge, and as acquired it is always mediated, relative, and limited. It is relative to the individual's sensitivities and reponsiveness (his somatotype), to his character as a species member, to his acquired experiences and meanings, to his nonhuman circumstances, and to his culture. The relativity of knowledge does not bar its objectivity. Our relations of exchange with things and persons take place as objective processes. The procedures for controlling the subjective elements in such relations are essentially twofold: to observe the object in question from different perspectives and to repeat such observations; and to integrate these with the observations of other persons. Subjective error is then corrected and corroborated by subject-object and subject-subject tests. Our relational knowledge, acquired in interaction with things and persons, is guided, checked, and revised by further relations, and by a consideration, comparison, and collation of data observed, communicated, and calculated. The social, relational character of knowledge is illustrated by such words as *correct, corroborate, communicate, conscious, consensual, content, convince, conclude.* Similarly, value is a contextual affair, a matter of effecting commerce with things, events, and persons so as to fulfill (or help fulfill) dispositions in a satisfying, unitary way. Again, value is consolidated or increased by certain processes of exchange with things and other persons.

When men do not communicate freely with those who differ, their opi-

29. The chance of a particular individual's being born (figured just before conception) is 1/300,000,000 (the denominator being the number of sperms deposited in the female at any given time). The chance of a particular individual's being duplicated has been estimated to be 1/70 million million. Garrett Hardin modestly estimates that there are 10^{3000} possible gene combinations for living things. *Nature and Man's Fate.* New York: New American Library of World Literature, 1961, p. 247. Serious contemplation of these figures should convince a person of just how fortunate he is to have been conceived. The good or bad "fortune" of his existence is for man's thought and action, not chance seeds, to determine.

30. Human "possibility" – from *potis*, able, plus *esse*, to be – means a capacity inherent in what *is*. Only what is is capable of further being. Possibility is not a Platonic "essence." It is what a concrete thing will do in another concrete context, and the actualizable power already resides in concrete things and their relations.

31. Aristotle and Chu Hsi are thus partially correct in attributing individuality to the physical body.

152

nion and values become rigidly non-adaptive. The secret of institutional creativity is an open channel of communication between leaders and led.[32] But either because of caste or class interest, or routine, or lack of imagination, or sloth, leaders tend to become isolated from the perspectives of the led. That this can occur under socialism as well as feudalism and capitalism has been recently illustrated. Leaders tend to screen out of their awareness perspectives that clash with their own, resisting communication more and more. Thus does pride overtake individuals and bureaucracy destroys institutions. The cure is open exchanges between leaders and led. The same cure applies to the hardening effects of isolation and enmity among peoples, and among national leaders.

3. *Unifying of differences.*[33] We are large and complex organisms. We have – each of us – some hundred million million cells.[34] All the DNA molecules in one human body if laid end to end would reach to the sun and beyond. Our body cells each contains twenty-three pairs of chromosomes, each of which contains or consists of many hundreds of genes; we probably have at least 10,000.[35] Within this large and differentiated body, structures and processes oppose and balance one another: dominant and recessive genes; endomorphy, mesomorphy, and ectomorphy; catabolic and anabolic forces; muscular activation and inhibition; afferent and efferent nerves; acid and alkali; positive and negative valences and charges; and so on. The mechanism of negative feedback, where the response counteracts the unbalancing effect of the stimulus, is an example of the process by which the conflict is maintained and controlled through unifying processes.[36]

At the psychic level of dispositions (energies formed and guided by symbols) the principle of unity of differences is evident: ego and alter, will and conscience, independence and dependence, expression and inhibition, unconscious and conscious, release and restraint, adventure and stability, emotion and intellect, individual differentiation and collective integration, construction and destruction, relativity and universality, means and ends, specificity and diffuseness, short-run interest and long-run interest.

Man is a plurality, a mixture, a *temper* of processes.[37] His nature is not a

32. George C. Homans, *The Human Group.* New York: Harcourt, Brace, 1950.
33. The metaphysics of "the unity of opposites" is well established (Brāhmanism, Sāṁkhya, Taoism, Heraclitus, Plato, Stoicism, Nicholas of Cusa, Hegel, Schelling, Marx, Engels, Lenin).
34. Julian Huxley, *Man in the Modern World.* New York: New American Library of World Literature, 1948, p. 89.
35. Garrett Hardin, *op. cit.,* p. 244.
36. Alfred E. Emerson, "Dynamic Homeostasis: A Unifying Principle in Organic, Social, and Ethical Evolution," *The Scientific Monthly,* vol. 78, no. 2 (February, 1954), pp. 67–85.
37. Cf. the Sāṁkhya *guṇas,* Plato's tripartite soul in the *Republic,* and those views which hold that man is a unity of opposites (Brāhmanism, Tantra, Heraclitus, Taoism, Stoicism, Marxism, and Sheldon, *op. cit.*).

homogeneous, necessary, completed, continuous, everlasting harmony of parts. Whatever harmony he has is generated in and among and between processes, real in their own right. And that harmony is pluralized, contingent, partial, broken, and sporadic. But while on the one hand the self of man is not uncompounded or unchanging,[38] neither on the other hand is the self a mere aggregation of elements devoid of any internal unity among those elements. Man's oneness is an emergent, unifying process in and among exchanging processes. Contrary to Kant, there is no transcendental unity of apperception prior to the act of synthesizing actual experiences. True, the possibility of synthesis and hence of an emergent self exists prior to the creation of the self. The possibility lies in the genetic structure and ordering mechanisms of the body to which we have already referred.

Psychosomatic unity arises when perceptual and motor processes of the body come under the control and direction of a structure of symbols. Such symbolic structure ("mind") normally remains more or less self-consistent from time to time, though broken by lapse of attention and interest, day-dreaming, sleep, the disruption of new and unassimilated symbols, the arrest of thought and action by blockages, etc. Psychosomatic unity is manifest in the activity of "interest," which unites the activity of the body, moving toward a goal, under the guidance of symbols. The interest may be in getting food or in composing poetry, in avoiding physical danger or in revolutionary social change. But the contingency of the unity of personality is evidenced by (1) its impairment in mental illness[39] and (2) its impairment or absence in the cases of defective bodies or bodies reared apart from all human society, symbols, and cultural life (feral children).

As the body of the infant is built up out of the selection and integration of relevant materials (food, oxygen, etc.) in its exchanges with the environment, so the psychic unity overlaid upon that is the consequence of a dialectical exchange of the symbolizing body with other symbolizing bodies or with non-symbolizing world. The person is never removed from such exchanges. As the *Gītā* says (ch. III), action is inescapable. The self and others (along with the "natural" world) are implicated in exchange and mutual change. In this mutually creative exchange persons more or less maintain their self-identity through time. Opposition underlies the unity and the reciprocal identifications, each balancing the other. Eventually, however, imbalance dominates the personal and interpersonal unities, as a result of changes internal or external to the participants. The relation then shifts

38. Uncompounded, static views of the self may be illustrated by Plato, *Phaedo*, Steph. 78 (but not altogether in the *Republic* or *Symposium*), and Descartes, *Meditations on First Philosophy*, VI.
39. For example, repression, isolation, and rationalization as means of coping with conflicting elements of experience.

from differences-in-unity, to ascendant opposition, to partial or complete destruction of one or both of the persons (or groups) related. But the interaction of processes and persons continues, and evolves new unities. "The unity of opposites is conditional, temporary, and relative, while the struggle of mutually exclusive opposites is absolute."[40] Thus the breakdown of personality, interpersonal relations, institution, and societies is not necessarily a disaster. It may, in fact, be the revolutionary transformation required to eliminate evil and open the way to a more human order of relations.

4. *Creating.* To create is to bring forth a new unifying relation between elements otherwise separate or antagonistic to unification. It is to integrate diverse parts into a whole, in a way that preserves the parts, enhances the vivid diverseness of each part, and introduces new relations between the parts in virtue of which the preservation and enhancement take place.[41] (Destruction may occur in the process.) Examples of man's creative acts are: the mixing of chemical compounds and electrical discharges (as in the Urey-Miller experiments) to produce many of the amino acids, the building blocks of protein; the breeding of plants and animals to obtain new stocks; the invention of tools, machines, and machines to make machines; the formation of languages and mathematics (a word or a number is a powerful unifying instrument); the development of social institutions, like the family, agriculture, and industry; the organization of diverse and even antagonistic perspectives into an ordered whole, as in creative love, friendship, religious intuition, diplomacy, art, science, and synoptic philosophy.

The major instrument for man's creativity is his languages – his mother tongue, mathematics, esthetic symbols, religious symbols, etc. While every organism, as temporal process with negative feedback, has some capacity to predict or prepare itself for the future, man does so pre-eminently through the use of sign-systems which he produces and controls. (When signs are produced and communicated by men, they are here called "symbols.")

40. Mao Tse-tung, *On Contradiction.* New York: International, 1953, p. 48.
41. Some philosophers have a theory as to the creation of the universe but do not deal with – or consider significant – the creativity within the universe. Deterministic philosophies (Augustine, Orthodox Islam, Calvin, Spinoza, Edwards) – indeed all forms of classical supernatural theism and pantheism – implicitly exclude the creativity of finite creatures. On the other side, some have taken creativity as a basic category: the Cārvākas (consciousness and other qualities are emergents of atomic interactions); the Buddhists and Nyāya-Vaiśeṣikas (the effect does not pre-exist in the cause); various Indians holding to the doctrines of the pure play (līlā) of the Mother Goddess, the productive *prakṛti*, the overflowing vitality of *Prajāpati*, māyā as God's creativity (Rāmānuja); Tantra; the Confucianists (*ho* is an emergent harmony arising out of the proportioned reconciling of differences); the Taoists; neo-Taoists such as Hsiang Kuo (*tu hua* or "self-transformation"); Dōgen, with his dynamic Zen; and, in the West, Ravaisson, Lequier, Marx, Peirce, James, Nietzsche, Boutroux, Royce, Alexander, Bergson, Dewey, Korn, Whitehead, Mead, Croce, Brunschvicg, Lenin, Hocking, Cassirer, Wertheimer, Vasconcelos, Wieman, Koffka, Hartshorne, and Sartre – to mention only a few.

A sign is a stimulus preparing an organism to act in a certain way toward an object. Such action may be checked or modified as other signs – perhaps self-produced – are introduced into behavior. Thus by means of his symbols man can foresee a plurality of possible actions and experiences in a short span of time. He can experience conflicting perspectives on a scale not possible to any other known creature. Further, this conflict is often inter-individual, for his use of symbols enables him to "take the role of the other"[42] by interpreting the other person's symbols as that person does. But symbols, while engendering conflict, may also provide the solution.[43] Symbolic systems are organizational and in principle provide a way or order-ing particular symbolic processes in a unifying way. Moreover, where con-flict of meanings is interindividual, destructive conflict can be forestalled. The way can be opened for creative conflict. As meanings are communicated, each party, internalizing the meanings guiding the behavior of the other, searches for ways of integrating his own symbolic meanings with the meanings of the other. In this way the two may evolve an interpersonal system of meanings that is new, that is common to both, that is systematically related to the personal systems of each, and that governs their interpersonal be-havior. Because symbolic conflict is not overt conflict but only the signal or portent of overt, physical conflict, symbols are the primary means by which conflict can be rendered creative among men.[44]

In the very process of his creative activity man realizes his true character. His reality is creative realization. Caught in the processes of exchange, change, uncertainty, and opposition, man's inchoate self struggles toward unification and identity. His creative activity, guided by symbols and con-summated in his exchanges with things and persons, is the means by which ihe achieves that unification. For his symbolic power enables him to resolve his conflicts with others, to form ideals and plans of action for himself and others, to discover the conditions for fulfilling those ideals and plans, and to appraise his actions once they have been taken.

Both in the life of the human species and the life of the individual person, symbolic meanings emerge in the struggle of man to adjust to his world of persons and things and to fulfill himself. The driving force of this struggle comes initially from particular physiological neeeds, lacks, or tensions in the organism, of such kind that if not satisfied the organism will not long survive – the need for oxygen, for food, for water, for a certain range of body temperature, for activity, for sleep, for micturition, for defecation, etc.

42. George H. Mead, *Mind, Self, and Society*, ed. Charles W. Morris. Chicago: University of Chicago, 1934.
43. *The Creative Process*, ed. Brewster Ghiselin. New York: New American Library of World Literature, 1955.
44. Mary Parker Follet, *op. cit*. The use of dialogue in philosophy (especially in Western and Indian philosophy) is illustrative of the creative use of symbolic exchange.

Though most of these needs as operating and as felt are localized in particular organs of the body, that localization is not sharp. For the organism functions as a whole, and when deprivation is acute the need may be felt all over the body. Other needs, such as the needs for bodily safety, pain avoidance, sociality, and creativity, are not localized. Such needs represent centers of "information" which send messages from particular parts of the body through the nervous system and brain to the musculature – i.e., they issue in felt restlessness and action toward the environment in an effort to relieve the tension (satisfy the need) and restore equilibrium. In the process of satisfying the need in the environment – in locating the food, the water, the shelter and clothing, etc. – the organism learns that one present object can prepare responses to an absent object leading to satisfaction, i.e., it discovers signs of satisfactory objects. Such learning of signs or meanings is the extension of a process that begins with a lack in the environment; the lack is communicated to the organism; a particular part of the organism communicates the lack to the nervous system and brain; the brain in turn sends messages to the muscles which move the organism into activity upon the environment in search of relief. In this searching, signs and sign systems develop – or the organism dies. Normally, the infants learns such sign systems from others, so that his survival is intimately dependent on them. Thus symbols are necessary instruments of man's drive to live and to fulfill himself.

Symbolic power must first be power. The use of symbols presupposes a formative drive – a disposition to unify the variety of processes, qualities, and relations into which the incipient self is thrown. The history of the species of man has been contingent, long, arduous, and imperfect. It has evolved potent social drives in the individual infant, drives expressive of its dependence on others; and at the same time reciprocal drives of protection and care have been developed in adults. This is not an absolute difference; for infants, children, and adults alike develop both the need to be cared for and the need to care for others. The symbiotic instinctual sensitivities of infant, mother, and father have evolved together. Observe an infant perceiving things or learning to speak and to adjust its behavior to others. It persistently drives toward the formation of "we-experiences,"[45] endeavoring to shape its responses and actions in accordance with its yearning for a unitary relation with others. Buber is correct in speaking of "the *a priori* of relation."[46] At this point the accumulated linguistic materials and skills

45. Fritz Kunkel and Roy E. Dickerson, *How Character Develops*. New York: Charles Schribner's Sons, 1940.
46. *I and Thou*. 2nd ed., trans. Ronald Gregor Smith. New York: Charles Scribner's Sons, 1958, p. 27. Infants possess innate dispositions to respond to certain visual patterns and these may be elicited and developed with experience. Since these are adaptive, we may presume they evolved through natural selection. See Robert L. Fantz, "The Origin of Form Perception," *Scientific American*, vol. 204, no. 5 (May, 1961), pp. 66–72.

of culture come to man's aid. As his drive to relate himself creatively and securely to others intersects the linguistic responses of others, that drive becomes lingualized. His behavior becomes communicative, socialized, and humanized.

At this point too man's career and destiny are defined. Symbols are projective. They refer to the absent, the distant, the yet-to-be. They are the mapping of man's journey and territory as he moves *en route*. They presuppose a prior movement and disposition toward some destiny or destinies. But to seek a complete map of the future, or to suppose that man's destiny is arrival at a finished destination – such are illusions. Man's only destination as man is his fulfillment as man. This task is constituted by a ceaseless struggle toward the creation of a self in growing unity with other creative selves and with the world. The way of man's fulfillment is not escape from the events of his experience (asceticism; modern *anomie*) or submergence into them (mysticism; "adjustment" to society, tradition, or the state) or defiant conquest over them (the effort to be supreme dictator or God). The way is creative transaction with those events.

Since we change and live in a field of changing forces, our knowledge must include knowledge of both relative permanencies and relative changes. When we grow a crop or bake a loaf of bread or catch a flying ball or converse with another person, we have knowledge of that other as we adjust our activity to its changes. We remember and predict. We infer. We take one sense datum to be a sign of another. In our exchange with this sequence of external changes, we develop a meaning or insight into its character and course of behavior. This insight is subject to correction by subsequent observation, experiment, and control. It is a hypothesis, a postulate to be tested. Such insights are creative syntheses of observations arising out of our exchanges. They are summaries of past tendencies and projections of future behavior. As insights into the course of a given change, they go beyond what is given to the senses: they integrate and extrapolate. In this sense they are creative.

As all knowledge is predictive, it imports planning. To survive in a world of change, man must respond to changes in the present in such a way as to anticipate future changes (induced by himself or another cause) and to adjust to them accordingly. This capacity to prepare responses to the future is the seat of man's responsibility. Because he can rehearse now possible responses in the future, man can control his future. He is free – free from the determination or unknown and uncontrolled events, and free for the creation of values, or disvalues. At the present stage of human history, individual planning does not suffice to solve men's problems. For those problems are social – national and international – in scope. Therefore large-scale, democratic planning is necessitated. Men must exercise their responsibility (freedom) collectively and creatively, if men are to be fulfilled. Such planning must be directed toward the maintenance of the ecological balance of nature and man's place in it and the ordering of individual and communal life in ways that promote individual and social creativity. Neither feudalism nor capitalism has been capable of such planning; and socialism, while in principle democratic planning, has not yet achieved this ideal, though it is on the way.

5. *Individualizing.* The term "man" refers not only to the generic characteristics which any individual must possess in order to be called a man. It refers also to each and every actual individual who possesses these characteristics. Further, every man is not a mere duplicate of a certain archetype of the pattern "man." Nor does he derive his humanity in virtue of "limitating" or "actualizing" some prior ideal form of humanity. Human individuals are real in their own right; they are not just appearances or copies.[47] They are created. They emerge into being as unique, creative syntheses.

Individuality of personality emerges when there is (1) control of behavior in relation to others and the world by means of a system or signs that is corrected by itself and by the systems of signs of environing persons; (2) the persistence and elaboration of this system of symbols from place to place and time; (3) the production of signs signifying relatively inclusive values (preferred personal states and contexts) taken as ideals or guides of conduct; and (4) the more or less successful pursuit of such values. The strong individual person displays these activities consistently and effectively. The weak individual person displays them sporadically and ineffectively.

Ordinarily, no person is preoccupied with becoming "human." Every one of us is confronted by particular need-drives, obstacles, conflicts, changes, uncertainties. We are driven to plan our day, to get along with others, to manage our affairs in an orderly way, to attain our goals or progress toward them, to find footholds of permanence in precarious situations, to become something worthwhile, to discover enjoyment in participation, to attain some summit of significance. Such creative, unitary becoming is a highly partic-

47. The sense of individuality, and of individuality as self-creative, has been throughout the history of philosophy, weak and sporadic until the modern period, when in fact the processes of the political, industrial, and scientific revolutions commenced to liberate the individual into an awareness of himself and his possibilities. Although at times they perceived the "equality" of individuals, the philosophies of India, China, the Greco-Roman world, and Western Europe did not fully grasp the dynamic interactional character of the life of individuals. They tended to picture a preordained harmony between individuals and other individuals and the ultimate (God, nature, history). Their sense of possibility, of becoming, of progress, was hazy. Thus, in accordance with status-determined societies, we find *dharma* and *Brahman*, *Te* and *Tao*, *yi* and *li*, justice in the individual and justice in the state, the good and the right, man and God. At the other extreme, individualism in Western philosophy – Renaissance naturalism and humanism, English empiricism and analysis, American pragmatism, continental existentialism, and revived Japanese Zen – has tended sometimes to go to anarchic excesses.

ularized, individual task. The achievement of significance, order, and purpose is inseparable from the achievement of individuality. There is no significance, order, or purpose apart from the doings and undergoings of particular individuals as they individualize their experiences through creative acts.

Individualization is our human way of becoming social. We define our identities as we choose to relate ourselves to others. We may choose relations of dependence, dominance, or detachment, or mixtures of these. But in no case do we escape social definition. The crucial measure of personality is how it relates itself to differences. A weak and thin personality is one who dissociates the differences and screens them out of consciousness. He pushes down opposition, challenge, and hence the possibility of growth and enrichment. The strong personality not only tolerates but actively searches for disorder, asymmetry, complexity, ambiguity, and tension.[48] In a planetary community of precisely this kind, can we – leaders and laymen alike – muster the courage to be ourselves, i.e., genuine individuals? Can we engage in vigorous, genuine interaction with other persons and societies who possess diverse political, social, economic, religious, and philosophical viewpoints? While this spells danger and risk, it also holds the promise of human enrichment. It is the only way to save the nations from the destruction of war and the individual persons from the annihilation of anonymity.

Solution: The Fulfillment of Man's Nature

Once we are gripped by the conviction that all that we are and might be is here and now, as we are thrown forward with others in our efforts to live and live well – then all the philosophical problems can begin to fall into place. Those problems become, in principle, susceptible of clarification and resolution. For it is the practice, the practical values of men, that become ultimately determinative. Thus the generic reality of *exchange* does away with the erroneous idea of atomic individualism of the "self-made man," of superior races, classes, nations, and religions. And the superior social and political system becomes that which most effectively produces creative exchange among men and systems of men. The reality of *change* shows that the dream of absolute, unqualified permanence is the prejudice of the privileged or apprehensive mind, that we *can* and *ought* to change human nature (since its nature is to change), and that the enemies of human progress are class dominance, special privilege, private habit, intellectual inertia, and institutional idolatry. The *unifying of differences* teaches us the necessity

48. Frank Barron, *Creativity and Psychological Health*. Princeton: D. Van Nostrand 1963.

160

of dialectical thinking and action, and the folly of segregations and dichotomies, in thought and practice. Truth and falsity, good and evil, growing and dying away, are always tendencies mixed and changing. And the man mindful of this changing mixture will seek through it to assimilate opposition and enrich human advance. He will seek to discriminate between what is helpful to man's fulfillment and what is inimical to it. In either case he will realize that the reality of his self and his society is a dynamic order that must be wrested and won day by day from a situation where differences constantly contest. *Creativity* gives the lie to the doctrine that man is impotent, unconcerned, or incompetent to change his destiny. It opposes all forms of fatalism – religious, economic, social. Man creates himself and his world. Finally, the reality of *individualizing* is a rejection of the ideas that the personal soul entirely pre-exists and post-exists; that the individual soul is a copy of a prototype; that the individual person "has infinite worth"; and that the individual person counts for nothing.

Such static and pessimistic "myths"[49] as are here opposed are reflections and perpetuations of the backward social orders in the world. They must be dissolved if the new order, dynamic and optimistic, in which man is to be fulfilled, is to come to pass.

The concrete problem of man is how he can fulfill his nature, i.e., realize his potentialities as a human being.[50] Man's nature is not a fully determinate form antecedent to his experience or a goal toward which experience moves but an emergent patterned behavior. Therefore the solution to the problem lies in finding ways to release and maximize this kind of behavior. Man's fulfillment is a way in which the person enters into creative exchange with other persons, things, and events, so as to vivify and enrich individuality and at the same time unify his differences with other persons.

Concretely, two of the three billion human beings now alive on the planet face the problem of survival. Thrust into the world by biological propulsions not of their own making, they blindly struggle, in the face of deprivation, to maintain life. Their life-expectancy is low; their fulfillment expectancy is still lower. Yet "fulfillment" is implicated in "life." The order of human life, even at the level of hunger, disease, and ignorance, displays some degree of fulfillment, and intimates the possibilities for a higher order of fulfillment. Born as a partially solitary being and destined to remain that way, man yet develops relations of exchange. Ever changing and uncertain, he effects patterns of relative permanence and security, patterns ultimately bound by the broad limits of genetic inheritance and environment. (Eugenics and the other sciences may yet widen these limits.) Diversified and individualized,

49. Barrows Dunham, *Man Against Myth*. Boston: Little, Brown, 1949.
50. This is not a tautology, because some will say that the problem of man is how to nullify or escape from his nature.

161

man yet manages to unify his dispositions, thoughts, and actions with those of others and with the demands of the world. Born indeterminate and acquiring a certain use of cultural instruments – skills in handling language, materials, tools, etc. – he becomes still freer through that acquisition. He learns to use his freedom in creative ways, strengthening and expanding the system of living relations between himself and nature. Born proto-human and dimly individualized, man does take on some color of human individuality.

Thus the objection that the foregoing description of "man" does not apply to the majority of men (who live most of the time near a sub-human level) is partially true. We have, in one sense, proposed an ideal. But it is an ideal only in the sense that it is proposed as a condition that ought to be. It is first a description of fact, of what men truly are when they are becoming fulfilled as men. It is a normative description, applying to all men both as fact and ideal. For men *become* men: they both are and are not yet human. Ideally they should become and be men. Factually they are in process of becoming fuller men, or can be in process. This fact is the ground of the human ideal, and its justification.

Thinking, theoretical men may always differ as to the meaning of "value" and the best "way to live,"[51] as well as to the concept of "man." But it is submitted here that while such perspectives, relative and different, will persist, there is a concrete process, absolute and unchanging in its essential structure, in virtue of which these perspectives exist.[52] This is the process by which man becomes man in any circumstances, maintaining, augmenting, and increasing the order and value of his life. Accordingly, men ought to discover and produce the conditions that conduce to men's fulfillment. This means efforts by individuals and groups to bring about:

1) Procedures in their interpersonal relations for discovering and providing the conditions of human survival and fulfillment;

2) More efficient education and government so that these institutions express and implement the emerging will of people concerning their needs;

3) Increasing democratic planning of the production, distribution, and consumption of resources so as to meet these needs;

4) Progressive negotiation between governments issuing in universal and complete disarmament;[53]

5) The break-up of the anti-human, military-industrial-scientific-ideological complexes and security systems in the nations, and the creation of national

51. Charles Morris, *Varieties of Human Value*. Chicago: University of Chicago, 1956.
52. Henry Nelson Wieman, *The Source of Human Good*. Chicago: University of Chicago, 1946.
53. Norman Cousins, *op. cit.*

and international institutions to serve and create man, not enslave and destroy him;

6) The strengthening and expanding of the United Nations and its agencies, and the development of still more effective agencies in peacefully solving international conflicts and in promoting friendship and reciprocity among nations;

7) Massive aid (U. N., national, private) in the form of capital, capital goods, and services from the more technologically developed nations to those less developed;

8) Increased efforts of international agencies to utilize, in the less favored countries, the skills of millions of persons from the more favored countries; and the pledging of a period of service on the part of those persons;

9) Action to increase cultural exchanges of all kinds (between scientists, artists, laborers, farmers, educators, etc.) at all levels (popular, governmental);

10) A series of meetings of governmental representatives and citizens from all countries to plan the graduated ending of the armaments race, the cold war, and particular international conflicts; and to discuss world-wide solutions to problems of producing, distributing, and allocating resources, international trade, population, the exchange and utilization of scientific information and technology, and education;[54]

11) Word-wide democratic socialism, as the economic and political base for building a truly humanized world for all people.

54. See the encyclical of Pope John XXIII, *Pacem in Terris*, 1963.

Chapter VII

MAN, NATURE, VALUE, AND RELIGION

As adaptable animals, we survive by interacting with persons and things so as to complete actions that satisfy vital needs – the needs for food, water, air, clothing, shelter, activity, rest, bodily safety, etc. (If you think that survival is not difficult, you are at best only one person in three on our planet.) Survival is possible under a variety of biological, social, and ecological conditions. People survive in unproductive terrains and harsh climates – in tropical deserts, in Arctic wastes, in mountains, in jungles and forests, on plains and by river and sea, under water and in air. Some day they will probably live on other planets and indeed in other solar systems. Members of *Homo sapiens* variously eat raw grubs, roasted snakes, bamboo shoots, raw oysters, living cheese mites, grass,[1] rotten meat and fish, vermin, and even putrefied wood and clay.[2] They can survive on less than 2250 calories a day, as most of the people of Asia, Egypt, Central America, and parts of South America do.[3] Or they may consume more than 4000 calories of energy per day, as does the average U. S. man at work.[4]

But to be *human* animals we must satisfy other needs as well – interpersonal needs (communication, nurturance, friendship, love, sexuality), social needs (roleship, familial needs, peer group needs, cooperation), needs of exploration and play, needs of dependence, dominance, and detachment, cognitive needs, esthetic needs, creativity needs, the needs of distantiation and independence, the need to orient the self to realities and values transcending the self, the need to know and fulfill one's place in history and nature (one's "vocation"), the need for a symbolized system of basic realities and values (the philosophical need).

A "need" or "need-disposition" may be defined as a lack or deprivation in the personality system. It is usually accompanied by a striving toward a goal conceived to be capable of completing the action and satisfying the need. If prolonged as unsatisfied, the deprivation will lead to impairment of health and even loss of life (as in the case of the biological needs like oxygen

1. Ellsworth Huntington, *Mainsprings of Civilization*. New York: New American Library of World Literature, 1959, p. 40.
2. Clyde Kluckhohn, *Mirror for Man*. New, York: McGraw-Hill, 1949, p. 96.
3. Harrison Brown, *The Challenge of Man's Future*. New York: Viking, 1956, p. 112. The calorie intake of the average Indian has been put at 1,880. *The Times of India Directory and Year Book, 1962–3*. Bombay and London: Bennett, Coleman, p. 279.
4. Huntington, *op. cit.*, p. 446.

hunger, thirst, and food hunger). The presence of needs may be suppressed from awareness, though not entirely. Likewise, because of lack of information about himself, a person may be ignorant of his real needs, and in such a case his wants or desires may masquerade as needs and be interpreted as if they were such needs necessary to life and psychic health. For example, he may have a real need to be recognized as worthy by others; but being ignorant of that need and being influenced by advertising to want a new car as a status symbol, he mistakes that want for that need.

The term "interest" is normally used to mean an activity signifying an idea of what conceivably will complete an action and satisfy a need or a want. We may be interested in what will satisfy needs or in what will satisfy wants apart from needs. Thus we can say that any object that satisfies any interest is a value, and call that *interest value*. But then we must discriminate between *need value* and *want value*. *Need value* has the character of categorical and intrinsic good; *want value* may or may not be good, depending on how it affects the satisfaction of human needs in the long run.

Needs and need values are not isolated, atomic entities. They come in clusters called personalities. A personality is an ongoing system of needs and need values. While a single need may be satisfied or "fulfilled," the term fulfillment also applies to the synthesized satisfaction of some or all of the real needs of personality. Needs of course conflict with one another: some, such as hunger and thirst, appear as earlier, more imperative, and more necessary to survival than others;[5] some cannot be satisfied simultaneously; and some when expressed may exclude or impair others.

The fulfillment of personality has been defined by various ideals: Apollonian, Buddhist, Christian, Dionysian, Mohammedan, Promethean, Maitreyan, Epicurean, Taoist, Stoic, meditative, active, yielding.[6] All of these have been analyzed into common factors: social restraint and self-control, enjoyment and progress in action, withdrawal and self-sufficiency, receptivity and sympathetic concern, and self-indulgence.[7] These in turn can be formulated as patterns of interaction of the body with the social and natural environment wherein the needs of the personality system are satisfied and the system is fulfilled. The presence of these constant factors signifies a common pattern of all personality fulfillment: the differentiation and integration of needs, actions, and satisfactions of persons in a system of interactions with other persons, with artifacts, and with the rest of the planetary environment.

The term "fulfillment" properly applies to the maintenance and development of the whole ecological system in space and time. It includes not only the life of feeling, thought, action, communication, cooperation, and commit-

5. A. H. Maslow, *Motivation and Personality*. New York: Harper, 1954.
6. Charles Morris, *The Open Self*. New York: Prentice-Hall, 1948, ch. 4.
7. Charles Morris, *Varieties of Human Value*. Chicago: University of Chicago, 1956, ch. 2.

ment of persons but also their growing integration with one another into a unitary planetary society and their interpenetration with non-human nature. Think of man's useful planning of natural resources, his preservation of wildlife and wild lands, his communication with dolphins, and his creation of space platforms and planetoids. Comprehensively, human fulfillment is the fulfillment of this whole natural system of interactions.

Society and nature set limits and provide opportunities for the fulfillment of various personality ideals. Class structure, institutionalized ways of getting food, and climatic factors, for example, influence which values are favored and which disfavored. In medieval western Europe a barter economy, scant food supply, and other-wordly Christian ideals were accompanied by an ascetic way of life for many When, later, a developing capitalism made food more abundant and opened up opportunities for action on the environment, an individualistic, promethean way of life emerged, accompanied by dionysian enjoyments. In order for future generations to fulfill their needs, it may be necessary for the present generation to forego optimum fulfillment of its needs, faced as we are with massive problems of poverty, armaments, and pollution. For whether we do or do not confront these problems, our living has consequences in society and nature that go far beyond us in space and time. For millions of years our ancestors participated in the cycles of water, oxygen, carbon, nitrogen, and minerals as these passed between the plants and animals and biosphere. Our species and other species evolved in the delicate balance of nature created by this evolution. But now our increased mechanized agriculture, irrigation, chemical fertilization, insecticides, herbicides, genocide, burning of fossil and nuclear fuels with accompanying wastes in the form of heat, carbon dioxide, water vapor, carbon monoxide, sulfur oxides, and hydrocarbons – have all interacted with those cycles, changed them, and adversely affected the living creatures which depend on them. In addition our production of metals, concrete, plastics, and other inorganic materials has created problems of waste disposal.

Man can be optimally fulfilled only as the ecological conditions affecting him are cooperated with so as to facilitate his fulfillment with them. A wise child not only does not bite the hand that feeds him; he honors and protects that mothering source from which he sprang and by virtue of which he lives. It is a narrow, vitiating, and foolish fulfillment that is achieved by ignoring the fulfillment of others, including unseen and unborn selves and non-human creatures. Though it may appear to be an affirmation of life to pursue one's own interests here and now, or even, with "enlightened" self-interest, for a lifetime, ignoring the two billion hungry and diseased people of the world – that is in fact a denial of life and an aid to death. He who strives to live for himself alone – or for his own family, race, religion, class, or nation – implicitly denies the existence and value of others and the world of nature.

And this is an indirect way of denying himself, since he is profoundly inter-dependent with others and the world. The truly mature and healthy person is biophilic.[8] He has the strength to affirm himself and hence the values, actual and potential, of our planetary world. He has the devotion to have and to hold that world of values, till death parts him from it; to be had and be held by it, to absorb its strength, and to live in the hope of contributing to it, in the assurance that it was here before him and will continue after him. The rich man in the Bible who built bigger and better barns to hold his goods, so that he could say to himself, "Man, you have plenty of good things laid by, enough for many years: take life easy, eat, drink, and enjoy your-self" – was answered by God: "You fool, this very night you must surrender your life; you have made your money – who will get it now?"[9] Here, under a myth, is expressed an ecological truth: individual man cannot take his wealth with him when he dies, as he must; since that is so, and since we are interdependent with one another, we ought to share our wealth in the unitary system of society and nature.

A common and serious error of some contemporary analyses of value is to neglect the contextual (social, ecological) and temporal (historical, evolution-ary) conditions necessary to create, sustain, and transform values. *Human value is by definition a phenomenon occurring in human beings as initiators, agents, and consummators of value.* And even those who attribute value to some nonhuman or supernatural power or being usually acknowledge that it has no value for man unless man *experiences* or participates in its value in some way. (Even Karl Barth, that once arch-supernaturalist, now says that God is an historical event.[10] "The Christian hope," he says, "does not lead us away from this life. . . . In the eschaton the light falls from above in our life."[11]) But for puposes of understanding, prediction, controlling action, and the facilitation of value we need to know as many of the necessary conditions of value as possible. The traditional way of acknowledging such conditions was the religious one: value is *out there*, as the Origin and Up-holder of the world, as determining and guiding Form, as the organic or per-sonal Order of the cosmos, as the ultimate abinding Thou, even as the great mechanical Designer. Modern thought, influenced by inductive science and its emphasis on experience, sense perception, and humanistic concerns, has rejected this way of thought. It is now the mode to speak of value as an experience of selecting, judging, and enjoying which is had by the individual human being. We accept this mode here. But we quickly qualify this by speaking also of pre-value and pro-value – namely, all those conditions,

8. The term is Erich Fromm's in *The Heart of Man*. New York: Harper and Row, 1964.
9. Luke 12: 19–20. A New English translation.
10. *Dogmatics in Outline*. New York: Harper and Row, 1959, p. 28.
11. *Ibid.*, p. 154.

from the beginning of the universe to the present moment, which demonstrably contribute to the human experience of value here and now.

Thus we may speak of value at four levels: (1) *need value*, the maintaining and fulfilling of a need-disposition (preferential action) of a single human being toward some chosen goal of action; (2) *personal value*, the maintaining and fulfilling of a personal system of need-dispositions toward some chosen set of goals; (3) *social value*, the maintaining and fulfilling of a social system of need-dispositions toward some chosen set of goals; and (4) *ecological value*, the maintaining and fulfilling of a system of need-dispositions of a human society and the actions of living and non-living nature toward some chosen set of goals.

If a pattern of interaction between a person and the world of things and persons contributes to the fulfillment of survival needs and distinctively human needs in the way described, then we shall call it bettering interaction. If the pattern of interaction does not contribute to such fulfillment (by leaving needs as they are, or by obstructing their fulfillment), then we shall call it worsening interaction. "Bettering" and "worsening" are comparative terms applicable to alternative actions and their consequences in the same context. Thus they may be variously applied to person's needs, to a society's set of needs or to the needs of all persons on earth – each considered in its temporal span. Whether a person's eating of bread or his enjoyment of a painting is a bettering interaction depends on the practical alternatives possible and the consequences of each alternative. For a hungry person, eating bread is better than not eating bread, other things being equal. But eating bread to perpetuate a system of personality within a system of society that continues or increases unfulfillment in the forms of poverty, war, and tyranny – where alternative courses of action with better alternative consequences are practically possible – is by definition a worsening interaction. Given the quality of values which most affluent persons enjoy in U. S. society today, the process of becoming affluent is in most cases a worsening interaction. Only those who are ignorant or dehumanized, who believe that a rich diet, prestigious clothing and homes, and conspicuous consumption and waste represent ultimate values, can hold that all this is a sign of "progress."

Things and persons are not here called "good" or "bad" in themselves. "Better" and "worse" (generically, "value," positive and negative) apply to things and persons as they enter into interaction with one or more systems of human need and thus produce consequences of fulfillment or unfulfillment. Strictly speaking, things and persons do not *have* value; they function or do not function as ingredients in the complex production of value, i.e., the fulfillment of any human need.

Value is thus felt as subjective, but it has an interactional and factual origin and framework. Where human need meets the world, interacts with it,

169

and a fulfillment is created, there is value. In the narrow sense value is the consummatory outcome of the interweaving of subjective purpose and objective fact. In the broad sense value is the whole process of needing, of initiating of interaction, and of satisfacting of need. Value-creating activity is the transformation of both subjective state and objective world together: value emerges into the world and adds a new fact to it; existing facts acquire a new relation and status of value.

These are but two different ways of viewing the same phenomenon, namely, the creation of value.

Because the process of value-creation is subjective judgment, needful selection toward the world of facts, and the factualizing of such judgment through fulfillment – the language of value is usually a mixture of value-language and fact-language. Where for purposes of analysis subject and object can be easily distinguished, so can the modes of a language. But if value is understood as value-creation, then for accuracy both modes must be employed. So far as the term "value" covers a complex interactional situation, it can variously refer to some subjective state (need-disposition or consummatory state); some property or properties of a thing or other person in virtue of which that disposition is fulfilled; the relation between subject and object in and through which the fulfillment occurs; or the total context of conditions determinative of the creation of value, conditions extending back in time and out in space. With partiality theories of value have variously singled out these different aspects of a complex situation.

Value is an actualization and enhancement of man's activity. As man is a creature of nature, actualizing his being in and through his relations with other beings in nature, it is necessary to understand man's being-in nature in order to understand his possibilities of value. This understanding must involve an understanding of evolutionary processes in nature and human societies.

In his palpable material form, man is a massive body of perpetually living and dying cells. Beginning with the union of two cells, the individual man at maturity consists of 100,000,000,000,000 cells, a huge coordinated colony which represents an epochal triumph over "the perennial antagonism of cell and cell."[12] This coordination is secured primarily by the nervous system with its large brain, an organ which also regulates the input of external information obtained through the sensory receptors and directs the body's response to the external world. The growth of the brain appears to be associated with the adaptive value of the social life and linguistic communication of the early hominids.[13]

12. Charles Sherrington, *Man On His Nature*. Garden City: Doubleday, 1953, p. 285.
13. Charles F. Hockett and Robert Ascher, "The Human Revolution," *Current Anthropology*, 5 (1964), pp. 135–168.

As in size man stands half way between atom and star,[14] so time-wise he is an in-between being. One recent estimate places the origin of the universe 18 billion years ago.[15] Another estimate places the end of the planet less than 10 billion years hence, when the increasing heat of the sun will make life on earth impossible.[16] Our planet is 4.5 billion years old, and life on it arose some 3 billion years ago. Most of that time has been needed to bring forth man, as he acquired his present general form 1/2 − 1 million years ago.[17] Man is a latecomer on the planetary scene, the fruit of a laborious and precarious process. He may take pride that, unlike any other nature, he knows his own nature and indeed many others, he knows that he dies, and he may soon overcome the limits of even this knowledge by his knowledge and manipulation of the atoms and genes. Still, a truly naturalistic view would lead him to the humility of George Wald's statement: "A physicist is the atom's way of knowing about atoms."[18] We can't escape from our skin – which means that we can't escape from the 3-billion year old atomic history packed into us.

Man is a living being composed of selected materials of nature, complexly synthesized: proteins (H, O, N, C), fats (O, H, C), carbohydrates (O, H, C), sterols (H, O, C), lipoids, cycloses, small but critical amounts of sea-salt ions (sodium, potassium, calcium, magnesium, and chlorine), and assorted substances, such as sulphur, phosphorous, iron, iodine, etc. – all held in an enskinned environment of water and maintained in elaborate dynamic equilibrium. All parts work in an interactive unit, performing the functions of "living" – metabolizing, growing, reproducing.

George Wald has pointed out the special significance of the character of H, O, N, and C atoms, which make up 99 percent of the living parts of all living organisms. They are the smallest elements capable of achieving stable electronic configurations by gaining 1, 2, 3, and 4 electrons respectively, i.e., they can share electrons with other atoms, bonding with them, and forming molecules. Moreover, they can form covalent bonds, in which a pair of electrons are shared, each atom contributing one electron, and they can form double and triple bonds, fulfilling all their tendencies for combination. The result is that, being small, these atoms are capable of forming tight and independent units, such as carbon dioxide molecules.[19] Moreover, the bond

14. Julian Huxley, *Man in the Modern World*. New York: New American Library of World Literature, 1948, p. 90.
15. By Allan Sandage, reported in *Scientific American*, vol. 226, no. 2 (February, 1972), p. 41.
16. George Gamow, *The Birth and Death of the Sun*. New York: Penguin, 1945, ch. 5.
17. Weston La Barre, *The Human Animal*. Chicago: University of Chicago, 1955, p. 92.
18. In Introduction to Lawrence J. Henderson, *The Fitness of the Environment*. Boston: Beacon, 1958, p. xxiv.
19. *Ibid.*, p. xx.

radii of C, N, and O as well as their bond angles are almost identical, so that the chains composed of them are almost identical in their geometry. Hence they can fit closely together and take the form of long helices, as in DNA, the stuff of the genes.[20] As these elements and their combinations represent only a small number of the possibilities, the chance factor is evident in the formation of life and of human life. At the same time the elegant, intricate, and variegated order generated by the genes in 3 billion years of evolution is evident in the known 10^6 animal species and one-third of a million plant species on the planet. The course of human evolution is unique, as Huxley says, and dependent on a vast number of propitious factors. It is also an impressive succession of successes, each building on its predecessors: multicellular animal structure, bilateral symmetry, blood system, vertebrate, adaptation to land and the development of limbs, sense organs, protective skin, temperature regulation, mammalian placenta, protected development, foetalization, family, social life, brainy and communicative primate, migration from the trees, upright posture, development of forelimb and hand, tools, language.[21] Man is a rational animal, but in order to be so, as species and individual organism, he must first be many other kinds of animals. *In utero* every man recapitulates certain past features of his animal ancestry – single cell, colony, notochord, gill clefts, tail, monkey hair. In creating the individual body today, the genes as in a dream replay and abridge significant portions of their past career, building on them before they get up to the construction of modern man. But a common base unites the divergent species of evolution. In the embryos of fish, salamander, tortoise, bird, calf, pig, rabbit, and man, as Ernst Haeckel showed, this common ground plan can be observed.

In the 5th century B. C. Empedocles said: "For I have been ere now a boy and a girl, a bush and a bird and a dumb fish in the sea." B. A. G. Fuller links this saying to an Orphic belief in reincarnation. But it may have derived from Empedocles' materialism and evolutionism. If he had observed human and non-human embryos, as is not unlikely, he might easily have arrived at the idea. A belief in spiritual progress through a series of incarnations would not have been for him incompatible with material evolution, and this Orphic belief was probably held by the Pythagoreans, with whom Empedocles was associated. The Pythagoreans in turn probably got the view from India and the Jainas, who had confused material and spiritual evolution.

In making the human embryo the genes do seem to remind themselves of certain selected designs that they have laid down in past billions of years

20. George Wald, "Determinancy, Individuality, and the Problem of Free Will," in *New Views of the Nature of Man*, ed. John R. Platt. Chicago: University of Chicago, 1965, pp. 21–22.
21. Julian Huxley, *op. cit.*, pp. 13–17.

of work, and they lay down once more these designs in abbreviated, recapitulated ways and in a sequence, as if the recapitulation of past patterns and their sequence were necessary as preliminaries to their being surpassed in the final stage. Thus the psychosomatic "I" is continuous with all other things in the universe made out of like building blocks, and it shares a special continuity with other living forms by reason of its evolved form in the scheme of evolving forms within embryonic development and by reason of its descent from a gene source common to all living individuals and species.

Educated people today in the West unquestioningly accept the fact that man is made out of the materials found in the earth and in stars and planets. But the full import of that fact is often lost on some; they dismiss it and proceed with their medieval mysteries about the soul and the supernatural. The fact that we are living matter has a double significance going both backward and forward: we are Nature's own children, stuff of her stuff and process of her process, as intimately and complexly related to her as anything yet created on the planet. And this emergent stratified structure of *Homo sapiens* – whose elements, in chemical bonds and interactions, undergird and envelope his biological life, and whose biological life is the material for his psychic life of symbolization – has reared up in Nature through billions of years of material evolution. Now surpassing its origins in certain respects, this mélange of molecules is an epitome of Nature and her unique organization; it is the dominant form of natural activity on the planet. The creative synthesizing of atoms, molecules, colloidal materials, organic molecules, nucleic acids, single-celled organisms, multicelluar organisms – all this has required favorable conditions for very long periods. And here we are – the compact summation of organic molecules, delicately adapted to a favorable environment which has evolved along with us.[22]

These large organic molecules (and hence the building up of organic bodies) are possible because (1) carbohydrates are synthesized by green sunlit plants out of the inorganic materials of carbon dioxide and water, transforming carbon and hydrogen into storehouses of energy; and (2) because carbon atoms have the capacity to form long chains and ring-systems. Accordingly, the living animals organism can use the stored energy by oxidizing (with atmospheric oxygen) the ingested substances. This symbiotic process of transforming, storing, and releasing energy is not found in inorganic nature. That is why one scientist described life as a tendency in the direction of the improbable. The common process in nature as we now understand it is change in the direction of highest probability, i.e., disordered motion, with consequent loss of available energy.[23] We are lucky. If we wish

22. Lawrence J. Henderson, *op. cit.*, p. 280.
23. C. F. von Weizäcker, *The History of Nature*, Chicago: University of Chicago, 1949, ch. 4.

to take pride in being God's chosen people or nature's chosen children, we ought also remember humbly our material origins and bodies and our tychistic and hazardous development.

Likewise, the formation of atoms, molecules, suns, planets, solar systems, and galaxies is contingent. Our earth is a solid body of iron, semi-molten basalt, and solidified granites and basalts[24] – but the universe as a whole is 99% hydrogen and helium.[25] As Harlow Shapley put it, "We are products of chaos in a universe of gas."[26] The relative solidity of *terra firma* and of our mammal bodies is even more startling when we consider that there is only one atom per cubic centimeter in our galaxy (one per cubic meter in the universe) and that an atom 10^{-8} centimeters in size, is, with the exception of the nucleus, highly attentuated energy. "If all the atoms of a man's body were so condensed as to leave no unfilled space, the man's body would become a barely visible speck."[27]

But we must not forget that the possibility of *Homo sapiens* – along with the possibilities for the myriad other forms of life in the various worlds of nature, our own and others, as well as the various lines of evolutionary development – must have been present in some sense from the beginning of the universe. Although the pathway of evolution leading to man is unique, we can still trace many of the orderly stages in this pathway, much as we might trace a climber's route up a rugged mountain or the zig-zag course of a ship across a chaotic sea. Man's course and his present conditions are both mixtures of chance and order. We are now told that conditions favorable to life prevail in 100 million planetary systems. Life is improbable, as are the conditions favorable to life. But in an immense universe with an enormous number of galaxies, an improbability does not perhaps appear so threatening as it does from a strictly terrestrial perspective wherein we have not long been freed from a geocentric cosmology.[28] The human species is not so central as we once proudly thought; nor are we so rare and alone (as forms of life) as we once, in recent scientific times, feared. We are not just lower than the angels, but neither are we only a cut above the flatworms.

Life is possible on planets like our own because they are situated at favorable distances from the right-sized, stable suns and because the building materials for living matter – C, N, H, O – are relatively abundant at the

24. George Gamow, *Biography of Earth*. New York: New American Library of World Literature, 1948, p. 92.
25. George Gamow, *The Creation of the Universe*, New York: New American Library of World Literature, 1957, p. 50.
26. Lecture at Coe College, October 16, 1957.
27. J. W. N. Sullivan, *The Limitations of Science*. New York: New American Library of World Literature, 1949, p. 35.
28. Harlow Shapley, *Of Stars and Men*. Boston: Beacon, 1958.

surface of the planets. Of course there may be ways of synthesizing and releasing energy in living forms of which we do not yet know.

Scientists are unravelling the evolution, structure, and function of living matter by genetic studies of how the macromolecules of the nucleic acids, DNA and RNA, variously duplicate themselves, manufacture proteins, and regulate growth. The evolution of living forms is likewise under study, including human evolution. Here we see the emergence of relatively constant, conservative factors, like instinct, natural selection, and culture. Chance factors also occur in evolution – the switching of the nucleotides in the genes (garbling of the message that determines proteins), geological changes, effects of radiation. Such chances may be turned to valuable uses. They introduce novelty and make progress possible. A universe without chance and experiment would be a perfectly secure universe – and an uncreative one.

The process of evolution is evident in diverse places, times, and levels, and is therefore best described diversely. (It is not always good; as Dobzhansky says, it is opportunistic and utilitarian, usually facilitates living, and sometimes produces miserably adapted creatures, like the man-o'-war bird of the tropics.[29] It also evolves toxic substances, disease-producing organisms and viruses, and parasites.) Generalizing, we may speak of constant factors (gene pools, customs), variability (mutations, new ideas), isolation (of breeding groups, cultures), interchange between groups, and selective synthesis resulting in experiment, waste, and more effective adaptation.[30] All these factors are themselves undergoing evolution; and indeed the process of evolution has itself evolved. The evolution of forms takes place in the context of an environment which is itself evolving; so we may speak of the whole of nature evolving. Physical and biological evolutions may be more or less finished on our planet, and the fact that psychosocial evolution is now dominant[31] (in the hands, instruments, and symbols of man) means that henceforth when nature changes it will change for good or bad primarily at the command of man. Nietzsche and Marx were among the first to grasp this. This fact frees man; but in equal degree it makes him responsible for the destiny of nature on his planet.

All evolution can be described as the interacting of some parts of nature with others to synthesize new patterns of matter and activity. Such synthesis is both internal (in organism and species) and external (in relations of organism and species to environment). While all interaction involves destruction

29. Theodosius Dobzhansky, "Man Consorting with Things Eternal," in *Science Ponders Religion*, ed. Harlow Shapley. New York: Appleton-Century Crofts, 1960.
30. Sewall Wright, "Evolution, Organic," *Encyclopedia Britannica*, Chicago: William Benton, 1959, vol. 8, pp. 915–929. George Gaylord Simpson, *The Meaning of Evolution*. New Haven: Yale University, 1950.
31. Julian Huxley, *Evolution in Action*. New York: New American Library of World Literature, 1957.

and the irrecoverable loss of energy, the revolutionary movement of life is one of expanding and coordinating power. Man is not an alien spirit intervening in nature; he is natural matter transforming natural matter in directed ways. Every (natural) thing – atom, molecule, plant, animal – interacts with and transforms its environment to some degree and exhibits a certain integrative directiveness. But man transforms his world more profoundly than any other being in nature. This transformation is possible because man is a *symbolizing-acting-social* being.

Huxley shows the evolutionary roots of "conceptual thought," one of the main consequences of symbolizing. Symbols are impossible in plants, as well as in single-celled animals; further, a blood-system is necessary, as well as independence (vs. parasitism) and bilateral symmetry (for a brain). Land life was needed to call forth perceptual development and organs of movement. The massing up of nerve cells essential to intelligence was lost to the insects (because of their efficient but limited method of breathing) and saved for the land vertebrates. Insects are small, and hence small-minded. Next, only two reptilian lines achieved stable bodily temperature, birds and mammals. But the birds specialized in flight (would Leonardo have exchanged flight for intelligence?) while the mammals prepared the young for independence and developed family life. But most mammals turned their limbs and jaws into specialized instruments and continued to produce their young in litters, encouraging intra-uterine competition and rapid growth. But the primates slowed this down, prolonging the foetal characteristics into post-natal and even adult life (e.g., nakedness – and, we should add, sensitivity). Our recent arboreal primate ancestors developed in the trees a true hand, binocular vision, and the coordination of the two; and they were gregarious. Down out of the trees, they acquired upright posture, freed hands, and a special motility. All these things together produced the mechanism we call symbolic behavior.[32]

Tools, then, must have followed quickly, with their stimulus to signification. Meanwhile, the voice mechanism was developing, with primate ears so placed that primates can hear their own voices. And the accelerated sexuality of intimate social life among the primates advanced speech greatly. Various features of communication can be found in animals that evolved prior to man.[33]

A symbol is a sign created by man. A sign is anything that prepares a disposition to respond to something not immediately a stimulus. Signs prepare responses to what is absent and future. The first buds of spring signify the coming of fruit; they are "natural" signs, enabling man to imagine the

32. Julian Huxley, *Man in the Modern World*, pp. 13–17.
33. Charles F. Hockett, "The Origins of Speech," *Scientific American*, vol. 203, no. 3 (September, 1960), pp. 89–96.

future and prepare for it. But symbols – such as words describing the sequence of sowing, cultivating, and harvesting – give man an active knowledge and control over things. Symbols are man's expressions and guides of man's propulsion to relate himself to an absent and future world, a world of crops or a world of art.

Signs introduce temporal structure into the perceived, spread-out, spatial world. By the use of self-created signs man foresees and hence controls things and events. Therein lies his great transforming power. But this power would be only visionary and detached if man did not *act* to change things, creating a (food) to cause b (life) and destroying c (bacteria) to prevent d (disease) and changing e (shelter) to change f (discomfort). Man's power to act arises because he *makes* things that extend his perception and manipulation – plows, microscopes, axes. These made things are material tools or *instruments*; they are extensions of his material body, instrumental to some signified end. Even a noise or a mark is a material thing and can get something done, triggering the actions of persons. While other animals make things (nests, dams, webs, etc.) most do not make things that make things: they do not have that much imaginative foresight (because they do not make symbols on the scale we do), they do not have prehensile hands, and they do not possess the freedom from instinctual patterns that we do. (Jane Goodall in Tanganyika observed chimpanzees stripping sticks, vines, and twigs and inserting them in termite hills for a snack, as well as the use of sticks to open boxes, the making of leaf sponges to drink water, and the use of leaves to wipe the body. A mongoose has been seen to throw and smash millipedes, and finches to use sticks to obtain food from crevices. A tool-using disposition seems to be there, and a tool-making disposition is evident in the chimpanzees, though limited by its hands.)[34] Man has and thus is a unique kind of natural power: he symbolizes the future, he hypothesizes what it might be, he observes and plans, he deduces consequences from alternative plans, he embodies and materializes plans and thus changes himself and the rest of nature.

What are we to make of this symbol-guided transformation of the world, which *defines* the human enterprise? Is there a Purpose in it, perhaps preceding the emergence of the directive human mind and even the emergence of living forms on the planet? Or is it all explainable by Chance and Mechanism?

Both of these are partial and poor explanations, for they are metaphors drawn from *human* experience. (Recourse to a supernatural explanation supervening upon nature is even more inadequate, for it suggests deriving

34. N. H. Pronko, *Panorama of Psychology*. Belmont: Brooks/Cole, 1969, pp. 125–143. See also Leslie A. White, "Use and Manufacture of Tools by the Lower Primates," *Antiquity*, vol. 22 (1948), pp. 210–211.

nature from non-nature, a pure contradiction.) Man's pre-human history long antedates his human, symbolic experience, his experience with conscious purposes and mechanisms. Man is a *natural* being in productive and destructive commerce with other natural beings. It is as true to say that man is evolving through Nature as to say Nature is evolving through man. Man is Nature humanized and given a voice and decision; and Nature is the material cause, means, and support of man. Man and Nature, in short, are evolving together: both Nature and man are agents, instruments, and ends in this joint process. It is as much a mistake to say that man alone creates himself and his values as to say that Nature or Deity alone creates values for man. Man creates and is created. True, man symbolizes and chooses and acts, and physical and biological nature often appears all passive and patient under the touch and intention of man. But man himself is an embodiment and creature of nature, an active and symbolizing natural body and process. Moreover, nature must hold and maintain man's creativity and his values or they will not be held anywhere. (An educational system requires buildings, cafeterias, fresh air, plants and animals for study, etc.) In addition, those parts of nature defined as other persons must be accommodated to the needs, demands, values, and purposes of the active man; what *they* need and demand and value and purpose confront us as immediate limits and opportunities in our creative activity.

If it is said that man is now the conscious agent and director of natural evolution on the planet, as Huxley emphasizes,[35] it should be added that the values and goals that man chooses are in large part determined by natural things and processes that man did not make or choose or control. The relations of mutuality in sex, the family, and common work are given as universal conditions of human survival. On the other side, natural evolution seems to provide no guarantee of automatic harmony among men and between men and nature, and no indication of an unambiguous goal toward which the whole of nature moves. Because he has an uncommon power of self-direction, man also has uncommon power to direct and hence disrupt the planetary order of nature. Man is not entirely free, isolated, and alone in nature; but neither is he the legatee of a preordaining providence or the hapless victim of blind forces. He is best defined, I believe, as a participant in a natural dialectic which at the present stage in the evolution of nature on our planet has man as the dominant power. Man is a seafarer in the cosmic ocean. Born in midpassage, in the ship of nature, he has only recently emerged out of the hold to fashion a rudder and assume the helm. He repairs his ship *en route*, and he steers the ship with the winds and the tide as best he can.

35. Julian Huxley, *Evolution in Action*, p. 10.

The question of *significance* or *value* for man in his cosmic setting is the question of the great religions. This is man's "ultimate concern." Tillich uses the term "being grasped" to characterize the state of faith or ultimate concern, an essential, necessary, and universal condition of man.[36] In principle I can accept this. But Tillich does not analyze what it is we are and ought to be grasped by. Indeed, he puts it beyond observation all form, space, and time. Moreover, he holds that man can do nothing about acquiring or influencing this ultimate concern.[37] Tillich, like Barth and others, is reacting to the extreme modern view that man is independent in his nature and creates his own values: he insists on the objectivity of value and God. Modern man follows in the tradition of the medieval mystics and idealists like Schleiermacher (who is both medieval and modern, since he puts God in the soul via "experience"). But once God then is located in man, there is no longer any need for the traditional term, and so modern thought tends to become anthropological – *nach Art von Feuerbach* – rather than theological. Yet a full anthropology, which sees man in society, history, and nature, in the full stretch of space and time, might bring modern humanism to affirm, in a new and qualified way, some of the assertions of ancient religion.

What am I "grasped" by, what am I dependent on, at the deepest root of my being? What stands under me there, that I may understand as the ground of my stance? I am grasped by the chair I sit in, the terrain I walk on, the gravitational field that holds me in place. I am grasped by my children, my wife, my parents and grandparents, my friends and enemies, my fellow citizens, and indeed the whole vast complex of this onrolling system of the human species, life, and, in its ever-widening horizons that escape the eye, nature. If deity is what ultimately grasps me, it must be this, or something intimately related to this – as Bruno and Spinoza saw. When the prophets spoke with flaming judgment and tenderest compassion, they evoked these concrete relations of man to man and man's duty in them and betrayal of them. And Jesus divided the sheep from the goats accordingly:

> For when I was hungry, you gave me food; when thirsty, you gave me drink; when I was a stranger you took me into your home, when naked you clothed me; when I was ill you came to my help, when in prison you visited me.[38]

Instead of choosing between extreme subjective or objective views of man and value (spiritualism or materialism, as erstwhile conceived) or extreme religious views (modern individualistic humanism or neo-orthodoxy), we can and ought to pursue and develop the interactional, dialectical view of

36. *Dynamics of Faith*, New York: Harper, 1958, p. 99.
37. *Ibid.*, pp. 11, 38, 109.
38. Matthew 25: 35–36. A New English translation.

man and value. In this, deity can then be variously defined: as those invariant conditions which make possible the creation of value; as the generic structure of all values; or as the power (process) by which values are generated in a way in which man cannot foresee or control.

We owe it to a naturalistic philosopher of religion, Henry N. Wieman, for calling our attention to this latter concept.[39] Historically, the gods have been seen as powers that work good in ways that we cannot, as when a poet like Lucretius, praying to "life-giving Venus... the guiding power of the universe," calls upon her for inspiration.[40] Are there such powers? Of course there are; but our modern empirical Humean eye, so sharp and clever, has led us to miss them. When I write, swim, or love, they come into play. We must look to the passive voice in grammar for indications that it is not subjectively deliberate action that determines our actions altogether. "I am being written"; "I am in swimming"; "I am in love – loving, being loved." By the unconscious movements of glands, reflexes, nerves, muscles, bones, pen, paper, water, air, etc., I (as will and intelligence) am enabled to contribute what I can to the organization of the whole complex. In love I experience perhaps insights and new mutualizing relations that I did not plan on or desire. In solitude, where social relations are internalized, profound transformations may occur, as in Tolstoy's great story, *The Death of Ivan Ilyich*. These transformations may not always be of value. Indeed, demonic unconscious powers may be at work, as Baudelaire recognized in that "special satanic grace" of the painter Brueghel.[41] But if they are of value, shall we not say they are divine activities? And if evil, then demonic? Of course we can control such activities, within limits, though history tells of some men and women "possessed" by them. Even Socrates speaks of the divinity within him, "which is a kind of voice" and first came to him as a child.[42] We can prevent ourselves, at least to some degree, from participating in the creativity that works, in love or in art, when conditions are right – or we can consciously promote it. But because participation is a transaction, we cannot, as the medieval alchemist would, extract gold out of lead or give up what we have without first being given to. The divine, as Martin Buber has reminded us, is most likely to be found *between* man and man – and, we should add, *between* man and nature and man and the movement of nature. Once insights and relations have emerged in man – as they may in solitude, where social relations still are – we still can cherish or reject them, develop or suppress them. Man rises or falls as he works or does not work with such creativity.

39. *The Source of Human Good*. Chicago: University of Chicago, 1946.
40. *On the Nature of the Universe*, trans. Ronald E. Latham. Baltimore: Penguin, 1951.
41. "The Satanic in Bruegel," *Curiosités esthétiques*. Paris, 1869.
42. *Apology*, 31.

Man is ultimately concerned about both life and death; he seeks the partnership of the gods and fights the powers of darkness. In his traditional religious orientation the balance of this concern shifted toward death and warding off its threats; in the modern view, the balance has shifted toward life and securing its promises. This does not mean that religion is born of fear and that when fear dies religion dies. It means only that the specific character of man's generic concern has changed from ancient times to the modern period.

So far as we know man is the only being who ceremonializes the fact of death.[43] He is the only being who shows sharp awareness of individuality, time, fulfillment, mystery, dependency, and death, and who endeavors to cope with the anxiety engendered by this awareness. He is the only religious animal; for religion is just this awareness at the level of deep concern, and man's reaction to it. It is false to say that such awareness, intermixed as it is with anxiety, is neurotic and illusory. Neuroses, which appear in every culture, naturally appear in religion, as they do in many phenomena of human existence. Man responds religiously to his condition when he puts his whole being in question and asks for the significance of his existence. He puts it into question and seeks an answer because he can signify to himself his own limits – in his knowledge, in his values, in his uncertain identity, in his smallness, in his loneliness and estrangement, in his frustration, in his impotence, in his change, in his old age and death, in his bereavement of loved ones and precious values. The traditional religious way of coping with such anxiety has called for belief in an individual soul, in the immortality of the soul, and in supernatural beings. (Gautama rejected these, and Jesus made them secondary; but religions have a way of not following their founders.) A scientific attitude does not as such dissolve this awareness; it only proposes to deal with it by understanding and control of natural things, events, and orders for the sake of human value. Such control, however, does not mean loss of nurturing contact with the world. On the contrary, it means opening windows upon that world, and walking out to meet it, and entering into personal relations with it, in such ways that what was otherwise dark now yields us strength, joy, and ecstasy. Most of traditional religion has confounded man's dependency on the capricious forces of nature and despotic social systems with superstitious ideas and myths. Most religious thought has deepened the darkness of man's natural and social enslavement. A humanistic science dispels that darkness by the light of knowledge. It proceeds in the spirit of Shakespeare: "there is no darkness but ignorance." But, as for Shakespeare, understanding and control do not diminish the sense of dependency, finitude, and wonder.

43. Clyde Kluckhohn, "Anthropology," in *What is Science?*, ed. James R. Newman. New York: Simon and Schuster, 1955, p. 344.

What is the origin of the awareness of which we speak? To seek the answer to this question is to seek what man is. The answer given by the traditional religions and cultures is that since man is oriented to a supernatural order his essence or "spirit" must be supernatural – and thus cannot be dependent on the body. That is why during the middle ages the Christian religion, like the Greek and Egyptian before it, forbade anatomical studies, and why, during the late middle ages when dissection was allowed on strangled prisoners, the subject's head was removed first – since the brain was held to be the seat of the soul – and the physician did not touch the body but instead read from Galen as the parts of the body were exposed by a servant.[44] The error here was to conclude that since man *believes* in spirits, he must *be* spiritual – or, as Plato put it, since man has ideas (like mathematical notions) that are not embodied, man must be a non-bodily spirit. The error persisted (and still persists) until it became plain that sign-processes constitute the underlying mechanism of all "spiritual" processes and states (memories, dreams, visions, voices, etc.); and that these arise in-the-body-in-transaction-with-things-and-persons. The slow discovery that mind or personality (*anima*, spirit, soul) is a *natural* activity occurring in space and time and subject to observation and analysis – a discovery accelerated about 1900, with Freud, Pavlov, Külpe, and Watson – ranks with the discovery of Wöhler in 1828 that organic compounds can be made out of inorganic molecules. Just as living forms are unique structurings of non-living forms and thus function uniquely, so the human form is a unique structuring of living forms and functions uniquely.

Man, as we have said, is a symbolizing being. To symbolize is to produce signs; and a sign is anything functioning to prepare behavior toward something at the moment not a stimulus. Thus man can symbolize to himself and others things remembered and things anticipated, things past and things to come, things dreaded and things hoped for, deeds done and deeds to be done, persons dead and persons yet unborn, values gone yet recollected in tranquillity, and the vast domain of possibilities that people the romantic imagination – all that might be, that is yearned for, and that may be tragically wept over. Thus man can symbolize his own self, separated from others and the world, integral and untouched; the passage of time, along with his own aging, his passing, and the passing of epochs and worlds; his own possibilities for fulfillment, emptiness, and death; the treacherous stretches of the unknown, within his depths and in the impenetrable beauty, darkness, and doom that surround him; his own transience and weakness as he stands under the starry heavens and sees the galaxies rush outward; and his own swift end and oblivion. The poignancy of these feelings is sharpened by his

44. Howard W. Haggard, *Devils, Drugs, and Doctors*. New York: Pocket Books, 1946, p. 149.

tender mammalian nature, gentled and nurtured in the bosom of a family, where in childhood time is unending play, and where he is deeply conditioned to develop needs for others in love, leisure, and work. That is why religion, as primitive man's response to these feelings of loneliness in a creature profoundly dependent and interdependent, has postulated father and mother gods in heaven and on earth: they are the man-child's rock, refuge, and everlasting arms.

The traditional religious response was matured, through centuries of myth and ceremony, to fulfill this deep human need for others. It was effective, in an indirect way, in putting man in touch with the sources of his being. But its mistake lay in a confusion about its symbolization. It mistook things symbolized for thing real, and sought supernatural answers to natural questions. Men have always known what they needed, even if through a glass darkly, but they have not always known how to find it. Moreover, religion became a natural response to an abnormal situation, namely, an oppression on earth that required heavenly gods, both as illusory relief from the oppression and as sanction for it. Religion has been "the spirit of an unspiritual situation."[45]

The blind alley of religious superstition developed not only from man's fears of natural forces and social conditions in class societies but also from man's peculiar biological makeup. The very brain of man makes possible the storage and recall of large amounts of qualities, forms, and symbols as well as, in imagination, seemingly endless combinations of these. Thus man has live in a greatly inflated symbolic sphere, much more populous with images and symbols than necessary for the meeting of his practical needs and often peopled with imaginary and horrendous beings, terrors, and hopes having no correspondence with the external world. Sensory practice and interaction with the world of existing people and things would test such symbols for their truth; but social convention, vivid imagination, and class structure militated against that. Hence symbols reverberating inside the heads of men proliferated their own internal systems quite apart from the external world. This "supernatural" world of religion, postulated as a real domain beyond the sensible or "mundane" world, has been no more than the world of images and symbols in the big and hyperactive brain of *Homo sapiens*. But just as some savages do not locate their headaches in their heads, so religious men have not located their symbolic systems inside their skulls and have reified and projected them in the form of a supernatural and alien world. Such men did in fact live in an alienated world of nature and society, but only indirectly perceived and signified that alienation in their symbolic systems.

45. Karl Marx, *Toward the Critique of Hegel's Philosophy of Right*, in Karl Marx and Friedrich Engels, *Basic Writings on Politics and Philosophy*, ed. Lewis S. Feuer. Garden City: Doubleday, 1959, p. 263.

Where then shall we look for the solution? Moses, Confucius, Gautama, and Jesus were correct in directing men's attention and action to the existential world where men live and move and have their being – to their familial and institutional relations, to their psychological life of motivations and values, and to their relations of dependency and interdependency with their fellow man and nature. But they did not go far enough. They knew nothing of the intricate mechanism of the body and its evolutionary origins in nature, or of its ecological relations to nature. They knew only vaguely, at best, the workings of the unconscious and the import of interpersonal relations for the health of the individual. They knew no science. Moreover, they lived and taught long before modern industry, technology, war, cities, and mass ideological revolutions.

Nevertheless, the historical religions, in the guise of myths, have carried within their traditions the conviction that man lives and lives well within the keeping of powers and relations that make him and give meaning to his existence. These have been located within the depths of man's soul: "Atman is Brahman"[46]; in man's relation to his fellow man: "the soul of my lord shall be bound in the bundle of life with the Lord thy God"[47]; and in man's relation to the universe: "only he who makes no distinction between himself and other things and follows the great evolution, can really be independent and "always free."[48]

If man's spiritual life is natural, the key to man's fulfillment lies in a study and control of his natural activity. If his profound need is for creative interaction and interdependency, detached and attached with others and the rest of nature – then his task and responsibility is to create the conditions by which that creative interaction can be released and fulfilled. If man feels anxious, alone, and impotent, the answer does not lie in the world of symbols abstracted from living intercourse with the world – though this is the answer which the mentally ill give themselves, since the world gives them no answer. The answer lies in a return to the sources of man's creation and growth, i.e., in man's relations to other persons, to nature, and to the whole evolving system which creates man and which he creates. Here man the Evolved Evolver is involved with that wider Evolving in the attitude of both freedom and responsibility. The broad lines of man's fulfillment and commitment are already indicated there. But they demand man's wisdom and courageous action to be made explicit and complete.

46. More exactly, "Tat tvam asi" ("That art thou!"), in the *Chandogya Upanishad*, 6.8.6. *The Thirteen Principal Upanishads*, trans. R. E. Hume. London: Oxford University, 1934, pp. 246 f.
47. I Samuel 25: 29.
48. Hsiang-Kuo *Commentary*. Quoted in Fung Yu-lan, *A Short History of Chinese Philosophy*. New York: Macmillan, 1950, p. 229.

Jean-Paul Sartre expresses a typical modern mood when he writes that the discovery that God does not exist and guarantee values, makes us forlorn.[49] How religious this reaction is – or rather, how post-religious! It assumes the old supernatural posture, in order to reject it. It laments a dead God. It still bears the weight of centuries of the religious superstructure of thought and feeling, even after that weight has been intellectually lifted. For modern man is like a slave, still bent from a burden that he has long since been liberated from.

If God is dead we have nowhere to go for our values except to our own choices; hence the anguish of "choosing all mankind."[50]

But the forlornness of modern man is in a sense the forlornness of historical man, i.e., urbanized man in class society. "Little we see in nature that is ours," said Wordsworth. That is the mood of industrial man, herded together in cities where his instinct of workmanship, his natural dispositions and needs to see and handle and transform natural objects, to deal directly and perceivingly and intimately with others, have been attenuated and starved. (Hence the compulsive, ritualistic cultivation of food and sex and mob activity.) We are forlorn because we have been robbed of our home in nature and society, the home that we grew up in for billions of years. This robbery that class urbanization has committed is compounded by the dissolution of our religious mythologies, which provided, in the absence of pre-historical, pre-urbanized mythologies, a distorted but still useful orientation to the sources of our being. On top of this, class society has split man down the middle of his being, divorcing him from himself and from even those closest to him in the family. With both Nature and Spirit dead, where shall we turn?

I have already indicated the answer. Sartre's own forlornness and anguish, which are the honestly faced consequences of an almost reckless courage, would be mitigated if he saw man in his natural setting, as a bio-social-ecological creature and creator. If we turn to the creativity of man and man, i.e., socialized man, constructing nature to suit his own nature – we shall have our hands more than full, and shall be situated in a place where man is not lost but is found.

Some immediate practical steps that need to be taken to this end are: the prevention of war and progressive disarmament; the manufacture, distribution, and use of a cheap contraceptive, along the lines of Lippe's loop or Incon; a collective effort by the wealthy nations to help solve world poverty by providing economic and technical aid to the poor countries (the U. S., with seven per cent of the world's population, consumes seventy

49. *Existentialism*, trans. Bernard Frechtman. New York: Philosophical Library, 1947, p. 25.
50. *Ibid.*, p. 22.

per cent of its resources); local, national, and international planning to conserve and develop natural resources, wildlife, natural beauties, and recreation sites; the preservation and cultivation of personal and ethnic variety; democratic ownership and control of the basic resources, processes, and techniques for maintaining human society; and the application of science for the relief and fulfillment of man's estate. While these steps need to be taken, they will not be taken save as large masses of people – one by one – themselves *consciously need* for them to be taken and begin to take them. In this, and hence in the fulfillment of man, education is all-important. To stimulate people to understand their needs and the conditions for the fulfillment and unfulfillment of such needs – such is the prize and pressing task of education today.

We have already said that religious concern in the past has directed itself to individuality, time, mystery, death, dependency, the divine, and fulfillment. We cannot dismiss these concerns as meaningless. But the responses made to them were for millennia conditioned by the prescientific orientation of man and the exaggerated emphasis on the spiritual life, i.e., the life of symbols. In the light of present natural knowledge, what can we say of them? We cannot hold they are wholly illusions; nor, on the other hand, can we accept them intact as they have come down to us in traditional form.

Human *individuality* is not ultimate but derivative. As a species we have evolved over millions of years biologically and over a million years under the influence of cultural processes (activities directed by social symbols). Our biological individuality is a matter of chance, and, at the present stage of indiscriminate mating, owes no credit either to parents or society. We acquire our psychic individuality through symbolic interaction with others and the rest of the environment, and throughout life it remains dependent in a profound degree upon others. Gautama Buddha, Hume, James, Whitehead, Sartre, and others have shown that the individual self is not substantial but is plural, episodic, and uncertain. And, even if we did not possess this insight, we would be driven by the nature of our condition to seek a wider and fuller reality than our particular bodies and private desires. We are individualized portions of reality, but our needs move us into trans-individual relations and actions. Preoccupation with an individual supernatural God, perfect and personal, is, as Marx, Nietzsche, Freud, and others have observed, a symptom of individual distress and mental confusion. It is a strategy for meeting the threat of death; and when death – which attaches to the individual – is a dominant concern, the life-affirming impulses of man suffer and go awry. In the West, this concern with death appears in the Exilic period of Judaism – it is indeed evident in all the great empires of antiquity – and continues through Roman times among the Christians and into the feudal period. In spite of the vigorous humanism of the early Renaissance, the deity of death is peculiarly adapted to the lonely bourgeois ego of rising capitalism. The libraries, churches, universities, and skyscrapers that the robber barons built are modern mausoleums, expressive of the individual's yearning for immortality. They are fashioned in the spirit of the Pharaoh's pyramids. A Calvin's God who selects, sanctifies, and comforts the man who exploits his fellow man is the answer to a capitalist's prayer. But he who seeks and finds his values in socially constructive and cooperative work will feel no such desperation of compulsion (for all selfishness and compulsiveness express despair and meaninglessness). If the man who loses his individual life in the larger living texture of a creative society has a god it will be a god of the living and not of the dead, a god of the common life, a god of history and nature. Dread of death shall not dog him by day, nor shall the hopes of heaven tempt him by night.

Time is the limiting measure of the space we live in. (Space flights are flights from time; those who lose themselves in such flights lose themselves in a kind of intoxication, wishing to forget the historical suffering of men and women and children on earth, who daily edge toward death.) Time signifies all there is for the individual and the species: beginning, need, opportunity, fulfillment, end. It measures our mortality, and defines us as links in an ongoing chain, inheriting from the past, bequeathing to the future. It indicates to us our debt and our responsibility, our smallness yet our significance in the stream of nature, life, and human culture. Time is the locus and process of our fulfillment. To take it seriously is to understand how rare and valuable each moment is and how dreams of eternity for the individual are exact reversals of his true destiny – which is realization here and now, in a gathering community of here-now's.

Mystery is everywhere in our experience and in nature. The "heaven" of traditional religion is our natural mystery deferred, displaced, and disguised, projected where it cannot be accessible, relevant, or exciting. Historically, "mystery" means that which is unknown and secret, that which is essentially unknowable and unexplainable, and that which arouses wonder, curiosity, or surprise. This has been a basic concept on which traditional religion has been built. As naturalists we must reject the second component of this definition, the idea that a mystery is something *essentially* unknowable and unexplainable. For the naturalist, it is self-contradictory to assert that something is existent and also essentially unknowable and unexplainable. Many things existing (in past, present, or future) are unknown and will probably remain unknowable. Accordingly we cannot make any intelligible assertions about them.

Naturalism, therefore, retains the fact of mystery. Indeed, the category of the mysterious is indispensable here. All of the necessary conditions of human value are mysterious in part. The needs and impulsions that drive us

187

toward value, the repulsions that drive us away from value, the responses of other persons to us, the whole complex of conditions of society, culture, history, and nature forming the matrix for human life and its valuing processes – all these are in great part non-rational and sub-rational and pre-rational. They were in the making and in operation long before reason emerged with its linguistic forms to discriminate and relate certain elements of experience and thought. What then is the proper function of reason in regard to such an underlying and enveloping mystery? It is not to limit and confine these conditions of value in some narrow and rigid scheme, either descriptive or ideal. But it is to search out their structures and activities, so far as possible; to understand, facilitate, and release their pro-value working; and in all ways to follow and serve the lead of these pre-existing processes (prior to man's reason) which sustain and create human life and value.

Death loses it power and poignancy when that to which it attaches, the individual, is correctly understood. Time entails death. It is an aspect of creation. The genes create cells and bodies as way stations in their advance; and the stations having done their work, die and are cast off, like the stages of a rising rocket. The creative process by which a need is satisfied and individuality structured is a process that moves from birth to death – a precarious structure maintained through changes. It is interlocked with many other processes. And as our lives are defined and linked in this way, so is the career of a society and the career of the enterprise of life on our planet. Death is a phase of every sub-process in this living process. Individual aspects of an electron die in the career of an electron; an electron dies in the career of its larger atom; an atom dies in the career of its molecule; molecules die in cells, cells in larger bodies, bodies in societies, societies in nature. And nature, the universe? It is everlasting.[51] The everlasting creativity of nature, the primordial ground of a creative universe, is what men have sought when they have sought deity transcendent.

Death is universal, and, among the human species, so is mourning. This is a deeply social phenomenon, and traces of it may be found among the higher mammals. In the form of intense withdrawal, anxiety, self-denial of pleasures, depression, guilt, and self-reproach, the mourner takes upon himself responsibility for the relation with the departed person and for his death. Since the lost person was so intimately related to him as a force and datum in his own self-definition, he mourns for himself, he mourns for the other, he mourns for the society and indeed for the whole of humanity. As all the world loves a lover, so all the world mourns with a mourner. We know that his situation is essentially our own; and all cultures make way for this and

51. *Lao-tzu*, ch. 7.

ritualize it. The mourner's expressions become forms of healing as they give release to feelings and meanings and lead him out to form new social relations and hence a new self: "Tomorrow to fresh woods pastures new." Mourning can become pathological if carried as reinforcement of an individual state of disruption and impotence – if the injury is favored. The healthy solution to individual death then is social life – as Gautama illustrated when he told Kisa Gotami, sorrowing for her dead son, to seek mustard seeds in all those houses where no one had died.[52]

Primitive religion acknowledged man's *dependency* and coped with it by magic. The religions of civilized man who is less subject to the arbitrary perils of nature, are less sure on this point. Prayer, for example, is employed by some only during crises. But some advanced civilized men become unequivocal again: they affirm man's independency, and they deny his dependency entirely. This is a great error, with grave consequences, and is contradicted by the whole natural history of life and of the human species. We need only look at the lifelong dependency of the human mammal on fellow human mammals. Our affection, wonder, reverence, and exhilaration in the presence of red sun, white moon, silver rain, and still night of swarming stars; the cool far blue sky and drama of the clouds; all gentle, wild weathers; deepest foaming oceans, torrents and brooks and roaming rivers; blue lucid lakes, green speckled ponds, and puddles silver struck by shafts of sky; reedy swamps and plains all furred in feathery grass; heaving prairies; rough-hewn, embouldered mountains; grain growing and wetmost fronds and meekest mosses and low triumphant lichens; all ugly sea creatures and exuberant orchids, and toads and flies; flowering leaves and twigs, turning to green tumescence from old age; dark cryptic forests; birds of air and song and violent plumage; all hairy, scaly, finny things, predaceous, croaksome, gauche, or graceful: aha! our love and fascination with all such is no accident but it is a disposition induced in us and now indigeneous. For we by time were generated with them, and made our way among such natural surrounds, as to be rock and lichen and green plant, enough at least to know our kindred there, all swarming with us in the habitats of verdure, mud, and sand, and running waters. We love our world and all the little worlds within it, even at times those most evil which transfix us though they destroy us, because of the long adaptation of our sensitivities to what we depend on for sight and sound, for touch and scent, for pleasure, strength, and stay, in body and in soul. This natural feeling of dependence is most evident in the adaptation of male to female, of parent to child, of man to man, and of man to nature.

The increasingly popularized science of ecology reveals to us the complex

52. E. W. Burlingame, *Buddhist Parables*. New Haven: Yale University, 1922, pp. 92–94. Cited in *The Teachings of the Compassionate Buddha*, ed. E. A. Burtt. New York: New American Library of World Literature, 1955, pp. 43–46.

order of interdependence which unites living things with one another and with their inorganic environment. People with strong economic and political interests tend to view this order instrumentally and to ask how it can be changed or adjusted to so as to benefit man. But while it can be modified for man's benefit, it also preceded man and comprehends him. While it is necessary to man's system, man's system is not necessary to its prior and more inclusive system. Books and films about birds, land animals, and sea creatures have made us conscious of the elaborately developed and autonomous worlds of our fellow creatures, with their own systems of life and of values quite apart from our own. At the same time they show us, as in Farley Mowat's *Never Cry Wolf*, our affinity with them. To read about the tenderness, courage, loyalty, communicativeness, playfulness, extensive social system, and resourcefulness of the gray wolf on the Canadian tundra discovers to us some of our own virtues, in a form established along another route of the evolution of life, and in ways distinctive and sure.

In this self-same matrix we must comprehend the idea of the *divine*. The word comes from *divus* (Latin, *deity*) and the Sanskrit *divya*, with its different Indo-European derivatives meaning day, heavenly, shining, shining sky, sky-god. The divine is something grand, commanding, exalted and exalting, numinous, and mighty in both reality and value. It is surpassingly worthy, and intrinsically evokes man's wonder and respect. Primitive man with his strong instincts went straight to the truth in deifying the sun and worshipping it; and it has modern science on its side now. All life on earth depends on this sun. But the idea of the divine was deviated by those who, worshipping a god of the heavens, "high and lifted up," looked *beyond* nature for the divine. Had they known science, and looked in the other direction, i.e., downward into nature, and outward into her transactions – they would have correctly divined the divine and its path, following it from the evolution of life into the social and symbolic life of man; and they would have been dazzled far more than those who gazed directly into the face of the sun-god.

Up until very recently in human history the idea of man's *fulfillment* has been closely associated with the divine. Some of the religions have claimed that there is a power (or powers) that creates values in ways that man cannot fully foresee or control. Is there such a power (or powers), and can it be experienced at work among us, in nature? (To assert that such a power is supernatural is meaningless, both rationally and empirically.) We have already indicated the answer to this. Man, in his dealings with other persons and things, creates values and relations that did not previously exists – as, trust, love, understanding, beauty. Is there, in this process of value-creation, an activity which is other than man's own conscious and purposeful activity and which contributes to the creation of value? There is – a mutualizing process (1) which links together in integral forms the items within the awareness of a single person[53] and (2) which integrates into mutuality the activities of two persons (as when an interpersonal relation grows in value over and beyond what the two persons contribute to it individually and collectively). If this relation is in nature and if relations can be experienced in some sense (as harmonies, tensions, loving, hating) – then it can be experienced. And if it can be called the divine, as I contend, then the divine can be experienced.

Here we must discriminate between (1) "experience" as the focussing of attention or selective perception upon some particular item in the manifold of qualities and forms which presents itself for such perception (as "I see red") and (2) "experience" in the sense of *undergo, live through,* or *enter into* (as "I experience love," or colloquially and more accurately, "I am in love"). In both cases the person or experiencer is *in* a relation (perceptive seeing, loving). But in the first case the experiencer is attending to one discrete item in the field of experience, while in the second he is sensitive to the relation itself, aware that the other person in the relation has, like him, the relation in himself and that it is internal to his being. What is being experienced in the second case is not experienced as something "out there" but as something ingredient in one's very being. For since such a relation is internal to the self, then to experience the self is to experience the relation, and *vice versa.* By the same token, to experience the self is to experience the other person in the relation of loving. In love, one cannot sunder the object of one's knowing – the relational loving and the person loved – from one's own being. Hence we do not "perceive" love as we "perceive" a red color; we undergo it, we are in it, and we are created and perhaps destroyed by it.

While we can experience the relations through which human fulfillment occurs, it yet requires an act of conscious awareness and analysis to understand the structure of fulfillment and to direct its course in human affairs. The concept of human fulfillment contains within it, analytically, the concept "human." This in turn can be derived from a description of the structures of behavior of human bodies in various societies, and a selective integration of such descriptive data that characterizes what man generically is. The sciences of human anatomy and physiology are well developed, and while they are not complete they are recognized as universal in their principles and valid for all investigators. The social sciences are not so well developed; nonetheless we can indicate examples of social studies that are moving toward the same universality as now enjoyed by the biological human sciences.

In sociology and anthropology, G. P. Murdock has specified more than seventy items which can be found in every culture.[54] Clyde Kluckhohn, at a

53. *The Creative Process*, ed. Brewster Ghiselin. New York: New American Library of World Literature, 1955.
54. "The Common Denominator of Cultures," in Ralph Linton, ed., *The Science of Man in the World Crisis*. New York: Columbia, 1945, p. 124.

more general level, points out that certain "invariant points of reference" must be used in describing human beings: a social system, psycho-biological individuals, external situations of living and acting, the functional roles of individuals, and the coordination in a social system as a whole.[55] The existence of two sexes, an ordinary life-span, and the dependency of infants lead to family life and the various relations of the young to one another and to parents. In such relations of human biology, human gregariousness, and external nature, we can find a certain "ground plan" for all human cultures. A. R. Radcliffe-Brown has specified three basic relations that define primitive and indeed all kinship systems and societies: the separation of the generations from one another, the equality of siblings so far as they participate in a common unity and loyalty, and some form of "filiation" providing for the orderly succession of sibling groups.[56]

Going still farther, Claude Lévi-Strauss has proposed that anthropology analyze the relations that subtend the phenomena of cultures and the systems of which these are part and which determine their changes. Structural analysis identifies the units of a social institution, defines their various relations of opposition and change, shows similarities with other institutions both in the same society and other societies, and formulates abstract models of interacting elements which can then be used to explain and predict the facts of human cultures. Such models would provide universal applicability.[57]

In the field of psychology, where the individual person is taken as the unity of study, much work has been done to display the invariant sequences of development of the infant and youth in the various modes of his behavior – perception, cognition, emotion, learning, etc. Arnold Gesell's studies are well known in the United States, and in Europe Jean Piaget was one of the pioneers in this regard. More recently the work of Jerome Bruner and others has called attention to the sequences in the cognitive development of the infant. In language study Noam Chomsky and allied sholars have maintained that linguistic evidence in the learning of children indicates the presence of "deep structures" innate in all human beings which generate models and systems of rules that determine perception and mastery of language.

In his studies of moral standards of children in various cultures, Lawrence Kohlberg has claimed to discover an "invariant developmental sequence" in children in all cultures: first, physical objects and the social status of their owners are valued; then a human life is seen as instrumental to the satisfac-

55. "Universal Categories of Culture," in *Anthropolgy Today: Selections*, ed. Sol Tax. Chicago: University of Chicago, 1962, pp. 304–320.
56. Meyer Fortes, "Primitive Kinship," *Scientific American*, vol. 200, no. 6 (June, 1959), pp. 146 ff. See also A. R. Radcliffe-Brown, *Structure and Function in Primitive Society*. Glencoe: Free Press, 1952.
57. *Structural Anthropology*, trans. Claire Jacobson and Brooke Grundfest Schoepf. Garden City: Doubleday, 1967, ch. 1.

tion of needs of its possessor or someone else; then the value of a human life is based on the affection or empathy of family members and others toward it; then that life is judged by its place in a moral or religious order of rights and duties, later in its relation to communal or a universal human right, and finally as representative of the universal human value of respect for the individual.[58]

Psychologists have described the pattern of the evolution of human needs and their fulfillment in the individual human being. A. H. Maslow, for example, has proposed a hierarchy of needs – physiological needs, safety needs, needs for belongingness and love, esteem needs, self-actualization needs, cognitive needs, and esthetic needs.[59] Erik H. Erikson has outlined a developmental scheme of tasks natural to the infant and youth and adult.[60] We shall not deal with the issues raised in such studies. For our purposes here, it will suffice to assert that the individual person always and everywhere develops into a *human* being in and through interactive processes between his body and other persons, the artifacts of his culture, and the inanimate and living things of nature. His needs and ways of satisfying them develop and become integrated in such interaction. As distinct from the development of other living creatures, this generic development occurs as symbols and symbol-systems, socially generated, form and direct the satisfaction of need-systems. It is an oversimplification to say that the human being first has bodily needs, satisfies these by thinking, and then proceeds to have and satisfy psychic or secondary needs. All needs and their satisfaction are bio-psycho-social-ecological. They emerge into being in interaction of body and environs. Hunger, biologically rooted, is acculturated; so is the need for beauty, which shows itself almost immediately in the infant's preferential responsiveness to certain colors and forms.[61] The later development of symbols builds on and facilitates these need-reponses; it is not superimposed on them or separated from them.

Man's fulfillment is not a final, finished state but a movement and a becoming, an integrative interaction with persons and things, an evolution with a whole system of persons and things in evolution, and with a mutalizing and creative process.[62] This process depends on man, as reciprocally, man depends on it. Formerly man relied excessively on powers external to his thought and action to produce his fulfillment. The result was massive impoverishment and misery, with exploitive earthly tyrants in fact ruling

58. "The Child as a Moral Philosopher," in *Readings in Educational Psychology*. Del Mar: CRM, 1967, pp. 37–43.
59. *Op. cit.*
60. *Childhood and Society*. New York: Norton, 1950, ch. 7.
61. Reference is made to research on the visual preference of new-born infants in Adolf Portmann, "The Seeing Eye," *Landscape*, vol. 9, no. 1 (Autumn, 1959), pp. 14–21.
62. C. Judson Herrick, *The Evolution of Human Nature*. Dallas: University of Texas, 1956.

men – a function reserved theologically for a divine and omnipotent ruler. (Theology has never been the queen of the sciences; it has usually been the handmaiden of politics.)

Although the masses of the world are still unfulfilled and miserable, the balance of thought has shifted: many men, and certainly most intellectuals, political leaders, and educated persons, believe that the principal way to man's fulfillment is not dependency but understanding and control. The hazard here, however, is that we shall swing excessively in the other direction, not only repudiating the age-old vices of religion (superstition, dogmatism, intolerance, fanaticism, cruelty, narrowness, arrogance) but also forgetting the religious virtues: faith, zest, compassion, charity, humility, reverence, gratitude, wonder, praise, responsibility, and a sense of depth, mystery, and dependency.

Is it possible to combine the best of the religious perspective with the power of scientific knowledge and control now in our hands? It is not only possible; it is necessary, if we are to be saved from a science determined by men who do not understand or appreciate the evolutionary role of man in nature and his responsibility toward it, and from religions that do not understand and even repudiate science. The first would give us man divorced from nature and from values grounded in nature; the second, values divorced from man and nature. In both cases, values become arbitrary and, in the event of conflict, subject to settlement by capricious preference and arbitrary power.

The tragedy of traditional religion is that it expressed important and universal truths about man's relation to man and nature but at the same time held man in captive to the blindest dogmas and blackest despotisms. Precisely because religion reflected man's condition, both his social and natural dependence on the sources of his being and his enslavement, it held and kept man in its grip. It suppressed the true situation of man; the divine was conceived of as the supernatural power, independent, impervious, and unpredictable, mediated by his priests and secular rulers with their "divine right" – not as the immanent relation of interdependence binding all men together as equals. It was the lay prophets who, representing the people, periodically protested against this first idea as idolatrous – and who were stoned to death and crucified. The idea of deity as alone and unreachable by the individual is an alienated idea because it reflects the actual social alienation of man. Since the divine can be found only in the relations between man and man, to seek it *beyond* such relations – in the mystic soul, in heaven, in the Unconditional above nature – means that man has already lost it because he has lost himself and others.

Someone may object that this account of man, nature, value, and religion is an expression of value and a proposal that certain values be chosen and adopted by others. That is so. But every proposition, whether in predominantly designative or syntactic form, involves a judgment and an implicit discrimination as to value and action. The proposition, "this is a table," or "the universe is material," selects out certain features of the environment, organizes them in a selected perceptual and conceptual fashion, and directs the active attention in a certain way with respect to certain purposes, proximate and remote. The purposes of "objective description" and "syntactic analysis" are derivative and abstract purposes that arise in the concrete context of solving problems and satisfying needs. They ordinarily subserve the more imperative and directly felt needs of survival and the pursuit of fulfillment. But even if they are isolated from such needs and such pursuit they are still value-enterprises. Description and analysis become valued and implicit standards of value begin to operate.

Nor does the assertion of the value-factor in our description of the world lead to an acceptance of an opposite objection, namely, that all views are ultimately a matter of faith and nothing more than faith. To be sure, faith as a form of value-commitment is there. But shall we then say that life must be at best a dialogue of faiths and at worst a war of faiths? The modern view, which sees need as the originator and determiner of value, is true; but to insist that this is the whole truth is an error that is of a piece with the ancient dogma that the faith that triumphed in a religious war must be by definition the highest. We must take account of the function of need in the context of a practical organism's action. In the first place, the environment is there before we ever come on the scene. It generates us. It sustains us. We then perceive, structure, anticipate, and act upon our environments as we are driven by our shaped needs to find there fulfillment of such needs. Existent things and persons have characters and resistive power of their own. They set limits to what we can and cannot do to them and extract from them in the way of fulfillment for ourselves. Accordingly, if we persist in our need-dispositions, we may revise the structure and direction of our needful activity and accommodate it to the external world. This mutual definition of need and environment, of subject and object, of valuation and fact, is called learning. It is, in fact, the way in which "instincts" are formed.[63] Of course, this definition of the need-environment relation is itself determined by need – whereas persons with other needs would define it differently (e.g., positivists, existentialists, ascetics, etc.). Are things then so arbitrary? Comparative anthropology makes it plain that cultures vary widely and that as individuals are acculturated they acquire the need-systems and value-systems of such cultures. The Zuñi Indians see the world as orderly and peaceful, the Dobuans as cruel and malignant, the Kwakiutl Indians as

63. T. C. Schneirla, "Psychology, Comparative," *Encyclopedia Britannica*. Chicago: William Benton, 1959, vol. 18, p. 697.

insecure and competitive.[64] But three considerations prevent us from asserting complete cultural or individual relativity: (1) people do appear in the psycho-social sciences to have a certain structure of common needs the world over; (2) a selected and effective technique (science) shows that the world has the same structure everywhere; and (3) for the purposes of living and living well, the methods of the sciences as employed by men throughout their history seem to be the most effective thus far discovered.

If we use the term "sciences" narrowly to mean the rational and empirical studies of early Egyptian astronomers in the fifth millenium B. C. or even of the Greeks almost 4000 years later, then within the span of human culture the career of science occupies a relatively short time. However, most of urban science built upon and refined the knowledge and techniques painfully acquired and carefully accumulated by primitive man during his million or more years of existence prior to the Agricultural Revolution about 8,000 years ago. While much of this existence was guided by supernaturalistic myth and reinforced by ritual, ceremony, and the instruments of magic and superstition, nevertheless the day-by-day practices of securing food, clothing, shelter, defense, and other necessities for survival required an attention, perception, thought, experiment, observation, and practice which resulted in a growing body of naturalistic beliefs and skills advantageous to the satisfying of men's needs both biological and spiritual. Primitive men accumulated intimate knowledge of local habitats, resources, plants, animals, birds, fish, and insects. They studied the stars, constellations, solar and lunar cycles, and seasonal changes. They invented virtually every kind of tool and the basic weapons and utensils. They created techniques of making pottery, buckskin, textiles, boats, and houses. In chemistry they developed paints, antidotes, the use of poisons, and ways of processing food. They domesticated plants and animals; modern civilization has domesticated no new plant or animal, nor has it discovered any new kind of food. Primitive men were skilled in the preparation and preservation of food, medical diagnosis and surgery, and the making of medicines, beverages, musical instruments, and means of ocean travel.[65]

These techniques and knowledge were quite specific, directed to the satisfaction of specific needs and the overcoming of specific obstacles in specific situations. At the same time such knowledge was interwoven with more general sorts of knowledge, answering such questions as: What are the nature and origin of man, his society, and nature? What is the relation between man and the world of nature, and between man and the world of the spirit

64. Ruth Benedict, *Patterns of Culture*. New York: New American Library of World Literature, 1953.
65. Leslie A. White, *The Evolution of Culture*. New York: McGraw-Hill, 1959, pp. 266–272.

(consciousness, values, the alleged afterlife)? What are the different roles of men in society? What ought man to do in relation to other men and to nature? What methods should man follow to secure reliable knowledge? Such knowledge, like the knowledge pertaining to specific things and techniques, was usually a mixture of the naturalistic and supernaturalistic outlooks. But this general orientation was not separated from specific and practical knowledge. As a framework of orientation for the individual to self, society, and nature, it provided a philosophy or more accurately a mythology for eliciting, sustaining, inspiring, directing, and organizing his energies. Both primitive man and civilized man seem to need a framework of orientation informing man about himself and his world, appraising the significance of man and his world, and promoting action toward the world and the values cherished and sought by man.

The answers to these general and basic questions – What is man? What is the nature of things? How do we know? What is value? – are ordinarily carried in the linguistic habits – grammatical, technical, economic, political, religious, esthetic, etc. – of the culture shaping the mind and personality of child and adult. As cultural artifacts and as structures of basic belief essential to the cohesion and continuity of cultures, mythologies have been accepted unconsciously, have been maintained by specialists (shamans, artists, musicians, priests), and have been slow to change. Yet, as structures themselves dependent on the underlying technology of their cultures, they have always shifted and responded to changes in the technological base. Thus, for example, when the Greek city-states were (relatively) freed from domestic and foreign tyranny by emperor and priest, thinkers went to work on these general questions, heretofore answered mythologically and supernaturalistically, focussed conscious attention and analysis on them, and sought to come up with antisupernaturalistic and naturalistic answers. "Philosophy" in the Greek and Western sense was born. But even in Greek philosophy we can sense the struggle between the Neolithic tradition, which emphasized the older, subjective, idealistic, religious way of explaining things, and the newer, objective, naturalistic, scientific way. For philosophy, the solution to its general questions is not so easy as the solutions in the sciences, which deal with either natural or human questions; for philosophy strives to deal with both the objective and subjective, the physical and spiritual, in an integrated way. It must find a method and a reality which, in unitary and dialectical fashion, combines an understanding of each. Accordingly, philosophies have veered either to mechanical materialism or to idealism. They either have gone backward to primitive spiritualism, subordinating science, or have idolized science and subordinated human concerns.

Philosophy that has maximum value for man begins with the prime fact of the unity and interaction of man and his world. As man's living is a dialectic of his needs with other persons and the things of nature, so philosophy ought to be an interweaving of subjective and objective strands, of evaluation and fact. Such philosophy is a proposal for action, for relating human purposes and actual conditions, so as to remake man and the world in the direction of new value. Such philosophy must be social, insofar as all human needs are social in their origins and require social action for their fulfillment. The "private" belongs to subjective fantasizing, a diversionary blind alley of the social process. In principle philosophy must work alongside science. It must appeal to public fact – common need-dispositions, common perceptions, common actions, a common source and terminus of perception and action. Questions of value, as we have suggested, can be resolved in this way. "Normative value" is a description of general human fulfillment, and can be developed as knowledge develops concerning man – knowledge from all fields of inquiry, since man is a human being set in a biological, social, and ecological context.

Still there are elements in the value-enterprise that are not now subject to description or inter-subjective agreement. We cannot now describe all the elements that go into individuality, creation, disagreement, and destruction. And even if we were able to do so, men would still diverge in their needs (individually different and culturally different) and in their ways of satisfying those needs. So we find ourselves in the midst of proposal and counter-proposal, of action and counteraction, of this faith and that faith. The most dramatic and dangerous exhibition of this is the clash between nations, divergent in their ideologies concerning class, each possessing thermo-nuclear bombs and the power to wipe out the whole enterprise of civilization. That is why the principle of peaceful coexistence among states of different social systems as a way of accommodating opposition is imperative for survival, and why the method of scientific inquiry, i.e., analysis and practice, is the most promising and productive way of preserving and even enhancing values in the midst of men's differences.

The method of domination or extermination of one group by another has been common to past religious mentalities in the West. It has been taken up by the virulent nationalisms of the West in the last 300 years. Under present conditions, it is self-defeating. We live in radically new times, and that is why we need a radically new commitment to value. Traditional religious thinkers argue that the pattern of values is already given objectively in the structure of the universe, of history, or of God beyond history. Essentially conservative, they want to return men to that – by coercion, in some cases. Modern existential and humanistic thinkers, having exposed the illusion and folly in that course, claim that all values are created out of man's internal freedom, and undertake to persuade others of this fact. The efforts of Christian orthodoxy to save itself, such as those summarized in John A. T.

Robinson's book *Honest to God*, cannot fully succeed, I think, so long as they ignore or set aside the findings of the sciences and reinstate in a new form the old self-evident position of revelation. Humanism in the narrow sense will also fail so long as it makes man the center of things – either individual man or man as race – and forgets his relations social, historical, and natural. The concept of "love" comes close to the latter, but the fact that thinkers like Tillich and Robinson repudiate naturalism suggests either that they are making war on an outmoded naturalism or that they really intend to oppose all efforts to ground faith on empirical evidence about man and nature, so far as they are possible. Such "grounding" of faith does not mean that man entirely makes and controls the ground of his faith; we have indeed argued all along that man is born into it. It means the testing and improving of faith by turning the tools of observation and analysis upon that prior ground of creation and thus putting man more fully in touch with it.

Both positions, modern scientific humanism (with existentialism) and religious orthodoxy, contain partial truths, I believe. The fuller truth – at least a more viable proposal – is a dialectic that extracts and synthesizes the truths and values in each. The evidence from evolution and ecology indicates an environment fit and favorable for man and his values. On the other side, it is plain that man, impelled by the dynamic of his own needs, does make his values and impose them on the environment. But each side here sets limits to the other, evokes the other, and helps to create, sustain, and transform the other. The method of such a dialectic is inherent in science and art, and when it becomes the method of man, as an overriding commitment for the fulfillment of man, we might soon approach those human values and human relations of which the great religions have dreamed. As for those who disbelieve that such a dialectic is the way by which to reach those goals – let us enter into the dialectic of discussion and common labor in behalf of man, and let the resolution of theoretical conflicts come, if it will, through that paramount practice. Short of total destruction, the method from now on must be man with man with the world.

INDEX

relativity, cultural and individual, 196
religion, 4, **14,** 121, 179–191, 194, 198,
 Chs. II, VIII
  defined, 181
Renaissance, 186–187
 naturalism and humanism of, 159
Revelle, Roger, 150
Ribble, Margaret, 142
Riesman, David, 3
Rig-Veda, 113
RNA molecules, 175
Robertson, Archibald, 26
Robinson, James Harvey, viii
Robinson, John A. T., 198–199
Rodo, José Enrique, 97
Romans, 120
Romantics, 77
Rousseau, Jean-Jacques, 145
Royce, Josiah, 147, 155
ṛta, 112
Rudra, 113
Russell, Bertrand, 60, 142
Russian Orthodox civilization, 1, 2

S

sage-king, 42
śakti, 35, 36, 83, 111, 127, 144
Sāṁkhya, 11, 36, 37, 76, 144, 146, 153

Samuel, 184
Sandage, Allan, 171
Śaṅkara, 35, 63, 147
Santayana, 10, 18, 24, 33
Sartre, Jean-Paul, 142, 155, 185,
 186
Satori, 71
Schelling, Friedrich W. J., 153
Schilpp, Paul Arthur, 59
Schleiermacher, Friedrich, 179
Schneirla, T. C., 195
School of the Middle Path, 58
Schopenhauer, Arthur, 145
Schroedinger, Erwin, 151
Schweitzer, Albert, 142
science(s), viii, ix, 7, 9, 22, 62, 77, 120,
 131, **150,** 163, 186, 196, 198, 199
 and technology, 65, 79
scientists, ix
self-interest, 167
Sellars, Roy Wood, 7, 76
sex (sexuality), 101, 145, 146, 147, 178
 division of labor based on, 108
Shakespeare, William, 30, 181
Shang dynasty, 43

Shang Ti, 41
Shapley, Harlow, 150, 174
Sheldon, **W. H.**, 6, 99, 114, 130, 132,
 133, 151, 153
Sherrington, Charles, 170
Shih Po, 95
signs, 155, 157, 159, 182
 definition of, 156
Simons, Leo, 67
Simpson, George Gaylord, 21
Śiva, 36, 37, 83, 100, 103, 105, 113, 125,
 136, 144
Śivaism, 146
Smithsonian Institute, 21
Snow, C. P., 139
social sciences, universality in, 191
social value, 169
socialism, 6, 9, 65, 122, 127, 159,
 163
Socrates, 180
Sol Invictus, 40
Soma, 113
somatotonia
 defined, 114
 temperament, 115
somatotype, 152
Somervel, D. C., 107
Sophocles, 125
Soviet Union, 2, 6, 127, 129
space flights, 187
species
 differences of, 151
 evolution of, 150
Spengler, Oswald, 127
Spinoza, Baruch, 70, 147, 155, 179
St. Francis, 30
Steichen, Edward, 141
Stoicism, 148, 153
Stoics, 25
Suffering Servant, 102
Sufis, 33
Sullivan, Harry Stack, 149
Sullivan, J. W. N., 174
Sumer, 2, 77, 83, 107, 108
Sumeric civilization, 3
śūnya, 35
supernatural(ism), 5, 38, 97–101, 105,
 115, 123, 148, 155, 173, 177, 182, 183,
 196
Suzuki, Daisetz Teitaro, 44, 132
syllogism, 53
symbols, 16, 143, 146, 153, 154, 155–
 158, 175, 176–177, 182, 183
 definition of, 155
symmetry, 144
Syriac civilization, 1

211